NORFOLK PUBLIC LIBRARY

# TWENTIETH CENTURY VIEWS

The aim of this series is to present the best in contemporary critical opinion on major authors, providing a twentieth century perspective on their changing status in an era of profound revaluation.

Maynard Mack, *Series Editor*
Yale University

# SAMUEL RICHARDSON

## A COLLECTION OF CRITICAL ESSAYS

Edited by
*John Carroll*

Prentice-Hall, Inc.   A SPECTRUM BOOK   *Englewood Cliffs, N. J.*

Copyright © 1969 by Prentice-Hall, Inc., Englewood Cliffs, New Jersey. A SPEC-
TRUM BOOK. All rights reserved. No part of this book may be reproduced in
any form or by any means without permission in writing from the publisher.
C-13-791160-2; P-13-791152-1. *Library of Congress Catalog Card Number 69-17372.*
Printed in the United States of America.

Current printing (last number):
10  9  8  7  6  5  4  3  2  1

PRENTICE-HALL OF AUSTRALIA, PTY. LTD. (*Sydney*)
PRENTICE-HALL OF CANADA, LTD. (*Toronto*)
PRENTICE-HALL OF JAPAN, INC. (*Tokyo*)
PRENTICE-HALL OF INDIA PRIVATE LIMITED (*New Delhi*)
PRENTICE-HALL INTERNATIONAL, INC. (*London*)

## Contents

| | |
|---|---|
| Introduction, *by John Carroll* | 1 |
| *Pamela*, *by M. Kinkead-Weekes* | 20 |
| Richardson's *Pamela*: the Aesthetic Case, *by A. M. Kearney* | 28 |
| From *Pamela* to *Clarissa*, *by William M. Sale, Jr.* | 39 |
| On *Clarissa Harlowe*, *by Dorothy Van Ghent* | 49 |
| Clarissa and Lovelace, *by Ian Watt* | 67 |
| The Plan of *Clarissa*, *by Frederick W. Hilles* | 80 |
| The Style and the Action in *Clarissa*, *by William J. Farrell* | 92 |
| Clarissa Harlowe and Her Times, *by Christopher Hill* | 102 |
| On *Sir Charles Grandison*, *by A. D. McKillop* | 124 |
| Epistolary Technique in Richardson's Novels, *by A. D. McKillop* | 139 |
| "Writing to the Moment": One Aspect, *by George Sherburn* | 152 |
| Richardson and the Bold Young Men, *by Morris Golden* | 161 |
| *Chronology of Important Dates* | *181* |
| *Notes on the Editor and Contributors* | *182* |
| *Selected Bibliography* | *183* |

# Introduction

## by John Carroll

### I

In *Aspects of the Novel*, E. M. Forster creates a mythical room where we are to imagine novelists of all eras writing simultaneously. The writers have been instructed to group themselves in pairs, and the first two we come upon are engaged in writing *Clarissa* and *The Ambassadors*. Henry James early apprenticed himself to the art of the novel (his first signed story appeared when he was twenty-one) with the declaration that "my work is my salvation." Samuel Richardson was apprenticed as a boy to a printer, handsomely reaped the rewards of the industrious apprentice, and not until fifty (when, in writing a book of "model letters," he recalled the story of a virtuous maid-servant who married her master) did he begin writing his first novel. *Pamela* (1740) was an immediate success, and *Clarissa* (1747-48) and *Sir Charles Grandison* (1753-54) burnished the fame which Richardson's first-born won in Europe as well as in England. By his testimony in letters and in the prefaces to the novels, Richardson hoped that *his* work would be the salvation of his readers. Despite their surface differences, Richardson and James sit side by side in Forster's room because each is "looking at life from much the same angle." Both are aware of suffering and appreciate self-sacrifice. "Each falls short of the tragic, though a close approach is made. A sort of tremulous nobility—that is the spirit that dominates them—and oh how well they write!—not a word out of place in their copious flows." Admittedly, James might be uneasy about his place next to a tradesman, and, Forster confesses, "I hear Richardson equally cautious, wondering whether any writer born outside England can be chaste."[1] Nonetheless, despite the hundred and fifty years that separate them, they sit in harmony—two ardent craftsmen who are born psychologists.

James himself found *Clarissa* "deeply interesting," though his in-

[1] E. M. Forster, *Aspects of the Novel* (New York: Harcourt, Brace & World, Inc., Harvest Books), pp. 14-16.

terest did not lead him to any extensive discussion of Richardson's art. But those critics and novelists who looked upon James as their master helped to prepare the way for renewal of interest in the technique of Richardson. Percy Lubbock illustrated his comments on the dramatic qualities of *The Ambassadors* by drawing a parallel between the presentations of Strether and of Clarissa. Lubbock writes,

> Little as Richardson may suspect it, he . . . is engaged in the attempt to show a mind in action, to give a dramatic display of the commotion within a breast. . . . [Clarissa's] emotion, like Strether's, is caught in passing; like him, she dispenses with the need of a seer, a reflector, some one who will form an impression of her state of mind.[2]

And in *The English Novel*, Ford Madox Ford (for whom James was also a hero) asserts that he has the "profoundest respect" for Richardson, a respect based not only on his "hearty and wholesome . . . sentimentality" but on his concern for craftsmanship. Ford argues that "you might call him an eighteenth-century Henry James and not go so far wrong." In that period, Ford concludes, "he stands alone as a modern novelist and had in England neither appreciable imitators nor rivals until the arrival on the scene of the author of the Barchester Towers series."[3] That Ford also describes Clarissa as a young lady who "permits herself to be seduced by a relatively commonplace Lothario" does not in itself disqualify his praise of Richardson's abilities.

Ford's misrepresentation of the action typifies the difficulties of many critics in remembering, or discerning, what Richardson actually wrote. Wondering at his own prolixity, Richardson exclaimed in 1756, "Nineteen or Twenty Vols. Closely printed! A Man of Business too!—Monstrous!"[4] His multi-volume novels not only daunt most readers in our own day but unmercifully stretch the attention and the memory of critics. A failure to remember all the details of the plots is forgivable, but when Leslie Fiedler says that at the end of *Clarissa* Lovelace is killed by his closest friend,[5] one thinks of Richardson's answer to a female critic, "Pray read, Madam, what you pretend to read."[6]

[2] Percy Lubbock, *The Craft of Fiction* (New York: Viking Press, 1957), pp. 152–53.
[3] F. M. Ford, *The English Novel* (Philadelphia: J. B. Lippincott Co., 1929), pp. 78, 80, 82.
[4] *Selected Letters of Samuel Richardson*, ed. John Carroll (Oxford: Clarendon Press, 1964), p. 329. This volume is hereafter referred to as *Letters*. For purposes of simplification, I have omitted the notations in this edition of verbal changes Richardson made in his letters.
[5] Leslie Fiedler, *Love and Death in the American Novel* (New York: Criterion Books, 1960), p. 30.
[6] *Letters*, p. 271.

## Introduction

As they attempt to deal with his copious flow, many critics feel that they must caution us against believing that Richardson knew what he was doing. Even while Lubbock, the idolator of James, bestows the high honor of comparing Richardson to the "master," there is an important qualification ("Little as Richardson may suspect it . . ."). To take a more recent example, after B. L. Reid nicely dusts off the forgotten virtues of *Pamela*, he still concludes that Richardson is a prime example of *"unconscious* genius." [7] And David Daiches remarks of a passage from *Pamela*, "This, and scenes like this, are admirably done, whatever Richardson thought he was really doing." [8]

Many readers obviously feel that the pen of the mild, benevolent, vain little bourgeois printer must have been, like that of Harriet Byron, "volant," "self-conducted." Or if the pen was guided, according to some modern critics, it must have been controlled by a tumultuous subconscious. We have on the one hand, then, Richardson the *"unconscious* genius" and, on the other, the writer who never misplaces a word in his "copious" flow. Whatever the critics' explanation of Richardson's artistic success may be, the briefest glance at the milieu in which he wrote shows that he had an extraordinary awareness of his audience and of the ways in which he could affect them.

When writing *Pamela*, he read sections of the manuscript to his wife and a young friend. Richardson tested out his work on them, he remarked, as Molière tried the success of his plays on an old maidservant.[9] The writing of *Clarissa* involved consultation with a wider audience; advice was solicited from experienced literary men such as Edward Young and Aaron Hill as well as from young ingenues such as Sophia Westcomb. The circle had grown even larger by the time Richardson began *Sir Charles Grandison,* and, in reading the manuscript aloud, he enjoyed teasing his auditors: "Many things are thrown out in the several Characters," he wrote to a friend,

> on purpose to provoke friendly Debate; and perhaps as Trials of the Readers Judgment, Manners, Taste, Capacity. I have often sat by in Company, and been silently pleased with the Opportunity given me, by different Arguers, of looking into the Hearts of some of them, through Windows that at other times have been close shut up. This is an Advantage that will always be given by familiar Writing, and by Characters drawn from common Life.[10]

There can be little question that the reactions of critics and readers

---
[7] B. L. Reid, "Justice to Pamela," *Hudson Review*, IX (1956–57), 522.
[8] David Daiches, *Literary Essays* (Edinburgh: Oliver and Boyd, 1956), p. 39.
[9] *Letters*, pp. 41–42.
[10] *Ibid.*, pp. 315–16.

outside his circle had notable influences on his work. The attacks on Part I of *Pamela* stimulated Richardson to defend and explain the actions of his heroine in the sequel, and the revisions he made in the third edition of *Clarissa* are partially intended to dispel misinterpretations and adverse criticism that reached his ears after the publication of the first edition.[11] Even more important and less easily defined, however, is the effect that his friends had on each work as it was being written. The private material he included in all three novels shows his consciousness of their presence. His great friend Edward Young is the favorite author of Harriet Byron, and Clarissa finds a copy of "that genteel comedy of Mr. Cibber, The Careless Husband," in the brothel, a subtle nod in the direction of Cibber himself, who followed the composition of the novel in manuscript and urged Richardson to provide a happy ending. Still another amusing example of this awareness of an immediate audience is the little bows he made to his wife in all three novels. Mrs. Richardson believed that Thursday was a lucky day for her; it is surely no mere coincidence then that Pamela argues at length for Thursday as her wedding day because of its luckiness or that Clarissa dies a saintly death on a Thursday and that Harriet Byron marries on a Thursday.[12] More significantly, some of the passages in *Sir Charles Grandison* are clearly aimed at his favorite correspondent, Lady Bradshaigh, as a continuation of their disputes on manners and morals.

Richardson sought advice and commentary partly because of his insatiable hunger for praise, but the variety of responses from his auditors undoubtedly made him aware of the ambiguities in his work. As he wrote to Lady Echlin,

> It is impossible that Readers the most attentive, can always enter into the Views of the Writer of a Piece written, as hoped, to Nature and the Moment. A Species of Writing too, that may be called New; and every one putting him and herself into the Character they read, and judging of it by their own Sensations.[13]

Whether he was particularly sensitive to the responses of his coterie or naturally adept at predicting lines of criticism, Richardson anticipated possible objections by placing them in the novels. Those who denounce Pamela as a designing minx hardly use more vehement language or find a more cynical interpretation for her motives than

---

[11] See M. Kinkead-Weekes, "*Clarissa* Restored?" RES, X (1959), 156–71 and Owen Jenkins, "Richardson's 'Pamela' and Fielding's 'Vile Forgeries,'" *PQ*, XLIV (1965), 200–210.

[12] On Mrs. Richardson's superstition, see *The Posthumous Works of Mrs. Chapone* (London, 1807), I, 170–71.

[13] *Letters*, p. 316.

do Mr. B., Mrs. Jewkes, and Lady Davers in Part I of the novel. Those who believe the immaculate Clarissa is preternaturally aware of sex are anticipated by Lovelace, who says, half despairingly, half ironically, that "Her senses . . . are much livelier than *mine*" and that "she seems sensible of liberties, that my passion made me insensible of having taken." And those who find Sir Charles an impossible prig have an ally, at least briefly, in Harriet Byron, who remarks that if he had been Adam in the Garden of Eden, Sir Charles would regretfully but conscientiously have declined Eve's offer of the apple "and left it to the Almighty, if such had been his pleasure, to have annihilated his first Eve, and given him a second."

Many critics peruse the novels with a humorless obtuseness because they allow the "editor" of these novels to put blinders on them. The truth is that writing in character freed Richardson's imagination; writing as editor confined it by making him vindicate his own creation. It was typical both of the age and of Richardson to relish a good moral, and he writes of his instructive sentiments with the gusto of Lovelace describing the tender beauties of Clarissa. But he has paid a high price for his loving reviews of the moral doctrines in his work. Taine writes of the prefaces and concluding notes,

> Do you know the effect of these edifying advertisements which you stick on at the beginning or end of your books? We are repelled, feel our emotion diminish, see the black-gowned preacher come snuffling out of the worldly dress which he had assumed for an hour. . . . Insinuate morality, but do not inflict it.[14]

Yet as William Lyon Phelps remarked of the prefaces, "However the orator may rave and moralise about the mountain, the mountain itself is objective. The moment Richardson leaves his damnable faces and begins, he is an absolute artist." [15] The "damnable faces" often excite either contempt or wisely ironic smiles in those who criticize Richardson by rewriting *Shamela*. Joseph Wood Krutch's essay on Richardson in *Five Masters* is an outstanding example of an inability to read the novels on their own terms rather than on those of the "editor." Convinced that Richardson is a simple-minded man, Krutch pillories him for moral fatuity.

Samuel Johnson was well aware of Richardson's failings, but he never made the mistake of underestimating the complexity of the novelist's work. When Johnson said that Richardson's heroines have

---

[14] H. A. Taine, *History of English Literature* (London: Chatto & Windus Ltd., 1920), III, 287.

[15] W. L. Phelps, *The Advance of the English Novel* (New York: Dodd, Mead, and Co., 1927), p. 48.

a "kind of obliquity in their moral vision" and observed of Clarissa that "there is always something which she prefers to truth,"[16] the great moralist provided an important clue to the kind of reading the novels demand, a reading that grants Richardson a knowledge of how people bend facts to justify themselves. In the novels (and in many of his private letters), Richardson shows that he is well aware of this "obliquity." Pamela may not want to see the truth about her emotions, but Richardson has her say of Mr. B., "What is the Matter, that, with all his ill Usage of Me, I cannot hate him?" (This is merely one of several hints that Pamela has feelings she dare not recognize fully lest they weaken her resistance.) In 1746, while still working on *Clarissa,* he wrote to Aaron Hill,

> As to Clarissa's being in downright Love, I must acknowlege, that I rather would have it imputed to her, (his too well-known Character consider'd) by her penetrating Friend, (and then a Reader will be ready enough to believe it, the *more* ready, for her not owning it, or being blind to it herself) than to think *her self* that she is.[17]

And the firmest evidence that he was completely aware of the dramatic nature of the epistolary form comes in a letter to Lady Bradshaigh. Defending himself against criticism of a character's pronouncements, he wrote, "It is not fair to say—I, identically, am any-where, while I keep within the character."[18]

The position of the editor is curiously like that of his exemplary letter-writers. All profess complete openness of heart; all proclaim their intentions of maintaining propriety, decorum, truth, and morality in the act of writing. Yet their stated purposes are curiously at odds with what they do and say. In the moment of writing or acting, intentions are refracted into a wider spectrum of behavior and feeling.

When discussing the theory of letter-writing with Miss Westcomb, Richardson praises the letter "because of the deliberation it allows, from the very preparation to, and action of writing," and, in another letter to her, he indicates that the best correspondent is unafraid to have her "Impulses *embody'd*."[19] This interplay between deliberation and impulse gives Richardson's novels their peculiar subtlety and ambiguity. The moment when one of his characters is in the writing closet choosing words that fix and evaluate the flow of thought and

---

[16] *Johnsonian Miscellanies,* ed. G. B. Hill (Oxford, 1897), I, 297.
[17] *Letters,* p. 72.
[18] *Ibid.,* p. 286.
[19] *Ibid.,* pp. 65, 68.

feeling is the heart of the Richardsonian drama. Richardson was well aware of the advantage of writing to the moment, when events and emotions are vivid. But even more important is the instant of writing itself, when deliberation and impulse are in continuous tension. Clarissa's reputation as the "Gloriana" of England, her desire to be an example to her sex, are, in a sense, the prefatory matter to all her letters. Behind the letters of Lovelace is his intention to be the most accomplished rake of his time. Yet the letters also embody the impulses of their hearts. Clarissa develops a conditional "liking" for Lovelace, which is absolutely opposed to her "role." Lovelace, who proudly declares his aversion to any shackles, eventually becomes a monomaniac about possessing one woman. The "intentions" of Richardson always have to be taken into account, but, like those of his characters, they may assume new forms under the pressure of imagination and emotion.

## II

Unlike Richardson's contemporaries, few twentieth-century readers willingly pay the price of a tear for a tender sensation. Nor do they give a warm reception to the black-gowned preacher who occasionally darts from the wings onto the stage. Despite these differences, the critics of the eighteenth and twentieth centuries who admire Richardson are surprisingly close in their appraisals of his technique and in their comments on his understanding of the dark, hidden drives of the human soul. The novels and criticism of James and Ford may stimulate our awareness of the value of Richardson's dramatic form, but this value was also clearly apparent to the novelist himself and to his contemporaries. In a letter published as part of the preface to *Pamela*, Richardson's friend J. B. de Freval commented that the

> Letters being written under the immediate Impression of every Circumstance which occasioned them, and that to those who had a Right to know the fair Writer's most secret Thoughts the several Passions of the Mind must, of course, be more affectingly described, and Nature may be traced in her undisguised Inclinations with much more propriety and Exactness, than can possibly be found in a Detail of Actions long past.[20]

Richardson echoes this comment in his preface to *Clarissa*: "All the Letters are written while the hearts of the writers must be supposed to be wholly engaged in their subjects (The events at the time gen-

---

[20] See *Pamela* (Oxford: Basil Blackwell, Shakespeare Head Press, 1929), I, iii.

erally dubious): So that they abound not only with critical Situations, but with what may be called *instantaneous* Descriptions and Reflections." [21]

Any action obviously differs in its experiential quality for the man who acts and the man who observes that action. Richardson immerses us in the moment-by-moment process of inner experience, while a novelist such as Fielding creates an observer whose voice suggests that he is speaking with objectivity, that he is concerned with establishing the relative significance of deeds and emotions. We are *within* Richardson's main characters as principles, intentions, impulses, half-realized desires engage in a free-for-all that may continue inertia or produce action. The acute self-awareness of all his main characters also means that there is a part of the character observing and judging this brawl, though the objectivity of the judgment is compromised by the role a character has assumed for himself. The epistle, then, is the arena Richardson provides for the interaction of these forces; it is the cockpit of the personality. This preoccupation with the *"instantaneous"* (an interest shared, for example, by Sterne and Boswell) attracted his contemporaries and continues to give these novels an air of modernity.

When Reid quotes James to the effect that "the air of reality (solidity of specification)" is the supreme virtue of the novel and argues that Richardson's work has this air,[22] the twentieth-century critic praises qualities discerned by eighteenth-century readers—and by Richardson himself. After asking for Aaron Hill's advice on how to shorten *Clarissa* (and being obliged by a severely cut opening of the novel), Richardson commented huffily that "all . . . I design'd by it, I doubt cannot be answer'd in so short a Compass without taking from it those simple, tho' diffuse Parts, which some like, and have (however unduly) complimented me upon, as making a new Species of Writing." [23] The same point is tellingly made by Diderot: "Sachez que c'est à cette multitude de petites choses que tient l'illusion; il y a bien de la difficulté à les imaginer: il y en a bien encore à les rendre." [24]

Richardson also impresses Mario Praz, Dorothy Van Ghent, and Leslie Fiedler, among many others, as a man familiar with the underworld of the psyche. But again this view of Richardson was an-

---

[21] *Clarissa* (London, 1751), p. viii.
[22] Reid, p. 519.
[23] *Letters*, pp. 75–76.
[24] ["Know that the whole illusion depends on the multiplicity of small details; it is difficult enough to imagine them—to render them is even harder."] Denis Diderot, "Eloge de Richardson," *Oeuvres Complètes* (Paris, 1875), V, 218.

ticipated by his contemporaries. Diderot remarked of Richardson that he

> porte le flambeau au fond de la caverne; c'est lui qui apprend à discerner les motifs subtils et déshonnêtes qui se cachent et se dérobent sous d'autres motifs qui sont honnêtes et qui se hâtent de se montrer les premiers. Il souffle sur le fantôme sublime qui se présente à l'entrée de la caverne; et le More hideux qu'il masquait s'aperçoit.[25]

Much of the modern criticism of Richardson has been a gloss on this text.

While continental writers such as Diderot, de la Clos, and de Sade were fascinated by the demonic forces in Richardson's novels, his English coterie were attracted to a novelist who touched the passions and yet taught them to move at the command of virtue. This power over readers' emotions continued well into the nineteenth century and is superbly illustrated by an anecdote Thackeray tells of Lord Macaulay:

> I spoke to him once about *Clarissa*—"Not read *Clarissa!*" he cried out: "If you have once thoroughly entered on *Clarissa*, and are infected by it, you can't leave it. When I was in India I passed one hot season at the hills, and there were the governor-general, and the secretary of government, and the Commander-in-Chief, and their wives. I had *Clarissa* with me; and, as soon as they began to read, the whole station was in a passion of excitement about Miss Harlowe and her misfortunes and her scoundrelly Lovelace. The governor's wife seized the book, and the secretary waited for it, and the chief justice could not read it for tears.[26]

This anecdote takes us back to the atmosphere of the 1740's, when Richardson was implored by his readers (as the book appeared in installments) to save Clarissa and, if possible, Lovelace.

Until the end of the eighteenth century, Fielding and Richardson shared honors as the foremost English novelists. But by 1785, in a novel called *The Recontre*, Richardson is already described as an "old fashioned author." [27] In *Fielding the Novelist*, F. T. Blanchard maintains that a precipitous decline in Richardson's eminence was well underway before *Waverly* appeared in 1814.[28] In his introduction to

---

[25] ["(He) carries the torch to the depths of the cave; it is he who teaches us how to discern the subtle, dishonest motives that are hidden and concealed under other motives which are honest and hasten to show themselves first. He breathes on the sublime phantom which presents itself at the entrance of the cave; and the hideous Moor hitherto concealed comes into view."] *Ibid.*, V, 215.

[26] W. M. Thackeray, "Nil Nisi Bonum," *Cornhill Magazine*, I (1860), 133.

[27] Quoted by A. D. McKillop, *Samuel Richardson, Printer and Novelist* (Chapel Hill: University of North Carolina Press, 1936), p. 239.

[28] F. T. Blanchard, *Fielding the Novelist* (New Haven: Yale University Press, 1927), p. 287.

the Ballantyne edition of Richardson's novels, Sir Walter Scott, whose fiction at once contributed to and benefitted from this shift in taste, wrote a generous and sympathetic critique of these works. And, in the same period, with the skill of a poet who was also a great critic, Coleridge caught the essence of Richardson's fiction by referring to its "self-involution and dreamlike continuity." While his reputation was going into partial eclipse, then, Richardson did not lack perceptive readers. Indeed, the critic who says the most about Richardson in the shortest space is William Hazlitt.

Hazlitt fastens on that blend of romance and realism which at once enriches the novels and creates so many difficulties in interpreting them. Those books, he suggests, have "the romantic air of a pure fiction, with the literal minuteness of a common diary." Hazlitt understood that Richardson, while attacking romances, actually used many of their conventions. He also discerned the hyper-awareness of Richardson's characters: "Everything is too conscious in his works. Everything is distinctly brought home to the mind of his actors in the scene, which is a fault undoubtedly: but then it must be confessed, everything is brought home in its full force to the mind of the reader also." Far from seeing Richardson as a clumsy craftsman, Hazlitt acclaims his structural skills. He writes of *Pamela*, "Taking the general idea of the character of a modest and beautiful country girl, and of the ordinary situation in which she is placed, he makes out all the rest . . . by the mere force of a reasoning imagination. It would seem as if a step lost would be as fatal here as in a mathematical demonstration."

In Hazlitt's view, the epistolary form is in some ways a disadvantage because it blunts and deadens actual objects and feelings (a position which is opposed to that of many modern critics). His most telling criticism is that Richardson "confounds his own point of view with that of the immediate actors in the scene; and hence presents you with a conventional and factitious nature, instead of that which is real."[29] This comment is too sweeping, yet the voice of the editor does on occasion drown out those of his actors.

Despite the generally laudatory comments of Scott and Hazlitt (and later of such writers as Ruskin and Macaulay), Richardson's readership diminished rapidly in the nineteenth century. When Leslie Stephen wrote a preface to a collected edition of Richardson's novels in 1883 (the first collected edition since 1824), he referred to them as slumbering works. Critical biographies of Richardson by Clara Thomson (1900) and Austin Dobson (1902) used unpublished letters in the Forster Collection of the Victoria and Albert Museum to give new

---

[29] William Hazlitt, *English Comic Writers* (London: J. M. Dent & Sons Ltd., Everyman's Library, 1910), pp. 117–20.

# Introduction

information on the writing and reception of the novels, but neither made startling advances in the evaluation or interpretation of Richardson's art and themes. Like the praise of many critics, Mrs. Thomson's laudatory comments on Richardson often contain a note of irritation, as though praise were elicited as a tax rather than as a voluntary tribute.

Richardson's admirers among novelists in the twentieth century have included Gertrude Stein, Andre Gide, and Theodore Dreiser, as well as Forster and Ford.[30] (Whatever his virtues and faults, Richardson has always appealed to a range of readers who differ widely in their tastes and interests; William Blake, for example, declared that Richardson "won his heart." [31]) We know of the admiration of these novelists mainly through passing comments rather than through extended commentary. There is little evidence that Richardson has had a profound influence on the technique of the modern novel, although John Malcolm Brinnin suggests that Richardson may have instructed Gertrude Stein in the use of the "continuous present." [32] Upton Sinclair wrote an amusing modernization of *Pamela* (in *Another Pamela*) with a California setting. And Kingsley Amis's *Take a Girl Like You* undoubtedly owes a debt to *Clarissa*. Interest in Richardson during the twentieth century has not, then, been restricted to academic critics, but, unquestionably, they have been more active than his fellow novelists in revaluating and reviving his work.

The most important studies of Richardson in recent years have been those of A. D. McKillop, W. M. Sale, and Ian Watt. McKillop prefaced his book on Richardson with the comment that "the work of Samuel Richardson needs not so much rehabilitation or ardent defense as candid reexamination." McKillop's work made this kind of reexamination possible. In providing a highly detailed history and analysis of the origins, publication, and reception of Richardson's novels, McKillop displayed the writer at work, provided details in the portrait that enabled us to see Richardson ruling his province in fiction rather than being ruled by a creative genius he did not fully understand. W. M. Sale's *Samuel Richardson: A Bibliographical Record* traced the stages of the novels in manuscript and print, thus providing another invaluable aid to the critic. Finally, Ian Watt's mastery of the social background as well as of the aesthetics of the novel not only

---

[30] Gide kept a running record of his reading of *Clarissa* in his *Journal, 1889–1939* (Paris: Librairie Gallimard, 1948), and Dreiser defends the length of Richardson's work in "The Scope of Fiction," *New Republic*, XXX (1922), 9.

[31] See Geoffrey Keynes, *A Bibliography of William Blake* (New York: The Grolier Club of New York), p. 64.

[32] John Malcolm Brinnin, *The Third Rose* (Boston: Little, Brown and Company, 1959), p. 61.

helped to restore a just perspective on Richardson's work but provided fresh insight into his characters and methods.

### III

In recent criticism of Richardson there have been three main areas of interest: Richardson as craftsman, as psychological novelist (carrying the torch to the back of the cave), and as commentator on the social and economic forces of his day. Among the most rewarding of these studies has been McKillop's essay on Richardson's use of the epistolary form.[33] As McKillop shows, the letter plays vital and diverse roles in the action of the novels, and, in terms of point of view, it is used for a variety of effects in each work. The essay is a valuable reminder that one cannot speak of Richardson's epistolary technique in a way that applies to all of the novels. The point of view in Part I of *Pamela* is largely restricted to the heroine's letters. This restriction increases suspense and contributes to the intensity of the portrayal; yet, as M. Kinkead-Weekes observes, it keeps us from seeing Mr. B. as anything but a black-hearted and rather bumbling villain.[34] The single focus thus undermines our belief in his conversion.

Richardson, however, compensates for these weaknesses in his apprentice work by skilfully using the letters to remind us that Pamela is an artist who shapes her material as she writes and that she is, moreover, a character at once creating and living her role. Mr. B. acknowledges this aspect of her imagination when he explains why he wants to see Pamela's journal: "There is such a pretty Air of Romance, as you relate them, in *your* Plots, and *my* Plots, that I shall be better directed in what manner to wind up the Catastrophe of the pretty Novel." Finally, Richardson uses the letters and the journal as efficient parts of the action, for it is the reading of Pamela's "pretty Novel" that brings about Mr. B.'s conversion. He at last sees her as we have seen her all through the action.

The conditions of the correspondence in *Pamela* and *Clarissa* (requiring elaborate devices for sending and concealing letters) emphasize the solitary battle waged by the heroines, but in *Sir Charles Grandison*, where we have a competition of virtue among the characters, there is, in McKillop's words, "an enormous expansion of social correspondence carried on without obstruction or threat, and usually intended to be shown about to a circle of friends." Here the shared read-

---

[33] See this volume, pp. 139–51.
[34] *Ibid.*, pp. 20–27.

ing of letters becomes symbolic of a community where little is concealed because there is harmony of understanding and feeling.

McKillop's essay illustrates the wide range of uses Richardson commanded for the epistolary form. In one of his last articles, George Sherburn also displayed how the epistles at once permitted and encouraged Richardson to use his strong visual sense.[35] Yet the handling of the epistolary form has by no means been completely explored. In *Clarissa,* for example, Richardson often links the letters by the use of repeated words or phrases. Thus, in the first volume, Clarissa discusses at length the pride of Lovelace, and, in his first letter, which immediately follows, he begins by calling *Clarissa* herself a "proud beauty" and then goes on to explain the role which his own pride plays in enflaming his desire for revenge. These repetitions show the central characters involved with the same conjectures at the same moments, show how closely they are gauging each other's actions and characters. Repetitions of this kind are frequent in the novel and often contribute to the dramatic irony, especially when they show Clarissa tragically unaware of the full complexity of Lovelace's character.

A complete understanding of the epistolary technique can come only through a careful analysis of style. A. M. Kearney's article on *Pamela* and William Farrell's on *Clarissa*[36] both demonstrate the value of analyzing the tone and diction of the voices assumed by the characters. The approach of Kearney is reminiscent of Hazlitt's statement that Richardson's point of view is confounded with that of the actors. "In reality," Kearney remarks, "we have two attitudes toward experience in the novel: Pamela's, and Richardson's own authorial one which he expresses through her." In Kearney's view the spontaneous voice in the novel is that of the heroine, the deliberate voice that of an observer rather than a participant in the action. Kearney's argument is persuasive and indicates why the character of Pamela has received such various interpretations.

In *Clarissa,* as Farrell points out, the varying styles of the characters are used to create a complex relationship between expression and action. Lovelace occasionally indulges in hyperbolical praises and conventional metaphors—in the tradition of romantic rhetoric scorned by Richardson and his heroines—but he moves away from this style in his early correspondence with Clarissa. Lovelace is aware of her belief that courtly rhetoric comes from a designing heart. Clarissa herself is occasionally given the rhetoric of the contemporary stage, a style that Richardson reserves for the most serious and pathetic scenes. Clarissa's

[35] *Ibid.,* pp. 152–60.
[36] *Ibid.,* pp. 28–38 and pp. 92–101.

grand style appears when she is most exalted, Lovelace's when he crows in triumph or is at a point of desperation. Style becomes, therefore, a means of dramatically noting shifts in attitude and situation.

The essay on *Pamela* by Kinkead-Weekes is particularly valuable in reminding us of the structural skill evident in Richardson's apprentice work. As Kinkead-Weekes comments, "However artless Richardson may look, his scenes are carefully related, often in cycles each of which reorchestrates its predecessor." Indeed, Richardson's care in blueprinting his works has been one of his most neglected qualities. Quoting Thomas Hardy's statement that "no person who has a due perception of the constructive art shown in Greek tragic drama can be blind to the constructive art of Richardson," Frederick W. Hilles shows how the division by volumes lays bare this careful design.[37]

As Hilles points out, the plot suggests a cycle, symbolized by the device on the heroine's coffin of a serpent with its tail in its mouth. To extend Hilles's argument is to see how astonishingly coordinated the incidents are. The basic movement takes the heroine from her earthly father, exalts her after the moment of her greatest degradation, and then returns her to her true Father—to the realm which places the proper value on the integrity Clarissa has maintained. The motif of departure and return establishes a pattern by which situations and relationships in the second half of the book provide reversals of those in the first half. The plot in its first direction, the downward course of Clarissa, ends with the triumph of Lovelace in recapturing and raping her. After that central episode, the hinge on which the novel turns, Clarissa's ascendance begins when she baffles another attempt to rape her and stuns Lovelace and his cohorts into silence by the vehement defense of her virtue. As Clarissa moves toward her triumphant death, incidents and themes continue to counterpoint those in the first half. Instead of being imprisoned in a brothel, she finds a haven with the Smiths. And as her refusal to marry Solmes conditioned the events of the opening sections, so the last part has as a central theme her refusal to marry Lovelace.

Another parallel is made explicit when Clarissa gives as the date of her death the day she left the family: April 10. The will of her grandfather had led to the possibility of economic freedom for Clarissa and had threatened the ambitions of the Harlowes; the heroine's will imprisons the family in guilt and sorrow for the persecutions arising from avarice. Finally, the pattern is completed when Lovelace, who had wounded James Harlowe in a duel, is killed by Colonel Morden. The reversals in the second part, unobtrusively present, satisfyingly suggest

[37] *Ibid.*, pp. 80–91.

Clarissa's eventual triumph over the world that tried to bend her to its will.

The real weaknesses of Richardson's construction have also yet to be fully explored. Many of these weaknesses arise from the shifts and dodges forced on him by the situations he chooses for each novel. His imagination worked only with heroines who are physically or spiritually imprisoned, kept in a state of continuous siege. He contrives endlessly to keep them there. It is true that the plot manipulations are often absorbed almost completely into the psychological portraits; Pamela's fears and her partially conscious liking for Mr. B., which keep her initially in her master's house, actually enrich the characterization. But when Anna Howe is barred from visiting Clarissa in her last days (for Clarissa must die without the comfort of her family or dearest friend), the manipulation of events becomes distracting. Harriet must also be kept in suspenseful agony over hundreds of pages—thus the necessity for the vacillating Clementina in the background.

Most fully discussed in recent years have been the sexual emotions and impulses that become apparent during these sieges. In the nightmare worlds where the heroines are under intense pressure, there are pre-Freudian revelations of hidden and perverse motives, revelations that assume the form of a sexual mythology. When critics begin referring to Richardson's mythopoeic power and to his insight into the mysteries of the human psyche, it is evident that the audience is being alerted to an author who speaks more intimately to a modern reader than does any other eighteenth-century English novelist.

Mario Praz was one of the first critics in the twentieth century to draw attention to the sexual themes in Richardson's novels. His discussion of Clarissa in *The Romantic Agony* as an archetypal suffering virgin, as the key figure in a drama of sadism and masochism that has haunted western literature, undoubtedly made many critics take a long second glance at Richardson. In the few pages he devotes to *Clarissa*, Praz lays bare the demonic element in Richardson's imagination, that awareness of evil which, as one becomes more familiar with the novels, removes them further and further from the sentimental tradition. Leslie Fiedler, in *Love and Death in the American Novel*, presents Richardson as the wellspring of the whole tradition of the bourgeois love tragedy in the English and American novel. Although Fiedler's chapters on Richardson are marred by egregious errors, they have probably brought *Clarissa* to the attention of a great many readers who knew the novelist only as the naïve celebrator of the rewards of virtue.

In one of the most stimulating modern essays on *Clarissa*, Mrs. Dorothy Van Ghent suggests that the heroine typifies a female debility that invites sadistic attack.[38] A broken-stalked lily is indeed one of the emblems for Clarissa in the novel, but it must be remembered that a far different woman first inspires Lovelace's passion. Here is how he describes her: "Such a constant glow upon her lovely features: Eyes so sparkling: Limbs so divinely turned: Health so florid: Youth so blooming: Air so animated—To have a heart so impenetrable." Mrs. Van Ghent, however, concentrates her vision on Clarissa as she appears under attack from Lovelace. The pale, fragile heroine who emerges from this part of the novel is, in Mrs. Van Ghent's interpretation, the product of the myths of Puritan religion, of social caste, and of bourgeois family life and its sanctions. One radical flaw in this essay is its tendency to discount the enormous energy, amounting to fanaticism, that makes Pamela and Clarissa supreme individualists, women whose instincts tell them they must not be used, must not be relegated to the status of objects. Ian Watt has most perceptively delineated this individualism in his chapters on *Clarissa* in *The Rise of the Novel*. And it is also Watt who shows how the conventions of Clarissa and Lovelace— the one of the decorous young lady, the other of the unfettered rake— serve to distort their visions of themselves and each other.

In "Richardson and the Bold Young Men," the opening chapter of *Richardson's Characters,* Morris Golden argues that the novels are records of conflicts of wills and that this aspect of his fiction "derives from Richardson's own nature."[39] Golden believes that the sadism of Mr. B. and Lovelace is a heightened version of Richardson's own tendencies. The heroes of these novels are, in Golden's terms, projections of Richardson's "dominance fantasies." Characters who exhibit sadistic tendencies also seem to be masochistic at times, bending to the glory of those they try to dominate.

There are recurring elements in Richardson—abduction, rapes or attempted rapes, totalitarian impulses by families or individuals, a willingness to abase the self before a stronger ego or a better person— that can be cast in terms of "masochism" and "sadism." But it is also worth saying that those relationships, or those fantasies of dominance and submission, reflect not merely the author's psychological tendencies but a view of man as constantly under seige from the evil in his being as well as from external evil. In *Clarissa,* the heroine sees one half of the world torturing the other half and being tortured in torturing. Whether in her father's house or in the brothel, Clarissa is in a kind of hell, surrounded by tormentors. And her own "secret Pride" and "busy prescience" have helped to put her there. Pamela is besieged by lust and the threat of violence—and fears to recognize the impulses

[38] *Ibid.,* pp. 49–66.
[39] *Ibid.,* pp. 161–80.

## Introduction

that come from her heart. Even in *Sir Charles Grandison,* a fictional world where virtue generally prevails, the hero says, "Men and Women are Devils to one another. They need no other tempter." Because of the sensationalism of the plots, it has been overlooked by most critics that in many ways the primary virtue in Richardson's novels is not chastity but charity. Benevolence is not an indulgence of the emotions but a necessary weapon against the darkness with which we are beset.

In the work of Mrs. Van Ghent and of Watt, social conventions are rightly seen as sources of psychological tension. W. M. Sale and Christopher Hill have examined the first two novels from a perspective emphasizing the social pressures on Richardson's characters. Sale's essay "From *Pamela* to *Clarissa*" has been particularly influential in its assessment of Richardson's attitudes toward society.[40] He writes that Richardson's "taste for aristocracy, like that of his heroines, is an index of his need to make common cause with a superior social class." But, as Sale remarks, Richardson learned between the writing of *Pamela* and of *Clarissa* that this taste "did not mean a complete absorption within its world was possible, however desirable in some respects such an absorption might seem." In many ways, Lovelace is attractive to Clarissa because of his freedom from the counting-house mentality of her parents. Yet, as Sale acutely observes, what Clarissa ultimately wants is a "chance to live life more completely in conformity with an ideal of conduct." Both her family and Lovelace (in their different forms of egoism) would deny her this chance. This trait aligns Richardson's heroines with those of Henry James and George Meredith.

Christopher Hill's article "Clarissa Harlowe and Her Times"[41] also illuminates the Richardsonian conflict between society and the unique individual. Hill argues that the true subject of the novel is "the effect on individuals of property marriage." Both Clarissa and Lovelace, in their various ways, struggle against the degradations of such marriages and the values behind them. One of the prime contributions of this article is to put *Clarissa* into the context of eighteenth-century politics and economics.[42] Through Hill's commentary we see that Lovelace is not only a rebel against conventional morals but a radical in his political views. Stimulating as it is, Hill's article, like so many others on Richardson, highlights some parts of the novel at the expense of others. His main argument works beautifully with the

---

[40] *Ibid.,* pp. 39–48.
[41] *Ibid.,* pp. 102–23.
[42] Hill believes that a title Richardson once contemplated for the novel—*The Lady's Legacy*—was intended to give added emphasis to the economic aspect of the novel. In fact, the "legacy" Richardson had in mind was Clarissa's letters. See *Letters,* p. 77.

two opening volumes but does not take fully into account the complexities of the later warfare—that between Clarissa and Lovelace in which the two individualists carry on the war between the sexes as well as class conflict.

Whether viewed from the perspective of psychology or of social history, the first two novels use imprisonment as a device which shows a person of vitality and integrity caught in a hostile world. The last novel is another study of the "divided mind," but in this case the hero is imprisoned only by virtues. Either Harriet or Clementina would make Sir Charles an excellent wife. Moreover, by his position in society he is free to exercise the benevolence that Pamela could practice only after her marriage and that Clarissa, in her last days, could exercise only spiritually.

*Sir Charles Grandison* has received little attention from modern critics. It does not lend itself to discussions of myth and symbols, but in this last novel Richardson shows an easy mastery of his craft that is well worth exploring. The flaw in the novel is, of course, the unflawed hero, who is so unfailingly reasonable and charitable, so secure in his own virtue, that he never really has to struggle with the world. He does not even have to make a decision between Harriet and Clementina; the Italian heroine returns him to Harriet because his very goodness would be a threat to Clementina's religion. Richardson continues to be haunted by certain situations: Sir Hargrave abducts Harriet, and, like the Harlowes, Clementina's family places her under extreme pressure. But in this novel Sir Charles is at hand to rescue Harriet almost immediately, and he is such a nonpareil that he can even be accepted as a potential husband for Clementina by the haughty Italian family. Difficulties nonetheless remain, principally caused by the love Grandison inspires. Again and again, as McKillop points out, the characters return to the question of how passion can be harmonized "with rational esteem and moral approval," how one can reconcile the rule to be open and truthful about emotions with the law that the lady must never display them before the man has confessed his love.[43]

Much as they may discuss the nature of love and propriety, the characters feel themselves to be within a settled system of values, and, in McKillop's view, this security encourages a lightness of touch in the narrative. A particularly significant character is Charlotte Grandison, who offers a running ironic commentary on all the young "lovyers." It is she who maintains that "love matches . . . are foolish things," who compares Sir Charles in his situation with an ass confronted by two equally appetizing bales of hay, who speaks in her free way of sexual

---

[43] P. 131 in this volume.

matters and thus reminds the other characters that they are not free of the flesh. And it is she who notes that the eternal friendship forged between Harriet and Clementina is a form of self-admiration, since each sees her own virtues in the other.

## IV

Despite the increasing number of articles and books on Richardson in the past several years, he is still in need of "candid reexamination." The air of moral earnestness in the novels has obscured Richardson's comedy for many readers. Sir Hargrave's proposal to Harriet is as absurd as Mr. Collins's proposal to Elizabeth Bennett. Pamela preens before the mirror after she dons her homecoming clothes (which are supposed to be more appropriate to her lowly status), and then she says, "To say truth, I never liked myself so well in my life. O the pleasure of descending with ease, innocence and resignation!—Indeed, there is nothing like it! . . . So I went down to look for Mrs. Jarvis to see how she liked me." The delight in her prettiness and the resultant feelings of superiority which she ascribes to "innocence and resignation" are also in a vein worthy of Jane Austen. The comedy in *Clarissa* is often heavy-handed—I refer particularly to Anna's treatment of Hickman—but the malign gaiety of Lovelace moves at a higher comic level.

Other aspects of Richardson's work that require further comment and elucidation are his use of "rhythm" (in Forster's sense of the term), his stylistic subtleties, his inclusion of critics within the novels of the characters and situations, his use of quotations and literary allusions, and his technique of brushing in minute details to create unity. Finally, good editions of all three novels are required.

The essays in this volume have been chosen for their quality and also for the ways in which they represent dominant themes in Richardsonian criticism. They are heartening signs that Richardson is receiving an interested hearing from excellent critics and that his greatest characters—Pamela, Clarissa, and Lovelace—live as fully and splendidly in the twentieth century as when Richardson first conceived them. Only *Sir Charles Grandison* could now be described as a slumbering work. For *Pamela* and *Clarissa*, however, the twentieth century has been a time of reawakening. They excite the kind of close, sympathetic reading that would have pleased Richardson even in his moments of most outrageous vanity.

# Pamela

## by M. Kinkead-Weekes

In 1740, at the age of fifty-one, Richardson was merely a prosperous printer whose few editorial performances only proved him an intelligent man of his trade with an eye to a new venture. Fourteen years later he reached the peak of his profession as Master of the Stationers' Company; but he had also written three novels which were to earn him a readership and literary influence spread across Europe. He had become arguably the greatest English novelist of his century, and certainly the inventor of a whole new way of writing—one of the most fruitful "kinds" of the novel.

The transformation began when two booksellers asked him to compile a letter-writer—a collection of letters which could both be entertaining and serve as models in all sorts of situations. The task was still humble; yet in several of the situations there was a new challenge to his dramatic imagination, his ability to put himself into the minds and the language of very different kinds of people. He also discovered how subtly the letter form can reveal character. In one situation, moreover, the correspondence of a father and a daughter whose master has tried to seduce her, there were dramatic and moralistic possibilities too fascinating to be confined to the letter-writer. So he laid it aside, and in only two months of intense creativity amongst all his everyday business he finished *Pamela: or Virtue Rewarded,* and published it anonymously. The story of the virtuous servant who resists her wicked master and is rewarded by his reformation and his hand may be based on fact, as Richardson himself claimed; but the novel which embodies it in a collection of letters and a journal was a brilliantly original invention.

It became one of the century's best sellers, going through five editions in its first year and being rapidly translated into most European languages. Fashionable ladies displayed copies in public places, and held

---

*"Pamela"* (Editor's title). Introduction to Everyman's Library edition of *Pamela* by M. Kinkead-Weekes (London: J. M. Dent & Sons Ltd.; New York: E. P. Dutton & Co., 1962), pp. v–xiii. Copyright © 1962 by J. M. Dent & Sons Ltd. Reprinted by permission of J. M. Dent & Sons Ltd. and E. P. Dutton & Co., Inc.

fans painted with pictures of its best-loved scenes. *Pamela* became a play, an opera, even a waxwork; and in a society suspicious of fiction had the distinction of a recommendation from a London pulpit. Yet the triumph was not unmixed. Even at its height harsher voices objected to the book's moral tendencies, and denounced its heroine as a sly minx far less innocent than she appears. Outstanding among these was Henry Fielding, first in the outrageously amusing and malicious parody *An Apology for the Life of Mrs Shamela Andrews,* and then in his novel *Joseph Andrews.* By mid-century opinion was sharply divided all over Europe. A Danish writer speaks of "two different parties, Pamelists and Antipamelists. . . . Some look on this young Virgin as an example for ladies to follow. . . . Others, on the contrary, discover in it the behaviour of an hypocritical, crafty girl . . . who understands the Art of bringing a man to her lure."

In our own time the Antipamelists seem to have won the day, *Shamela* is vindicated, and there is widespread agreement that Pamela's conduct is hypocritical, whether consciously so or not. Indeed, critics are less concerned to proclaim this now than to point to the psychological realism of Richardson's creation, and to seek the source of both this and the moral confusion in his unquestioning identification with his heroine. By tapping her author's unconscious, on this view, *Pamela* reveals to us not only Richardson's confusions, but a typical and significant ambivalence in the whole Puritan ethos. As Steele pointed out, prude and coquette are alike in that they have "the distinction of sex in all their thoughts, words and actions"—this is why Pamela can seem to be either. The more indeed the moralist and his heroine proclaim their rejection of sexuality, the more they can be seen to be obsessed by it. We may also recall Mrs Peachum's observation that "by keeping men off, you keep them on."

Yet only four years later Richardson completed *Clarissa,* about whose power and moral stature there is no less widespread agreement; and while there is much evidence of technical development, the moral and spiritual concerns of the two novels are remarkably similar. There is certainly no evidence of re-thinking deep enough to account for the radical discrepancy the critics discover between them. Disturbing, too, is the assumption that Richardson was an unconscious artist with little idea what he was doing, when it is coupled with a failure to examine the implications and complications of the new form he invented. For although Richardson wrote no formal essay on his art, he did scatter through his published and unpublished letters a large number of statements which show a surprisingly acute understanding of his problems.

What he invented was the dramatic novel, not merely the idea of writing in letters. The epistolary form is a means, not an end. It is an attempt to gain something of the immediacy of a playgoer's experience; of getting to know characters directly, not through a narrative filter, and of watching an action unfold now, while one looks and listens. Richardson called his invention "writing to the moment." As often as he could he made his characters write during the crises of their affairs. Where this was impossible they write immediately afterwards; either in letters largely composed of dialogue and description of action and gesture, to convey the effect of watching a dramatic scene; or in letters of immediate self-analysis like extensions of dramatic soliloquy. Because these are written "to the moment" and not collectedly later, consciousness can be caught on the wing, and one can discover things about the characters that they do not yet know themselves.

Drama, moreover, is not merely a technique of writing. It is a kind of imaginative vision that is quite different from other kinds. In narrative the author tells you directly in his own words what he has conceived. In drama he has to see and communicate indirectly, by projecting his imagination into characters who reveal themselves without his mediation. The author himself is not there at all—he has become all his characters. Some are obviously closer to him than others, but we can only establish his own views when we understand the whole meaning that results from the conflicts he has created. The moment we identify him with one character, we begin to blind ourselves to that meaning.

Since we are given no direct guidance, it is more than ever important that we become alive to the full implications of the conflicts; that we enter the "points of view" of all the characters; and that we build up a much fuller understanding than any of them possesses. Indirect forms are much more difficult than direct ones, and demand closer, more subtle and sensitive reading. This is particularly so with Richardson because his moral world is one in which the minutiae of speech, dress and behaviour may be important revelations of the state of the heart and mind that prompts them. We have also to be sensitive to the implications of different styles, for "styles differ, too, as much as faces, and are indicative, generally beyond the power of disguise, of the mind of the writer."

We should also be very wary of treating dramatic characters as though they were real people. It is ironic that the more successful a dramatist is in putting one directly inside the minds of his characters the greater becomes the danger of distortion through analysing them as one would an acquaintance. For we tend to forget how crucially our knowledge is limited by and dependent on the method and form of the work of art. It may be unjustified to see incurable vanity in Pamela's continual repetition of the praise she receives; or evidence that her delicacy about sex is hypocritical when she details the attempts made on her, or passes on dubious jokes; or morbid introspection in her prolonged and brooding self-analysis. For these are all *formal* matters. There are several dramatic points of view, but only one of them "writes" the novel; so Pamela has to tell us all there is to tell and carry the whole burden of analysis. We on the other hand ought to distinguish what is genuinely self-revelatory from what is narrative or analytic, and know when psychological inferences are appropriate and when they are not. We may point to the formal crudity which creates such difficulties, but this is quite a different criticism. (It is here that Richardson's great formal development, the multiplication of foci in *Clarissa,* itself removes many of what had appeared to be moral objections to *Pamela.*) Again, our knowledge of characters must be controlled by the development of a novel's formal patterning, the artful relationship between its scenes. However artless Richardson may look, his scenes are carefully related, often in cycles each of which re-orchestrates its predecessor. So the gift of clothes on which the novel opens is related to the important "clothes scene" of Letter XXIV. This in turn is parodied by B. in Letter XXVII, redeveloped in the "bundle scene" of Letter XXIX, given a new symbolic twist in Pamela's garments floating on the pond, another reorchestration on page 270, and a final pointing on page 449.[1] Examples could be multiplied, but in all the psychological speculation about Pamela and her creator the meaning of this patterning has played no part.

Most important of all, the fact that the dramatic "kind" is the most exploratory type of novel has not been understood. As well as formal crudities there are several crudities of attitude and value in *Pamela.* Yet what is really significant is not that these exist, but that in so many cases Richardson is able, in developing his novel, to feel his way towards far deeper and finer values which he carried over and extended in *Clarissa.* While we identify him with his heroine, and pay no attention to the structural and textual development of his work, we shall fail to see that its significance and its achievement lie precisely in its *criticism* of the mental and moral world of the little girl of fifteen we meet at the beginning, even if—as may be the case—that world was Richardson's when he began to write. For a dramatic writer not only has to become several very different points of view; he also is forced to imagine how these look to one another, and has to try to resolve the conflicts that arise. Whatever values he may have held are likely to go through what Blake called the fire of thesis and antithesis; they are tested, realized, criticized—and they change.

[1] [Page references are to Everyman's Library edition.]

The novel's first movement, up to the abduction of Pamela, is concerned with the day-to-day fluctuations of her struggle with her master. In this first conflict Richardson obviously uses her values to expose the implications of B.'s amoral world of pride and power; but in the process he discovers dangerous weaknesses in Pamela too. Hypocrisy is not one of them. Richardson saw the possibility of such a charge perfectly clearly—it is actually made by B. in Letter XXIV. But to Richardson this could only spring from a failure to understand how diametrically opposed to the world of the sex war with its laws of attraction and seduction the behaviour of Pamela is, as soon as one grasps what her new clothes symbolize. In that letter B.'s moral sensibility begins to be awakened. We have to be alive to the implications of what B. says and does to realize what is happening, but when we do the charge of hypocrisy is effectively refuted. What Richardson does discover about his heroine are the dangers that lie in her innate suspiciousness, which blinds her to the complex realities of other people; in her calculating prudence; and in her vanity and her inability to achieve real humility, social, moral or spiritual.

In the second movement Pamela is imprisoned. This is a period of "persecutions, oppressions and distress," but it is also a period of spiritual growth. It lasts, pointedly, for forty days and forty nights, and the presence of biblical language in the prayer which opens it, and in the scene by the pond at its heart, should indicate that the new conflict within Pamela herself has a religious dimension. Her greatest temptation in the wilderness has indeed nothing to do with B. Behind all her faults there lies a stubborn pride and self-reliance, and to be like this, for Richardson, is to court despair when one's human fallibility is inevitably exposed. Pamela's battles against despair, her struggles to regain true faith not only in God but in Man, lie at the very centre of the novel's meaning. At the first scene by the pond she discovers in her temptation to suicide the core of a new self-knowledge and humility. "And how do I know, but that God, who sees all the lurking vileness of my heart, may have permitted these sufferings on that very score, and to make me rely solely on his grace and assistance, who, perhaps, have too much prided myself in a vain dependence on my own foolish contrivances." In the carefully related second pond scene she adds faith in Man to faith in God, even though this means acting imprudently. For the first time she and her persecutor really meet and communicate as human beings.

Pamela's suspicion and timidity are not overcome in a day, but her happiness will depend on her ability to continue in her new-won faith. At first she fails disastrously. Her fear of a mock marriage makes her reject a genuine proposal from B., and at last she is given what she has constantly begged for, and is angrily dismissed to her parents. Now, however, she discovers (what the competent reader should have known from innumerable hints long before) the depth of her feeling for her persecutor. When he begs her to return, against all the dictates of pride and prudence, she does so in love and faith and makes her happiness and his regeneration possible.

Apart from the angry scenes with Lady Davers and the discovery of B.'s illegitimate daughter, the drama ends here. The rest of the novel consists mainly of social visiting, in which the happy pair discuss their history in public while Pamela is deluged with choric praise and blessing; and of long discussions of the duties and proper behaviour of man and wife—or, rather, largely of wife. This spinning out of the novel is further evidence that Richardson was not primarily interested in pursuit and capture, but one can see why readers find it tedious. Yet it was important, for Richardson, to demonstrate the consistency and integrity of Pamela's behaviour before and after her marriage; and also to enforce the validity of her values over a wider field than her struggles with B. could provide. The novel becomes a "Whole Duty of Women," a fictional counterpart to the *Whole Duty of Man* which Pamela sends to Farmer Jones. Her humility and obedience, her piety, her capacity for love, forgiveness and gratitude, her charities, and the regulation of her married life all throw out the challenge of an old-fashioned morality to a frivolous and lax society. The scenes of choric praise enact Richardson's hopes for the educative power of his story. They also prefigure the idea of moral community which is central to *Sir Charles Grandison*. The living example and the public discussion of virtue awaken the latent good nature and moral sensibility of all who meet them. All are "improved," and in joining the concord of praise all find their true selves, and the true sense of fellowship binding them to their neighbours.

It remains unfortunately true that it is not merely the overt didacticism of all this that prevents Richardson's readers from making the same response. For the novel, although it is not a case-study of hypocrisy, still fails in several important ways.

The most central of these concerns not Pamela but B. Once one has learned to read with the sensitivity to implications that Richardson demands, it becomes clear that after markedly crude beginnings B. does become a complex character in the grip of acute conflict. But if Pamela and B. are both on the stage, and we are required to understand and judge them both in their opposition, the fact remains that we live always in her mind and never in his because the novel is told from a single point of view. Not only is it fatally easy to miss the exact fluctuations of B.'s conflict through superficial reading, but we inhabit so continuously a mind in which he appears simply as a "black-hearted wretch" that we tend to oversimplify him too. (It is always a danger in point-of-view writing that we are tempted to adopt the viewpoint of one character instead of holding them all against our own greater knowledge.) At important points we need the same direct experience of B.'s heart and mind that we have of Pamela's; but the single focus cannot provide this. The result is disastrous when we come to B.'s reformation. If we are reading carefully enough we should understand perfectly clearly why and how it happens, but we cannot *experience* it. It is not proved on our pulses, it cannot have the imaginative reality of Pamela's transformation. If we do not grasp the technical origin of this, or are reading carelessly anyway, our response is likely to register itself in doubts of the quality of Pamela's forgiveness, her return, her gratitude and meekness, which ought never to have arisen. Critics who believe that it is not the man she objected to all along, but his terms, ought to be discussing not Pamela but B., and not B. as Richardson intended him, but his realization. Yet, however technical, this is a serious failure that affects one's whole response to the novel.

There are also flaws which are the result of crude moral vision, and most have to do with Richardson's attitude to sex. He is frequently accused of prurience. Any honest reader knows, however, that the sexual scenes are anything but inflammatory. Yet there is something strange about them, and this is that they are not *about* sex at all. They are intensifications of a study of pride, theatrical attempts of the male to subjugate, and they result in humiliation. They remain unsatisfactory, not because Richardson gives too much treatment to sex, but too little; because he treats it too narrowly in its brutally egotistic and violating aspects, and sees too little of its full human potential and significance. There are, however, once again interesting signs in Pamela's reactions to her wedding night, and in her attitude towards Sally Godfrey and her child, of the dawnings of more liberal attitudes.

Again, in putting virtue on trial in a sexual arena, Richardson has a tendency to confuse virtue with physical virginity. Towards the end Pamela becomes clear that her integrity would be untouched by violation, but earlier Richardson had allowed her to speak of the attempts at rape as though these had been her worst trials. This could only be true physically and emotionally; the hardest tests of her whole being come in the scenes where her own unacknowledged love and B.'s gentleness combine to trouble her. In these scenes Richardson's vision is clean and sure; but his tendency to give undifferentiated praise to her "resistance" too often leaves the assumption open that he places as much emphasis on resistance to force and finance as on the far deeper values which first send Pamela into the wilderness, and then bring her back to her master in love and faith. There is a similar crudity, less of the imaginative creation than of the author's attitude towards it, in the concept of virtue rewarded which gives *Pamela* its subtitle. Though calculating prudence is one of Pamela's faults, perhaps the greatest achievement of the novel is the way in which the fault is transcended. Yet in this subtitle and the moral summary he appended, Richardson does fall back into crudity, and appears to argue as though the reasons for being virtuous had something to do with the calculation of rewards. Pamela is not a hypocritical politician, but she could legitimately blame her creator if readers are tempted to foist upon her the idea that virginity is the best policy.

Indeed Richardson's value is vitally dependent on his dramatic imagination. The significance of *Pamela* is precisely the way in which he was able to feel his way imaginatively towards deeper and finer attitudes. Flaws remain, but they are less important than the growth. Yet the sequel to the novel shows again how fatally easy it was for him to relapse as soon as his dramatic imagination no longer predominated. He had finished his work, but to meet the challenge of an unscrupulous hack who advertised a sequel, he forced himself to continue. Apart from some technical experiment and a wholly proper realization that the reformation of B. had come rather too easily, the book is a product of the didactic will rather than the creative imagination. It shows all too clearly the pressure of the rigid, calculating morality he had inherited. Yet it also shows, by contrast with the first novel, the great value of the imagination which had enabled him to transcend himself as long as it continued to operate. What we watch in *Pamela*, despite its flaws, is the invention of a kind of novel which can help its author to find his way to a deeper sense of human integrity and a nobler idea of how human beings can attain true relationship with one another and with God. This seems more important than the faults of his first attempt.

# Richardson's *Pamela*: the Aesthetic Case

## by A. M. Kearney

Few novels have suffered so much at the hands of the critics as Richardson's *Pamela*. Its ambivalent moral attitudes and prurient content attracted plenty of abuse in its own day, and Arnold Kettle probably echoes a majority opinion in our own time when he writes: *"Pamela* remains only as a record of a peculiarly loathsome aspect of bourgeois puritan morality." [1]

This kind of verdict doubtless arises from a close preoccupation with the character of the heroine herself, and certainly her case is by no means a simple one either psychologically or morally as is testified by the extraordinary amount of interest shown in her. But this attempt to sabotage the motivation behind Pamela's conduct, set in motion by Fielding and other contemporary satirists of Richardson's work, provides only the narrowest and most dubious approach to the novel, which, as a highly original mode of writing in a new genre, deserves another kind of treatment. In fact *Pamela* turns out to be a much more interesting achievement than might be thought, and illustrates for us many of the problems inherent in the art of fiction itself and, in particular, the special problems of style and narration that exist in the epistolary technique. If the vexed question of Pamela's psychological motivation can be laid on one side and the novel can be regarded as an artistic whole we may, by looking at *Pamela* afresh in this way be able to disentangle Richardson's version from Fielding's.

Perhaps the most crucial problem raised by *Pamela* and certainly one which exercised Richardson throughout his life as a novelist, concerns the relationship between the "experience" of the novel—i.e. what actually takes place—and its emergent literary shape. While this may present all writers of fiction with a special problem, to none is it so acute as to the epistolary novelist, where literature is created on

"Richardson's *Pamela*: the Aesthetic Case" by A. M. Kearney. From *The Review of English Literature*, VII (July, 1966), 78–90. Copyright © 1966 by Longmans, Green & Co. Ltd. Reprinted by permission of the author and *The Review of English Literature*.

[1] *An Introduction to the English Novel* (1951), I, p. 69.

the spot and out of the moment itself. In epistolary fiction, we watch the actual process of literature being made as private experience is transmuted into public knowledge. In this way, literary style becomes much more than surface manner, and the way the narrator treats of her experience is revelatory to a high degree, thus giving an interpretative power to epistolary style. In *Pamela,* particularly, the whole problem is heightened by the fact that the bulk of the writing is carried on by the chief participant herself, and the reader is placed in the position of not knowing the degree of correspondence between what is written down, and what actually happened. With a novelist like Fielding, of course, the problem does not arise: the author is always on hand to supply an authoritative commentary. When Tom Jones, for example, gets drunk on Allworthy's recovery, he has Fielding to explain away his behaviour, but when Pamela returns to Mr. B.'s after he has let her go, she has her own explaining to do. The result is that while Tom's character is an open book to us, Pamela's, as the critics have always insisted, is not. All this perhaps is fairly obvious, but it serves to show the particular narrative problem which faced Richardson in *Pamela,* and provides us with a convenient starting point for examining the complex relationship between experience and the literary product in the epistolary novel.

In reality we have two attitudes towards experience in this novel: Pamela's, and Richardson's own authorial one which he expresses through her. Pamela, in fact, is both "character" and "author" and the effect of this double function tends to make Pamela real at one moment and unreal the next; as an early critic claimed, she talks "like a *Philosopher* on one page and like a *changling* the next." [2] Corresponding with this double role, therefore, we have in effect two voices: the first manifesting itself in a direct and spontaneous manner, coming from the centre of experience itself, and the second a much more deliberate one, suggesting the impressions of the observer rather than the participant. In short, we have a voice which is recognizably Pamela's own, and a commentary which is often palpably not. But, before going on to consider the implications of this in greater detail, it will be as well to take a closer look at these voices in action and see the effect they have on the actual tempo of the novel.

The liveliest writing in the novel occurs in the early part, where Pamela's fear of physical outrage produces an almost instinctive recoil into words. This is where we have Pamela as distinct from the author speaking. Her descriptions of Mrs Jewkes and Colbrand for example, are nightmarish to the final detail: "she has a huge hand, and an arm

[2] Cited by A. D. McKillop, *Samuel Richardson, Printer and Novelist,* Chapel Hill (1936), p. 67.

as thick as my waist, I believe" (I, 99).[3] Colbrand's repulsiveness is similarly detailed: he had a "sword on, with a nasty red knot to it . . ." (I, 148-9). This is the least sophisticated of Pamela's styles —the instinctive *cri de coeur*—and comes from the field of action rather than the study. In the description of Colbrand, running in pursuit, "with his long legs, well nigh two yards at a stride" (I, 161), there is something elemental, and we have in its very "unliterariness" the suggestion of the experience itself rather than a delayed retrospect as elsewhere.

In marked contrast to this kind of thing, at other times even in the early part, we have a much more deliberate literary recording of events where, at first sight anyway, the style seems to distort rather than reflect the dramatic situation. In part this can be accounted for by recalling that Pamela's head was full of allusions culled from her wide reading, and these quite spontaneously take shape on the page as she writes. Thus she instinctively falls into Miltonic phrases like "brown nodding horrors" when describing the gloomy Lincolnshire trees (I, 94), or more frequently the biblical, as when comparing her chastity to the city assaulted by the sons of Edom (I, 293); particularly when she feels the need to relate her problems to a wider and more comforting context. In a similar way, her quoting *Hamlet* (I, 20), and her describing the edge of the carp-pond—in which she nearly drowned herself—as "these perilous banks" (I, 155), and Mr B.'s falling into a stream whilst hunting as "the peril of perishing in deep waters" (I, 172), can be related to the kind of therapy effected by hyperbolic utterance. But such explanations quickly break down when we try to relate many of Pamela's reflections to the dramatic context which inspires them: no one similarly situated, we are forced to admit, would express themselves thus.

In these cases we have, quite unmistakeably, the voice of Richardson himself, and the result is a kind of blurring in the characterization. (The same effect occurs in *Clarissa* as Richardson increasingly uses Belford as his mouthpiece.) At the same time, a sense of dramatic proportion is also lost on such occasions, and sometimes the effect is one of unconscious parody. (See, for example, the passage where Pamela likens herself to Queen Hester, II, 305.) Sometimes, indeed, Richardson seems to counter his own intrusions into Pamela's writings by using other characters as critics of Pamela's style: Lady Davers, for example, takes Pamela to task when she neglects "truth and nature" for "studied or elaborate epistles" (II, 33), and Polly Darnford cau-

---

[3] All references to *Pamela* and *Clarissa* in this article are to the Everyman editions: 2 vols. 1914, and 4 vols. 1932, respectively.

tions her on the danger of "falling into a too thoughtful and gloomy way" of writing (II, 215). But the real fact of the matter is that Richardson was prepared to sacrifice the strict demands of characterization in the interests of his own entry into the novel. He was prepared to stick to a psychological realism only so far, and his main concern was to impose a deliberate and literary commentary upon the "raw event" and, as a result, control it. Thus the second voice counters the first.

One of the chief reasons for this controlling technique can be related to the subject matter of the novel. Obviously the main theme is a delicate one and Richardson found himself in considerable difficulties when trying to reform "young and airy minds" by attracting them sufficiently in the first place. The danger was that they might take away the wrong impressions. On the other hand, as he put it in a letter to George Cheyne, "If I were to be too spiritual, I doubt I should catch none but Grandmothers," though there were plenty about "who cou'd find Sex in a *laced shoe,* when there was none in the Foot, that was to wear it."[4] The alliance between the "inflaming" and the "spiritual" in *Pamela* is perhaps an uneasy one, but certainly one reason for the reaching after the formal style in Pamela's reflective letters is an awareness on Richardson's part of its value as an intellectual counterweight. The effect on the reader is one of being involved in the experience and then abstracted from it and, ideally, one has the best of both worlds.

In practice, of course, this is rarely the case, and Richardson found that many of his readers were more taken with his villains than his heroines. Nevertheless, the very literariness of the epistolary style, which strengthens as the novel develops, tends to distance the "inflaming" content and to refine much of the pornography out of existence. No one in fact was as conscious of indecency in literature as Richardson, though his very preoccupation with it suggests some ambivalence. Both his letters and his novels are full of scathing references to "low" authors (see, for example, his remarks on Pope and Swift, *Selected Letters,* p. 57, Clarissa's on Swift, IV, 504 and Pamela's on the "vile epilogue" which concludes a particular performance of *The Distressed Mother,* II, 259) and he obviously intends his own fiction as a corrective to such writing.

Richardson's own writing however reveals a deep-rooted conflict over this. The epistolary technique in his hands became a subtle probing instrument which sometimes opened the mind too far for comfort. Lady Mary Wortley Montagu perfectly stated the Augustan case when,

[4] *Selected Letters of Samuel Richardson,* edited John Carroll, Oxford (1964), pp. 46–47.

with Richardson in mind, she remarked that "fig-leaves are as necessary for our minds as our bodies." [5] Richardson is pulled in both directions: his own inclination, and indeed talent as a writer, prompted him to release the (uncensored) contents of the mind in a flow of consciousness but, at the same time, he is pulled away from the subjective pulse of experience towards the authorial and the objective which finally places him on the right side of the fence.

*Pamela* is especially interesting in that we can watch Richardson's first attempts to resolve these tensions in didactic art. In the early part, as we know, there is a wealth of lively involvement, but as the novel progresses a very different tone appears in Pamela's writings. She is still the sentient and moral centre of the novel but the author increasingly takes over. Her comments on masquerades, operas and the stage, as well as her lengthy treatment of Locke's theory of education, not only fairly represent Richardson's exact views, but indicate that the controlling voice is well inside the world of the novel. This shift in perspective from subjective to objective clearly suggests a change of function for the heroine, a change which parallels her elevation from low to high life.

While it would be untrue to say that Part II is nothing more than a weighty moral tract, what does happen is that much of the quickening power is lost as Pamela is more consciously "used" by the author. Richardson obviously found the lengthy process of retrospection that takes place in Part II a congenial task, and the whole performance is rather like the sermon in shape, where the *exemplum* is followed by an appropriate summary. But Part II is also in a sense an apology for Part I. As he takes pains to point out in his letters, "the poor scenes" —by which he means parts, especially in the early pages of the novel, likely to stimulate the passions—were intended "only for a *first Attractive*." [6] The apology is rather a facile one, but Richardson clearly felt happier about the novel after completing the last two volumes, and was pleased to defend the lack of vitality in the second part by stating that in the interests of instruction, "I labour'd hard to rein in my Invention . . ." [7] The term "invention" came to have unlawful connotations for Richardson as his sense of caution strengthened, and he was very grateful to the "kind Anonymous Gentleman" who vindicated scenes in *Pamela* which appeared too "deep" for nice readers, by pointing out in Milton "Passages full as strong if not stronger." [8]

[5] *Letters*, Everyman edition (1906), p. 466.
[6] *Selected Letters*, p. 47.
[7] *Ibid.*, p. 54.
[8] *Ibid.*, p. 50.

The tensions that lie just beneath the surface in Richardson's novels are an interesting manifestation not only of the conflicts which existed in the author's own mentality, but of tensions that can be found at large in the literature of the period. "The Copernican revolution in epistemology," as M. H. Abrams has termed it, which took shape as a conflict between objective and subjective theories about art, and between the respective claims of imitation and originality in authors, obviously affected far more than the poetry of the period, though this has received the most attention with reference to aesthetic theory. Richardson's influence in this debate was of course minimal, but his ambivalent attitude towards originality in literature, clearly highlighted in the novels themselves, makes him something of a test case. As Ian Watt points out, he was responsible "for a general sharpening of Young's polemic (that is, in the *Conjectures*) in the direction of a new anti-classical hierarchy of literary values." [9] But while his own strength as a writer lay in the direction of the expressive and self-taught, he was clearly not prepared to take his originality very far: he saw the dangers in his path.

His real achievement in fiction rests on his ability to do brilliant portrayals of the mind under duress, calling forth its deepest fears and primitive associations, and connecting the reader with these in a remarkably effective way. His use of the dream or dreamlike associations, in suggesting significant hallucinatory effects, anticipates the interest shown by later novelists in unconscious association. (See, for example, *Pamela*, I, 135, and *Clarissa*, I, 433.) There is little point in speculating how far Richardson might have taken fiction had he been writing in a different aesthetic and moral climate, or if he had decided to use the potentialities of the epistolary technique as a mind-opener to the full. But it is relevant in passing to note his attitude towards *Tristram Shandy*, the most original novel of the day. As he wrote to Bishop Hildesley, he approved of the sentiments of a certain lady who concluded: "Unaccountable wildness; whimsical digressions; comical incoherencies; uncommon indecencies; all with an air of novelty . . . But mark my prophecy, that by another season, this performance will be as much decryed, as it is now extolled . . . and yet another prophecy I utter, that this ridiculous compound will be the cause of many more productions, witless and humourless, perhaps, but indecent and absurd . . ." [10] Indecencies apart, he is not impressed by Sterne's bold experiment and is alarmed by the example he may have set for would-be authors. While he may approve the spirit of Sterne's rebuttal of

---

[9] *The Rise of the Novel* (1957), p. 247.
[10] *Selected Letters*, pp. 341–42.

Horace—"for in writing what I have set about, I shall confine myself neither to his rules, nor to any man's rules that ever lived" [11]—Richardson shies away from the real implications of originality in fiction, which Sterne exploited so brilliantly.

Such ambivalence tends to make Richardson's own performance an uneasy one. Unlike Fielding and Sterne who were able to rest their fiction on established and learned traditions, Richardson's own approach to the novel is a hesitant one. Despite the speed with which *Pamela* was written, he was never quite happy about either his own qualifications as a novelist, or the finished results. (See, for example, *Selected Letters*, pp. 158 and 245.) His frequent requests for advice during the actual course of writing—advice rarely accepted however —betray his need to bring things out in the open, to discuss and abstract what in reality is the author's private concern. We can see therefore, that with all his *penchant* for the individual and subjective conscience in art, Richardson's ultimate concern was to relate this to the plane of an acceptable impersonality: in the end, the personal voice in his fiction—insistent and pleading though it is—is always replaced by the frankly authorial one.

The formalization that takes place in the second part of *Pamela* is precisely this process in operation and the epistolary medium, which tuned us in to the inner rhythms of the heroine's experiences, becomes increasingly an instrument of reflective commentary. The action continues, but the present is always seen against the background of the past in a mood of increasing retrospection. Here Richardson was aided by the extreme adaptability of the epistolary medium itself which can vary between wide shifts in tempo: both personal thought and public statement find their proper level of utterance in the letter form. Moreover, by applying certain stylistic criteria Richardson is able to bring the whole body of writing that forms the novel into correspondence with the nature of the lessons communicated.

In adapting what is in essence a folk archetype to the existing social conditions of his time, Richardson carefully preserves a balance between the ritualistic and the familiar concerns of daily life. On one level, Pamela develops rather like an allegorical quality—as Miss Goodwin sees it, the figure of Prudence itself (II, 480)—but on another, and more satisfactory, level perhaps she emerges as an exemplar of various social types: "the prudent Wife, the affectionate and tender Mother, . . . the sincere Friend, the charitable Steward to the Poor, etc." [12] Pamela's trials, in so far as they continue in Part II, therefore come to have a distinct social flavour: the area of hostile confrontation

[11] *Tristram Shandy*, Bk. I, ch. IV.
[12] *Selected Letters*, p. 46.

has been shifted from bedroom and closet to the drawing-room, and Pamela's various demonstrations of superior strength are increasingly public. The point of these rituals is to prove a right to recognition on Pamela's part; a right not only moral, but social. Pamela's moral superiority is amply highlighted in the first part of the novel, now she must be accorded another kind of recognition: her claim to be called "sister" and "Mrs B." is a well-founded one, and Richardson insists upon the connexion between her social and moral qualities. This is the point of the rather drawn-out scene where Sir Jacob Swynford, refusing to meet Pamela as Mrs B., is deceived into thinking that she is Lady Jenny (II, 163-8). His final recognition of Pamela's real identity leads him to acknowledge her full right to her "exalted condition": "I don't wonder at my nephew's loving you!—And you call her sister, Lady Davers, don't you?—If you do, I'll own her for my niece" (II, 169).

Richardson's chief claim in *Pamela* is that not only can virtue be transferred to good effect from one social context to another, but that without civilized recognition virtue is powerless in terms of influence. He lays considerable stress therefore on the value of social status—and in doing so placed an unfortunate second meaning on the phrase "virtue rewarded"—though he carefully tries to distinguish between the superficial and the well-considered implications of the concept. Hence the public and ceremonious nature of much of the second part where Pamela and Mr B. play out their privileged role in social life, and Pamela's critical observations are increasingly adapted to the wider scene. What she has to say, however, at this later stage of the novel, appears in a stylistic form which itself takes root in the social milieu to which she now belongs. Epistolary style in fact provides Richardson with a unique reflector of social and moral circumstance.

In an age which attached such importance to the notion of literary decorum, endless opportunities were afforded for stylistic exploitation of one kind or another. *Tom Jones,* of course, amongst other things, is a brilliant exhibition of rhetorical extravagance carefully adapted to certain dramatic ends. Like Fielding, Richardson is also aware of the value of style as dramatic function. Unlike Fielding, however, who utilized his stylistic excursions to point various comic incongruities, Richardson was mainly concerned with the literary style as an expression of moral being. His interest in this relationship is indicated by the many discussions of it in his letters and novels. The whole thing seems to turn on the question of unaffected deliberation, and Richardson's demands for epistolary style are as strongly realized as his rigorous requirements for any other form of conscious self-expression. We have in his novels therefore an insistence on a relationship between literary expression and moral value that hardly exists elsewhere.

In a world where such criteria exist, it is hardly surprising to find that Richardson's heroines have much to offer on the subject. Pamela is quick to censure Miss Stapylton's "allegorical or metaphorical style" because it strays too far from what is "easy, natural and unaffected" (II, 456) while Clarissa in connecting epistolary style with "judgment and discretion" goes so far as to detail several kinds of stylistic abuse (IV, 494–6). However, perhaps the clearest statement which concerns this relationship comes in *Grandison* where Charlotte Grandison, having been disposed to accept the advances of Captain Anderson, is gradually disabused by watching the man emerge through his letters: "When he came to write, my judgment was even still more engaged in his favour than before. But when he thought himself on safe footing with me, he then lost his handwriting, and his style, and even his orthography. I blush to say it, and I then blushed to see it." (1754, II, Letter XXIX) There is a certain priggishness perhaps in this, but what Richardson is really after in epistolary terms is not a classical elegance or conscious adornment—in fact he satirizes these in Brand's letters in *Clarissa*—but an unaffected naturalness of style, mid-way between the performances of Brand and the semi-literate Jackey in *Pamela*.

Literary values thus figure strongly in Richardson's novels, and he is able to make extensive use of epistolary assumptions in the treatment of character. Pamela's qualifications for her role as commentator, as it develops through the novel, are far from being those of an untutored and illiterate virtue; her improvement gained from her own experiences, and her ability to influence the lives of others, originates from a development at once intellectual and moral.

Pamela's "itch of scribbling" then, which in sheer bulk tends to strain the credulity—for example she writes six letters on her wedding day, beginning at six a.m.—has a twofold purpose in the moral scheme of the novel: first it brings Pamela herself to public recognition, and secondly it propagates her thoughts as influence. Lady Davers states this plainly enough when she writes to Pamela:

> But I'll tell you what has been a great improvement to you; it is your own writings . . . So that reading constantly, and thus using yourself to write, and enjoying besides a good memory, every thing you heard and read became your own; and not only so, but was improved by passing through [your] more salubrious ducts and vehicles . . . Really, Pamela, I believe, I, too, shall improve by writing to you . . . for already you have made us a family of writers and readers; so that Lord Davers

himself is become enamoured of your letters, and desires of all things he may hear read every one that passes between us. (II, 34-35)

The person is quite consciously submerged under her writings and what takes place is significant only in so far as it can be turned into epistolary comment.

Pamela's role thus defined is that of the novelist himself: by bringing literary ability and sufficient reflection to bear upon the crude stuff of personal experience, he shapes it as didactic art. At the beginning, Pamela's energies in the literary sense are taken up with appeals of one kind or another (to possible sources of aid, including Providence), and the personal voice, as we have seen, is often a frantic one. But soon the value of experience as an object lesson is learnt, and Pamela develops a keener critical sense, enlarging the particular to the level of the instructive and general. Thus, after her marriage, she views her earlier unhappy experiences as part of some providential scheme fitting her for a special role: "Great and good God, as thou hast enlarged my opportunities, enlarge also my will, and make me delight in dispensing to others a portion of that happiness which I have myself so plentifully received at the hands of thy gracious Providence! Then shall I not be useless in my generation!" (I, 333) Such "enlargement" is a conscious process throughout, and Richardson is careful to emphasize the connexion between Pamela's emergence from obscurity and her formation of a consequential style (see *Selected Letters*, p. 250).

All this accounts for the peculiar shape of the novel. The endless *résumées* of Pamela's past, the enormous concern with education and the discussions about the art of writing, all of which take up a large part of the novel and which seem to stifle the lively action of the early parts, in fact have a direct bearing on what has gone before, and indeed are its sole justification in the Richardsonian scheme. Briefly stated, his purpose is to render significant what is privately experienced, and to do this by a literate self-awareness expressed and refined through the epistolary form.

Here one can see that Richardson's strength and weakness as a novelist spring from the same source. On the one hand, he narrows the gap between art and life by allowing his characters to create their own literature but, on the other, he widens it again by intruding as commentator regardless of dramatic context. The conscious deliberation that develops in Pamela's writings, as we have seen, is that of the artist himself seeking to objectify the emotional content of experience, and to interpret what goes on below the surface in a series of unambiguous moral statements. Richardson, however, pays the price of the epistolary technique in this: he asks the reader to accept Pamela as both participant and commentator. The result is scarcely successful, and Pamela, convincing enough as sensory sounding-board in the earlier part, is much less convincing as an external commentator later on: the two voices are never successfully fused.

The epistolary technique therefore presented the inexperienced novelist with some knotty problems. Some of these Richardson never properly solved; others he did, including the question of authorial commentary. When he wrote *Clarissa*, he had learnt the value of having several commentaries, and no one character is burdened to the same extent as in *Pamela*. Yet, despite its technical crudities, Richardson's first novel represents a brave attempt to harmonize the two worlds of fiction: the internal and the external narrative viewpoint. He goes further than Fielding does in acquainting the reader both with the reality of the situation and its moral implications and, on the whole, his attempt to intellectualize, in effect from the nervous centre itself, is much more impressive than Fielding's preservation of a conscious externality. Thus, despite its stringent moral tones, *Pamela* remains of compelling interest as a complex work of fiction, but only by stripping away its aura as a *cause célèbre* for the moral satirists will we be able to get to grips with the thing itself.

# From *Pamela* to *Clarissa*

## by William M. Sale, Jr.

During periods of history in which men have felt a sense of disrupted society, a sense of class differences, the novelist has usually been quick to respond to this feeling. If the disruptive forces are held in check, if they seem only mildly active, the novelist will usually content himself with recording the contrasts that are evident in the intermingling of classes. His mood will be in the main good-tempered as was that of William Dean Howells. On the other hand, if the disruptive forces are—or are felt to be—violently active, the novelist may accentuate class differences and move beyond contrast to the point of conflict—to such conflict as is clearly evident in the novels of Zola. Samuel Richardson, whether or not he was the father of the novel, was certainly the first novelist deliberately to show in his fiction an awareness of the disturbing forces at work in his society, for he was, both as man and novelist, acutely sensitive to class differences. During the two hundred years since he wrote *Pamela,* and especially during the last hundred years, many men, feeling somewhat as Richardson felt, have turned to the novel as a particularly effective form for the expression of this feeling. They sometimes elected to show how the representatives of an older culture received the impact of the "new" man or woman, as in such markedly different novels as *The Age of Innocence* and *The Sound and the Fury.* At other times they showed the "new" man or woman either embarrassed, confused, or hurt in mind and spirit, as George Meredith and Henry James have done. Some novelists have seen the contrast or conflict in terms only of the immediate conditions that confront their characters; others have seen these conflicts in the perspective of time where the fate of their characters may seem analogous to the fate of man.

Patterns evolving from the interpenetration of classes have undergone such various and subtle mutations since *Pamela* was published in 1740 that Richardson's simple pattern may now seem unbelievably

"From *Pamela* to *Clarissa*" by W. M. Sale, Jr. From *The Age of Johnson,* edited by F. W. Hilles (New Haven: Yale University Press, 1949). Copyright 1949 by Yale University Press. Reprinted by permission of Yale University Press.

naïve. Those critics of Richardson who have found his pattern too simple have been led to call him a snob, but to be called a snob is the usual fate of any novelist who makes some degree of common cause with a social class superior to his own. Howells, James, Scott Fitzgerald are names that come at once to mind. Furthermore, the critic's motives in accusing an artist of snobbery are not above question. The accusation frequently represents the exercise of the critic's prerogatives in the service of convictions that are only remotely related to those he has about the art of fiction.

When not criticized for the simplicity of his pattern, Richardson is taken to task for having defined the problems of his characters too explicitly in terms of his age. But the critic who can see his novels only as time-bound documents may be a man as hopelessly rooted in his own era as he would argue that Richardson is rooted in the eighteenth century. Moreover, critics so disposed frequently seek to validate a novelist's work by referring it to other sources of knowledge about an age, without realizing that we frequently understand what the other sources mean only by reason of the light thrown by an age's fiction. To say that Richardson reflects his age is a manner of speaking which is sometimes useful, but if it results in setting him apart from his age, we may fail to see that his age was, among other things, Richardson and his fiction.

To propose these counterthrusts to Richardson's critics is not, however, to deny that in one sense Richardson's novels are inextricably bound up with the conditions of his age. It is the critic, not the novelist, who cannot afford to be provincial. The more conscientiously the novelist devotes himself to the exact rendering of his material, the greater the chance he has of finding in that material the measure of common humanity and the meaning of human life. It is, then, the purpose of this essay to urge a close examination of Richardson's novels in their own terms, though this examination is to be made from a somewhat different point of view than that of the critics who have found little in his fiction but historical significance. If we can see more clearly how his fiction rendered the conflicts he saw in his own society, we may see more clearly the meaning that his fiction had for his century and that it may have for ours. The inadequacy of his pioneering technique should not blind us to his intention, or result in our failure to see what his subject was. Through such an examination some light may be thrown on the tradition of the novel. Though we know that his "influence" can be found only in the second-rate imitations of his novels in the latter half of his century, we can find analogues to Richardson in the modern novel—the novel which began to be written after 1850 when English fiction escaped from the domination of Richardson's more vigorous contemporaries, Smollett and Fielding.

Literature is not a transcript of life but life rendered at the remove of form. To secure this remove the novelist must, among other things, create the images, the symbols, by which he can indirectly communicate his ideas and emotions. With the passing of time a wider and wider gap may open up between the image and the idea it is designed to communicate. To the extent—and only to the extent—that we can close this gap can the literature of the past become available for us. If the symbol can be apprehended only as literal fact, then literature does become merely a transcript of life: the *Divine Comedy* is read as apologetics, Chaucer's Criseyde is thought to be a facile opportunist, and Hamlet a victim of Elizabethan melancholia. It is not always easy to close this gap in the fiction of Richardson, but if the imagination does not fail us we may perhaps be able to recover his novels for our century.

We know that Richardson's characters and incidents were effective symbols for his contemporaries; this fact is attested by the avidity with which they were seized upon. He was providing new insights. He was realizing for his generation the emotions engendered by the conditions of life that defined his generation's hopes and that set limitations upon the fulfillment of those hopes. Before his novels appeared, however, eighteenth-century Englishmen were sufficiently aware of the fact that their vital social problem was the interpenetration of the emergent middle class and the surviving aristocracy. His contemporaries had read authors who sought to educate the middle class in the manners and decorum of the disappearing aristocracy; they had been amused by authors who pointed up the gaucherie of the new man and woman, the new peer. They had their Emily Posts who offered instruction in manners and their Henry Menckens who bumped the boobs. Satire flourished, and when class conflicts were observed with sufficient detachment, the comedy of manners was achieved. The problem was considered in many moods, prevailingly optimistic. But Mandeville treated it cynically, and Swift, beset by some of its aspects, was driven at times to seek the relief of the sardonic. Even the elegiac mood might have found expression, had the aristocrats possessed an able spokesman and had the age been less optimistic. Had not the more violently revolutionary element in society been drawn off into America, the social conflicts might have given rise to a genuinely revolutionary literature. But despite these lacks, there was no dearth of literature to reflect an interest in this social problem. Richardson caught the attention of his readers not by introducing a novel subject but by defining the subject in a new way and by rendering it in a different spirit.

Before the appearance of *Pamela*, fiction of two sorts existed. The eighteenth century kept the romances alive after a fashion, but by their flickering light the aristocrat and his world seemed little more than an artifact. Defoe introduced a fiction which, by contrast with the romances, was vigorously alive, but his characters, like their creator, lived outside the social pale. They "accepted the universe" and fulfilled their destinies in a defiance of society which called forth little soul searching. Though Defoe always took care to tuck them into the orthodox social structure in the final pages of his novels, he produced in so doing a conclusion that stood at odds with his central action. With the romances dead and with Defoe's pirates and prostitutes living outside the pale, it remained with Richardson to bring the heirs of a seventeenth-century Church of England piety into the world of the fatally attractive and profligate aristocrat.

Like James and like Meredith he preferred women for his central characters—the new women, products of a time when a new freedom seemed attainable but was certainly not attained. Richardson brought his heroines into the orbit of the aristocrat, just as Henry James brought the morally sensitive products of a new American civilization into the ancient and enchantedly evil gardens of Europe. He chose, as central symbolic incident, the real or threatened seduction of his heroines, just as Meredith chose the curious psychological violation of his heroine for the central incident of *Diana of the Crossways*, and just as James again and again exposed his heroines to a violation of the spirit, a deflowering of the human soul. Like James's heroines, Richardson's sought union with, not opposition to, those aristocrats who threatened their integrity. In the exploration of this subject lay the novelty of his fiction for his generation. In this respect his fiction shows an affinity with the modern novel.

Because Richardson chose physical seduction as his important symbolic act, he has been accused on the one hand of trying to satisfy vicariously desires which his circumscribed life denied, and on the other hand of a coarseness of moral sensibility. The former charge is irrelevant; the latter is more serious. It is interesting to speculate on why we are so unsympathetic with a heroine who seeks to preserve her virtue. It is true that we have often been confronted in our own fiction with the paradox of the unchaste virgin and of the chaste prostitute. Perhaps such paradoxes have effected a healthy reorientation of our sympathies; they need not, however, lead us to denigrate all virgins who cherish their chastity. Certainly all readers are not completely above "worldly" considerations, or in dire need of the flattery of being allowed to think that they are. But our difficulties with Richardson probably stem from the fact that we are the heirs of romanticism, which made the intensity of an experience the measure of its worth. It is somewhat provincial to impose upon his art the strictures of the romantic aesthetic. He clearly wants to measure the importance of his heroines' experience by the effort that it calls forth to measure up to a standard, however distressed they may be in mind or in spirit during the experience. Furthermore, his heroines meet the threat of seduction while seeking a union with those who represent— or are thought to represent—a way of life more gracious and more distinguished than that to which they were born. Were they made of the finer stuff of earth, they would not feel their lives incomplete, or be seeking to complete them.

The representatives of two modes of life are brought into conflict in Richardson's novels. The men and women are attracted to each other; they seek union, but they seek it on their own terms. The mode of life of these characters in conflict must be realized for us, but in effecting this realization Richardson is not altogether successful. He is reduced to blending romantic material with the realism of Dutch genre painting. This blend disturbed his Victorian biographer, Clara Thomson, who professed to be reminded of "rusty armour hung on the staircase of a semi-detached villa." It is true that the blend is not always happily achieved, but Miss Thomson's metaphor discloses her lack of a sense of history while it records her aesthetic distress. Richardson's heroes are no more knights in armor than his heroines are Victorian suburbanites. Eighteenth-century society, despite the shock that it caused in Miss Thomson, tolerated its Lovelaces; and Richardson's correspondence shows his excited interest whenever the doings of young aristocrats percolated down to him through the letters of girls who were on the fringes of the society in which such men moved. It is obvious that Richardson knew little at first hand of the life of the English aristocracy. But this lack of knowledge is not fatal. His taste for aristocracy, like that of his heroines, is an index of his need to make common cause with a superior social class. This need of the author is no more apparent in Richardson than it is in Shakespeare or in James.

But the need to make some sort of common cause with the English aristocracy did not mean that a complete absorption within its world was possible, however desirable in some respects such an absorption might seem. This was what Richardson learned between the writing of *Pamela* and *Clarissa*. The subject of the two novels is not radically different, but for many reasons he was unable to realize this subject in *Pamela,* whereas in *Clarissa* it had taken full shape. Had he come to the writing of *Clarissa* without the experience provided by the earlier novel, he might well have failed to preserve the sharp outlines of his subject and might indeed have never discovered its real importance. It is in the importance of the subject, fully grasped in *Clarissa,* that Richardson differentiates himself from Fielding. *Tom Jones,* for all its display of talent and for all the ingenuity of its construction, has a subject which is not fully worth the care and attention that Fielding lavished on it. It is Fielding himself and not the subject of his novel that continues to win our admiration, whereas all the irritation that we may feel with the author of *Clarissa* should not prevent our seeing that its subject is of the first importance.

In both *Pamela* and *Clarissa* Richardson chose to see his world in the microcosm of the family. Families were, as he said, but "so many miniatures" of the great community of the world. Tyranny, treachery, loyalty—duty and responsibility, right and prerogative—all these aspects of life he sought to comprehend within the world of the family. His concept of the family was never quite broad enough for the uses to which he wanted it put, but this constricted vision is more apparent in *Pamela* than in *Clarissa.* The master-servant relationship in the household is not so flexible as the father-daughter relationship which he uses in *Clarissa.* In order to maintain the conflict in the earlier novel, Richardson had in some degree to sacrifice the character both of Pamela and of her master. In eighteenth-century England a servant is not bound to her master as Pamela seems at times to feel that she is bound; nor do we find it easy to accept the highhanded fashion in which Mr. B. abrogates the laws of his country in carrying through an abduction. In the earlier sections of *Pamela* the heroine seems to be trumping up excuses in order to keep Richardson's novel going; in later sections, she is a prisoner with her freedom of choice so restricted that the novel becomes in large part an adventure story. The dual role of master and of lover which Mr. B. has to play clouds the main issue of the novel. Were he cast solely as lover, we could see more clearly that his dilemma arises because he falls in love with the girl he should seduce. Were he not Pamela's master as well as the man she wants to marry, Pamela would seem far less the schemer than she too often shows herself to be.

Richardson encountered these difficulties—and others to be mentioned later—because the main outlines of his story were determined before he started to tell it. He chose to follow a story from real life in which a master finally married the serving girl he tried to seduce. When Richardson turned to the reworking of his theme in *Clarissa,* he created his own story and held to it in spite of the advice and entreaty of his friends who sought to reshape it for him. Again he chose the microcosm of the family, but he wisely placed Lovelace outside the domestic orbit of the Harlowes. Furthermore, he idealized the Harlowes just as he idealized Lovelace. The Harlowes, if you will, are essentially London middle-class tradesmen with the tradesman's narrowness of soul and smallness of mind. As Tucker Brooke said of *Lear,* Shakespeare's characters in that play are those whom he could only have understood "from sympathetic observation of the life before his windows and which few have been able to reproduce save by means of the closest transcription." Brooke shrewdly observes that Lear and his daughters are essentially bourgeois types. So are the Harlowes. But Richardson moves them from the city to the country; he wants us to see not the fact but the essence of their materialism, of their penny pinching, their selfishness. If we compare the idealized treatment of the Harlowes with the more direct transcription that Richardson employs for the middle-class Danbys of *Grandison* or for the tradesmen's daughters, Sally Martin and Polly Horton, of *Clarissa,* we can see clearly that the Harlowes are larger than life. The stultifying atmosphere of Harlowe Place is so pervasive that even the kindly instincts of some of the clan prove abortive. Clarissa alone is a free spirit, struggling desperately to preserve her integrity and her independence of mind and soul. She is set apart from the Harlowes more significantly than Pamela is set apart from her parents or from her companions belowstairs.

To make this distinction between Clarissa and her family a sharp one is only part of the task that Richardson had to accomplish in the first two volumes of his novel. Though her father's inhumanity seems intolerable, we must see that Clarissa can never escape from the fact of his fatherhood. She cannot, as Pamela could, quit her master. Though she finds it imperative to incur her father's curse in following the law of her own being, this curse lies upon her like a leaden weight, and Richardson takes pains to make clear that she cannot free herself from its weight until her soul speeds its way to heaven. Pamela's power of choice was removed, but choice is given to Clarissa. To make us see that she cannot escape from the consequence of her choice is a responsibility that the novel accepts and which it continuously makes clear. The burden of this curse is analogous to the burden of the traumatic experiences which pursue Diana Merion relentlessly and which result in her betrayal of both Warwick and Dacier. Both Diana and Clarissa are, by contrast with the other characters of their world, emancipated; but Diana, so often the ally of the Comic Spirit, is also its victim. Clarissa, despite the clarity of her mind, is the victim of the curse incurred when she defies her father and elopes with Lovelace. This aspect of the situation, so dimly grasped in *Pamela*, is clearly realized in *Clarissa*.

It is her fate to defy her father; it is also her fate to be attracted by the free spirit of Lovelace, who stands in such marked contrast to the Harlowes. Lovelace moves in a world of larger freedoms, of wider spaces. His values, however reprehensible, are not the countinghouse values of the Harlowes. Clarissa allows herself to hope that in union with him she will in some way complete her life. She knows and tells us in so many words that in marriage with Solmes, her family's choice, her life will stop. So this passionate pilgrim, like Isabel Archer, is driven to link her destiny with her Osmond. In our century the slackening of family ties has perhaps resulted in making less effective Richardson's symbol of the parental curse. In like manner, the steady democratization of modern society may make it difficult for us to accept an aristocratic rake at Richardson's evaluation, equivocal though that evaluation may be. Aristocracy meant to Richardson a distinction of personal existence. That he should have seen this distinction only in the acts of the attractive libertine is a commentary on his age. In their pursuit of women these energetic sons of the older families perpetuated a mode of life which had flourished during the Restoration. With political action frequently denied them, they flagrantly asserted the *droit de seigneur,* flinging their tattered banners from the falling walls. These gestures both attracted and repelled the creator of Lovelace. He caught fleeting glimpses of them outside his windows, and he idealized them as he did the Harlowes; he heightened the qualities that made them both attractive and repellent. But with them he had to make some kind of common cause if his vision of human potentialities was to extend beyond the narrow confines of his own middle-class world.

The degree to which he could make such cause and the success which could attend the attempt were matters that Richardson had not clearly thought through when he wrote *Pamela*. When he allowed the marriage to take place between Pamela and Mr. B. he did not really resolve his conflict. He merely put an end to it. It is true that he postponed marriage as long as his inventive genius would permit; he even borrowed all the antiquated machinery of romance to keep his story going through the long Lincolnshire episode. But, following his story from real life, he had eventually to bring his characters to the altar. It is difficult to see how Richardson might have avoided the marriage, but to include it is to suggest that a large part of the antecedent action is much ado about nothing. Richardson, of course, recognized the specious optimism implied in the marriage and tried to recover his subject. He devoted his second volume to the conflicts experienced by Pamela because she was the maid who had become the mistress. But the mood of the second volume is that of social comedy, and despite all his efforts the effect is that of anticlimax. To ignore the second volume, as so many critics of Richardson seem to do, is to fail to see, however, the efforts that Richardson made to preserve Pamela's integrity.

Richardson saw clearly what both Pamela and Mr. B. had lost when he turned to Clarissa's story. He would not allow his friends to persuade him to close her story with a wedding. In the course of the action Lovelace tried by several sets of arguments to persuade himself that he should and that he should not marry Clarissa. But he knew that such a marriage would represent a compromise with his own world and its values. If the pressure of opinion or the force of circumstances juggled him into marrying Clarissa, such a marriage would compromise his principles. Accommodations of this sort were possible in the world of the Harlowes but not in his world. In like manner, Clarissa knew that marriage with Lovelace was no resolution of her dilemma, though she found it very difficult to make the Anna Howes of her world understand this. Marriage was not the reward her virtue deserved. This pair cannot be tucked into the social structure as Defoe tucked his characters. There are moments when both Clarissa and Lovelace are tempted by the thought of their union; and marriage, as a symbolic act, is kept constantly in the forefront of the novel. But this story is no "love" story. It is not love for which Clarissa's old pious world is well lost; it is for a chance to live life more completely in conformity with an ideal of conduct. Clarissa is no more a girl in search of a husband than is Isabel Archer. She is—if I may risk a dangerous abstraction—humanity desperately if futilely seeking freedom in a world where duty and responsibility are constant limitations upon that search.

The theologians of Richardson's day were busy accommodating the new science to a world which many of them still believed was ruled by the God of their fathers; the political thinkers were accommodating a new constitution within the framework of the theory of divine right. Even the new industrialism was seeking to accommodate itself within the antiquated structure of the guild system of master and apprentice. Pamela, the embryonic new woman, is fitted somewhat too easily into the older social structure. But Richardson, like Swift and Johnson, finally saw that the optimism of his age was a facile optimism, that the attempts to preserve the old faiths by accommodation were sure indications that these old faiths were moribund. Clarissa can find no hope in this world; she must depend on heaven.

It is her dependence on heaven that is the final cause for the disturbance of many modern readers. The central irony in *Clarissa* is easily recognized, but her faith in heaven is felt to mitigate the sharpness of this irony. And indeed it does. We accept more readily James's secularized versions of a similar theme in which at the end the heroine receives the kiss of death. His heroines have fulfilled their tragic fate as inevitably as has Clarissa, but they have not her hope of heaven. In the closing sections of James's novels his heroines are frequently above or beyond life, even as Clarissa is during the last two volumes of her story. They are beyond earthly considerations; they live in an atmosphere as rarefied as that of heaven itself. The secularized version may be more acceptable to some modern readers, but the intent of the two novelists is not markedly different. Certainly in the charity of our imagination we should be able to understand Richardson's intent, despite his pious vocabulary and his pious symbols. He wants us to see that Clarissa is a child of heaven, finally removed alike from the world of the Harlowes and of the Lovelaces. The need of heaven was imperative. In this world Richardson could not, as did many of his contemporaries, find room in which to fit everything and a place in which everything might fit.

# On *Clarissa Harlowe*

## by Dorothy Van Ghent

Clarissa is the antithesis of Moll Flanders, as heroine. In the earliest episode of importance in *Clarissa Harlowe*—the attempt of the Harlowe family to force the girl into marriage with "rich Solmes"—we see her in revolt against that materialism to which Moll "adjusted" so nicely and with which she so tirelessly collaborated. The central action of Clarissa's story is a rape, an experience which might have assumed a position of minor importance among Moll's adventures in adultery, bigamy, and incest—conceivably an incident that Moll might even have forgotten to make a "memorandum" of. But Clarissa is sent to her grave by it, and not only does it cause her death, but upon it are made to hinge the sanctions of family life, the structure of society, and the power relationships between the orders of the divine and the diabolic. The chief idiosyncrasy of Moll Flanders' world is the tendency to externalize life, to convert all experience into measurable material quantities and cash; the chief idiosyncrasy of Clarissa's is exactly the reverse: it is the tendency to convert the external forms of life—social customs, physical action, material quantities—into subjective quality and spiritual value. This, at least, describes a striking difference between the two heroines and the two books at the literal level; though we must hesitate, at this point, to decide how deep the difference in values lies.

With materials whose tendency is so strongly subjective, the form of this novel will be one that allows a careful sifting of motives and a sensitive representation of emotions. The technical problem with which we are confronted here is that of the "point of view" (or "focus of narration"), a problem which may be phrased thus: given a certain kind of subject matter, how can it be brought into focus for the reader? From what "angle," what point of observation, can the drama

"On *Clarissa Harlowe*." From *The English Novel: Form and Function* by Dorothy Van Ghent (New York: Rinehart and Co., Inc., 1953). Copyright 1953 by Dorothy Van Ghent. Reprinted by permission of the publisher. Reprinted in 1966 by Holt, Rinehart, and Winston. Published in paperback by Harper and Row, 1967.

best be seen? From the author's own? or from that of the chief character in the novel? or from that of one of the minor characters? or from the points of view of several characters? or from some presumably automatic and mechanical point of view (like that of a camera)? Both of Richardson's protagonists must, for the full evolution of the tragedy, die in its throes, without that calm distance and settled state of health required for the writing of memoirs. Furthermore, the dramatic impact of the material lies in the vital immediacy, not of only one person's motives and emotions, but of those of at least two persons—Clarissa and Lovelace. If either of the protagonists had been allowed to tell the tale from his own point of view alone, neither would have been able to penetrate into the subjective life of the other. Richardson could not, therefore, solve the problem of point of view as Defoe did, by using the "seeing eye" of a single character. Nor could he use the point of view of the "omniscient author," as did Cervantes, which implies a removed standpoint, disinvolvement on the part of the observer, and a godlike sweep of vision and knowledge of the meaning of events. The reader must be as implicated as Clarissa herself, or as Lovelace, in false hopes, disappointments, expectations, torments, with as little foreknowledge of the way out; he must, moreover, be able to follow the drama from day to day, as it takes place within the minds of both protagonists. Thus the event must be recorded as if at the moment of its taking place; it must be recorded from a subjective point of view; and—additional problem—a certain amount of information must also be allowed to come to the reader concerning a number of other people's attitudes and activities. Richardson used the vehicle of a series of letters, written by major and minor characters, and representing a variety of points of view, all subjective.

The epistolary form of the book slows down the pace of the story almost intolerably, for we are dependent for information upon the mechanics of the postal system and the finger-and-elbow mechanics of the pen wielders. Certain significances attach to this slowness of pace. Before the reader can find out "what has happened" at any one point in the action, he must wait until a half dozen people have had time to write letters, receive answers, and reply; for no one in the story himself ever knows precisely and objectively "what has happened," inasmuch as "what happens" lies not in the objective event but in a multitude of subjective reactions. It is only by the mixed evidence of a number of letters that the "action"—being of a subjective character—can receive clarification. A psychological node, or system of interconnections and cross references, dense, complex, and life-resembling, is thus contrived from the operations of a group of minds on a single event, each mind offering its own fractional information or insight as to what the event is and signifies. Illumination is suspended until each of the fragments falls into place in the slowly accreted group, and meanwhile the action is kept under the pressure of doubt, hope, indecision, misconception, and fatality.

The central event of the novel, over which the interminable series of letters hovers so cherishingly, is, considered in the abstract, a singularly thin and unrewarding piece of action—the deflowering of a young lady—and one which scarcely seems to deserve the universal uproar which it provokes in the book. There is very little subplot. The rape is in the offing, it is at hand, it is here, it is over, Clarissa sickens and dies, and that is all. Against this simplicity of event, one thinks of Moll Flanders' "three score years of continuous variety." And yet *Moll*, with its long roll of statutory crimes and broken taboos, offers a flat fictional landscape, uniform, unaccented, horizontal (though fascinating in its own quality as are some flat physical topographies, such as the southwestern deserts or the Florida Everglades); whereas *Clarissa* is a dramatically vertical world of fabulous heights and rank profundities, with God the Father at the top, and, at the bottom, the lurid gleam and the foul stench of hell. The epistolary form of the novel provides us with a partial explanation for the fact that Richardson has been able to create so dramatic a world with so simple a theme. This slow and hovering form endows the physiological event—the rape—with profound attraction and significance by holding it up slantwise to view in a murk of shadows, turning it mysteriously, allowing it to emerge slightly, withdrawing it, allowing it to emerge again, and so on. It is as tantalizing and evasive as a trout. Only at long length are we permitted to get it into clear focus, while, in the meantime, we have been steadily bombarded, page after page, with an imagery deriving from various submerged but exceedingly powerful impulses and attitudes.

We have spoken of images and symbols to some extent in our previous studies. With *Clarissa,* these become of primary concern. An image, in its technical psychological sense, is a mental representation of a sense impression, visual, tactile, aural, gustatory, olfactory, thermal, or kinesthetic. In life, the image is frequently bound up with the actual sensation; but in speaking of imagery in a poem or a novel, we should be carefully aware that what we are referring to is the mental representation alone, quite divorced from sensation. Furthermore, an image is rarely single; a whole setting, or a moment of drama in which several characters participate, may form "an image," but it will be an image of a very complex kind, actually a construct of images acting as a unity. Again, a relatively simple image, like that of a porcelain teacup, or a green silk purse, or a parasol with the sun shining through it, though we may speak of it as "vivid," does not necessarily derive its vividness from imagined sensory impressions associated with such a teacup, purse, or parasol. It may be "vivid" as an image while the sensory impressions associated with it are extremely thin and vague. Its "vividness" will be a function of the context in which it finds itself, the way it is spoken of by the author, associations of attitude with the object that may not be sensory associations at all. There are many optical images of this kind in *Clarissa*: for instance, Clarissa in white clothes, kneeling in prayer, seen through a keyhole. What makes this image sharp and vivid are associations of purity and piety with whiteness and with prayer (most particularly in the dramatic context of Clarissa's captivity in a sordid house by a man of foul intentions); also the keyhole frame sharpens the image for us, as if we were looking at her through a telescope, for it focuses the eye on the single figure, cutting off any surrounding area, at the same time that it puts her at a distance like a person in a picture, removing her from any approach except the optical approach (this removal contributes, of course, to the "vividness" of our sense of her purity and piety).

By reiteration and accumulation, and by other always specific contextual conditions, an image may act as a symbol. That is, it may automatically begin to stand for a complex structure of feelings and values that are of great significance in the total structure of the book. We [can see] this happen in *Moll Flanders*. So insistently does *Moll* bombard us with gold watches, gold necklaces, gold rings plain or fancy, gold guineas, that when the Bath gentleman opens the drawer full of gold guineas and asks Moll to scoop up a handful, we are—even perhaps without framing the thought deliberately—under the strong impression of a symbolic action, an action that focuses the predilections and values of everyone in the *Moll Flanders* world. Let us consider the evolution of a symbol in *Clarissa Harlow*: that of the "Clarissa-symbol" itself. In the early scene when Clarissa is brought down into the parlor for a family conference, we are given a picture of the girl as she sees herself in the mirror beside her chair—pale, debilitated, and distraught, with heaving bosom, and most interesting and attractive. Cumulatively, many similar images reinforce this picture of attractive, desirable womanhood: Clarissa wilting like a broken lily on its stalk, Clarissa resting her lovely pale head on the motherly breast of Mrs. Lovick, Clarissa lifting her eyes in gratitude to heaven for a simple bowl of gruel or glass of water, Clarissa on her knees in prayer in miraculously dirt-resistant white garments, or Clarissa in torn clothes and with streaming eyes, prostrated at the feet of her demon-lover. The womanly quality which Richardson has made attractive in these images is that of an erotically tinged debility which offers, masochistically, a ripe temptation to violence. Thus the image of Clarissa achieves, under construction in the context, the status of a symbol, a focus of feelings and attitudes, rich, dense, and deep, however strange and even perverse.

In understanding the Clarissa-symbol, we should add to its associations the effect of the optical framing. Naturally, given the point of view that Richardson has adopted, we must always see Clarissa through someone else's eyes or else as she sees herself in a mirror. This would seem merely an exigency of the letter form of the book; but when we consider, along with this natural optical tactic, the fact that special devices (such as mirror or keyhole) are so often employed to emphasize the *seeing* of Clarissa by someone, and usually under conditions where she must be unconscious of being looked at, we begin to feel that the optical tactic must be "working" in a somewhat complex strategic way. The most extreme case in point is, of course, the episode of the rape itself, when the door of the room is left open and "female figures flit" across it, watching. One effect of this strategy is to make of the reader a Peeping Tom, to make him share in the dubious delights of voyeurism. Also, as strategy, it is consistent with that of the letter vehicle: as the letters "tell all" and the letter writer exposes all, turning himself inside out to his confidant, so the handling of the images offers all—not particularly to be experienced (in imagination) at first hand—but to be *seen*. Paradoxically enough, though the material of the novel is so largely subjective, "inner," yet a definitive quality of the *Clarissa* world is its publicity: no one is alone, can ever be alone, in *Clarissa,* not even in the most private performances of prayer, sex, and death. *Clarissa* is not a world of the individual soul, but, in the most extensive sense, a social world, a public world. We shall perhaps see, in a later consideration of this novel as myth, how the publicity tactics of *Clarissa* are technically coherent with its mythical significance, its significance as a projection of a social dream.

An immense number of the Clarissa-images occur in an erotic context; but Clarissa's whiteness, her narrow range of stances and gestures (she kneels, she prostrates herself, she tears her neck ruffles and exposes her bosom, she wields a key or penknife or scissors), and the distancing and framing of the image for the eye, exclude a large number of associations that might operate in an erotic context—as color modulations, tactile impressions, nature sounds, and so forth. In other words, the erotic situations that are dramatized are excessively simple and abstract, limited to suggestions of bodily violence or violence done to clothes (stabbing or tearing) and the converse, suggestions of violence suffered (weeping, fainting, dying). Clarissa herself is offered as the ideal woman in her purity and debility—and these qualities, too, are extraordinarily limited abstractions from the complex of qualities that might be conceived as making up complete womanhood; at the same time, pure and debile as she is, paradoxically she offers an ideal of the sexual woman (in the world of this book), the physically desirable woman. She is a kind of love goddess, a Venus. She is not the Venus of the Renaissance, with an erotic apparatus of Mayflowers, delicately tinted veils, sinuous tresses, zephyrs, lutes, and cupids, suggesting many enjoyments for the senses, suggesting also the aesthetic act of contemplation.[1] She is much more abstract than that. She is the love goddess of the Puritan middle class of the English eighteenth century, of the bourgeois family, and of mercantile society. She is pure (to be paraded for the sight as an expensive chattel—or, in later generations, to show herself voluntarily as "career girl"), and yet to be violated (for in a society that has desexualized its professed mores, sex is a violation), but still to be seen while she is being violated (for sex insists on perpetuating its attractions, but they must be enjoyed by proxy, as in the movies, or *sub rosa*). The lover to whom she deploys her attractions is the lover as narcissist, as voyeur, as sadist—all abstractionists. Her mythical features still appear to us—for it would be a mistake to think that the Clarissa-myth does not still have deep social and psychological roots—in her two chief aspects: they appear on the covers of *Vogue* magazine, in the woman who is a wraith of clothes, debile and expensive, irrelevant to sense-life or affectional life, to be seen only; and they appear on the covers of *True Confessions* and *True Detective Stories,* in the many-breasted woman with torn dishabille and rolling eyeballs, a dagger pointing at her, a Venus as abstract as the *Vogue* Venus in her appeal to the eye and the idea alone, but differing in that she is to be vicariously ripped and murdered. Clarissa is a powerful symbol because she is both.

Similarly, an image of "the man" begins its evolution into a symbol when Clarissa has her private interview with "odious Solmes." She speaks of his splay feet, his posture "asquat" (like a toad), and his "ugly weight" that presses against her hoop. Perhaps no single word with emotional resonance occurs more frequently in this novel than the word "man." Solmes's own function in contributing to the symbol of "the man" is rather quickly over with; all he has to do, as suitor, is

[1] In one of his erotic fantasies, Lovelace visualizes Clarissa in a situation bearing some pictorial resemblance to that of the Renaissance Venus with her bevy of cupids, but the difference is significant. He sees her "with a twin Lovelace at each charming breast . . . full of wishes for the sake of the pretty varlets, and for her own sake that I would deign to legitimate; that I would condescend to put on the nuptial fetters."

to be repellent; his real status is similar to that of the Harlowe males with whom he is hand-in-glove in action—that is, he is economic man, desexualized man. "The man" proper, as this symbol is deployed, is the man as lover, as the sexual threat. Clarissa screams, when she sees Lovelace in the garden, "A man!" "Ah, this man, my dear!" she exclaims to Miss Howe. "The man, my dear, looked quite ugly!" she tells her friend, after a predatory approach on Lovelace's part. She speaks of his "savage kiss" reddening her hand. Miss Howe confirms her notions of men: they are a "vile race of reptiles." Somewhere Joseph Conrad speaks of "the fascination of the abomination," a phrase which applies nicely to the image of "the man" in *Clarissa;* for as the image grows by reiteration and variation into a symbol, attractive elements are fused with the repellent elements, so that the abominable toadlike reptilian "man" becomes demonically fascinating: a creature obsessed with the desire to violate virginal, high-minded, helpless womanhood, and so single-tracked in his passion to destroy this divinity that he, too, assumes divine stature: he is the evil divinity, the devil himself. It is no wonder that even Miss Howe, after being present at a party where Lovelace has fluttered the dovecotes, confesses to Clarissa that she has begun to see him in her dreams.

The modern reader may fail to see at once in Lovelace the Satan, the archfiend, which many generations of readers have found in this character. Magnificently projected as Lovelace is, we may be inclined to see him as a study in psychopathology, or as a portrait of an egotist, or as a portrait (as one critic has said) of an "overgrown schoolboy." All these he may be, but, to read *Clarissa* in its fulness of implication, we should also be aware of the mythical resonances of the character. There can be no doubt that Richardson and the contemporary audience saw him as an embodiment of "splendid sin,"

> of the pride of life (as reproved by medieval theologians), of irresistible and pernicious fascination, the eighteenth century Lucifer, in fact, a worthy antagonist to his paragon of virtue, Clarissa.[2]

Lovelace himself, as he thinks of Clarissa as "divine," certainly considers himself to be one of the damned. In a dream he sees her angelic white-clad figure rising in a company of angels to the abode of the Seraphim, while an abyss opens at his feet and he falls headlong into it. Nor is this notion of the mythological significance of Lovelace, in relation to Clarissa, confined to Lovelace's own idea of himself, or to Richardson's intention, or to what older generations of readers may have found in the book. André Gide puts the matter succinctly when

---

[2] Brian W. Downs, *Richardson* (London: Routledge & Kegan Paul, Ltd., 1928), p. 116.

he says that "in the pages of *Clarissa,* heaven is continually being offered cheap to hell."

We have, in the preceding paragraphs, frequently spoken of *Clarissa Harlowe* as myth, and it is through the conception of this novel as myth that we are able to explain more fully to ourselves the strange fact that, though the book reflects an essentially perverse psychology, it is nevertheless a great and powerful piece of fiction. But let us first of all divest ourselves of the idea that a myth is something "untrue." A myth cannot be "proved" logically or by the observation of physical fact. Whatever "truth" a myth may hold is not susceptible of this kind of proof. Myth is a dramatic vision of life, and we never cease making myths, accepting myths, believing in myths; even in our own positivistic age, we see life dramatically through the myths offered us by Hollywood, by the commercial advertisements, by the detective story, by local politics, by international diplomacy, or by the physicists. Myth appears in a novel when the action and the particular set of manners represented in the book are organized in a total symbolic construct of such a kind that it not only reflects the aspirations and ideals, the attitudes and customs, of a large social group, but also seems to give to these attitudes and customs the sanction of some "higher authority," perhaps the authority of ancient tradition, perhaps supernatural authority, perhaps the authority of some vaguely defined power-and-knowledge concept such as "law" or "government" or "science" or even "society" itself. Finally, this total symbolic construct is, in myth, projected dramatically. We shall need, for greater clarity, to differentiate myth from allegory. . . . The differentia of allegory is the fact that its elements are, in gross, to be read off in point-to-point equations into an abstract, discursive, intellectual system. Myth does not offer an intellectual system. What it offers is the dramatization of powers that are assumed to have universal authority over the actions of men. The dominion of allegory (as a total system) is the intellect; the dominion of myth is the irrational.

We shall speak of *the* myth of *Clarissa Harlowe,* but we must be prepared to see it in several different aspects, or as several different sets of mythological ideas which have been mingled and fused by Richardson and given coherence in the large, simple dramatic shape of the story, but which can be singled out as sub-systems for examination. An analogy may help us here. It is as if the *Clarissa*-myth, as a whole, were a universe described by a number of different planetary orbits; the different sets of "mythological ideas" are the different orbits, but these orbits have interrelationships in the larger system of the *Clarissa*-universe, and the whole is held together by complex magnetic correspondences. The analogy helps us to visualize both the strong internal unity of the major system and the distinct existence of the sub-systems. For convenience, then, we shall be speaking as if of a number of different myths ("the Puritan myth" in *Clarissa*, for instance, or "the myth of class"), but we should continue to think of them as not actually independent or self subsistent, but as operating only by virtue of the magnetic laws binding them in the unit of the whole.

Certain of these we have already touched on, but we must see them now in fuller articulation and in their correspondences with others. The most evident, and one which had Richardson's own conscious deliberation behind it, is the Puritan religious myth, which was alive in Richardson's culture and which he used to give edificatory significance to his materials. His aim, as he expressed it, was to teach the "highest and most important doctrines of Christianity," and his success in this project is witnessed by the comment of a contemporary Dutch Mennonite divine, who said that if *Clarissa* had formed one of the canonical books of the Bible, it would have furnished proof positive of divine inspiration. The Puritan myth, as it is inflected in *Clarissa*, is a daemonic view of life. Deity and the evil spirit are deeply concerned in the affairs of men. Through charm of body and other lures—wit, worldly graces, worldly power, mobility, uninhibited freedom—and with the most cunning deceit, the evil spirit tempts the woman as he tempted Eve. The ultimate obsession of the devil is, of course, sex, for in the Puritan mythology sex is the culmination of all evil, the unmasked face of fear. Like the Satan who tempted Job, this Lucifer is not interested in small fry. Job was "the greatest of all the men of the east," there was "none like him in the earth," he was "a perfect and an upright man." Similarly, Clarissa is a paragon of virtue, a "divinity of a woman," which is the reason why she holds any interest for the prince of evil spirits. She is virtuous in many ways, she is charitable "to the industrious poor," she disciplines herself to deserve 144 merit marks for virtue every week, and if she omits to earn one of them she has to add it onto the next week's budget. But above all she is chaste. As the devil's evil obsession is sex, so the woman's virtuous obsession is her chastity; but it must be observed that chastity is here a physical attribute (quite as it is in *Moll Flanders*), that innocence of spirit is not distinguished from bodily intactness, that the two are identified as one. Therefore, when the devil has succeeded in befouling the woman's body, he will have obtained a victory over her soul—save for the intervention of the Deity. The woman's will for purity makes her subject to an inspiration of Divine Grace. As Job was selected from among all men for the severest trial of faith, so Clarissa has been selected from among all women for unique travail as preparation for sainthood. Potent as the devil is, the universe is well loaded against him, and when the crisis is over, Providence begins distributing rewards and punishments with remarkable accuracy to everyone in the book, thoroughly satisfying poetic justice. Lovelace is, as Richardson puts it, "condignly punished"; the infamous Sinclair dies in incredible torments of a vile disease; Miss Howe, Mr. Hickman, Belford, the worthy Norton, are all made "signally happy"; the Harlowes themselves are so deeply afflicted in conscience that they take the backstairs the rest of their lives to avoid passing the martyred Clarissa's room; James becomes involved in insupportable financial difficulties; Arabella's husband is unfaithful to her and her wedded life horrid; even the servants are paid off with minute attention to their respective deserts. As for Clarissa, she has received the crown of all joys: her bridegroom is Christ. We may observe that, far from being the tragedy which Richardson, as a literary man with some knowledge of the traditional structure of tragedy, worked hard to make it (Clarissa's "tragic flaw," for instance, is designed with high deliberation), the novel is really a comedy—a "divine comedy"—if we use as the generic distinction between comedy and tragedy the happy and the unhappy ending. It has a "happy ending," the good are rewarded, the evil are punished; and it has this ending by virtue of the Puritan world view whose powerful outlines dominate the novel.

We turn now to another mythological aspect of *Clarissa,* and if, for the sake of clarity, we must pin labels on each of these, we shall call this one a myth of social caste or class. We have said that Lovelace, who has the place of the devil in the Puritan myth, offers the lures of wit, worldly graces and power, mobility, uninhibited freedom; but these are qualities and privileges of aristocracy, and Lovelace himself is a member of the aristocratic class and heir to a title. By contrast, the woman he woos is the daughter of middle-class parents. The Harlowes are London tradesmen, representatives of the prosperous bourgeoisie that has been supreme in society and politics since the consolidations of the seventeenth century. It is a class not distinguished by the social refinements and gallantries or by the intellectual graces, a class that has acquired power through hard work, cash calculation, and sobriety, a class therefore by definition unable to afford aristocratic freedoms such as impulsiveness, enthusiasm, idleness, extravagance, debauchery (as these freedoms are conceived in Richardson's middle-class fantasy on the aristocratic theme).[3] Just as Lovelace, the aristocrat, is drawn larger than life, both as to his vices and

[3] The discussion of this aspect of the book owes much to the essay "From Pamela to Clarissa," by William M. Sale, Jr., in *The Age of Johnson* (New Haven: Yale University Press, 1949). [See pp. 39-48 in this volume.]

his charm, so also the Harlowes are drawn larger than life: not only Clarissa—who is the epitome of that virtue of virginity which, besides a fortune, is the best trade commodity of the middle-class woman, determining her price bracket—but the others as well, the mother and the uncles, and particularly Mr. Harlowe and the son James, with their concentration on hard cash and the consequent brutalization of their feelings. Clarissa herself is powerfully attracted to Lovelace. Possible marriage with him is kept constantly in the foreground of the novel; indeed, even after the crisis, when she has excluded that possibility, it is still kept in the foreground by the other characters, by Miss Howe, for instance, who sees the marriage as a sensible way to settle the hullabaloo and make everybody happy yet. Marriage with Lovelace would be a symbolic act, uniting middle class and aristocracy, bringing the middle class within those delightful open ranges of freedom that are the aristocratic privilege, and endowing it with the refined talents and the graces that it lacks. Clearly, in reading *Clarissa* in this way, we are reading the whole action as "larger than life," larger than a private family's adventures. We are reading it as a symbolic construct reflecting the ideals of a whole culture—that is, we are reading it as myth. A modern commentator has said that Richardson realized

> for his generation the emotions engendered by the conditions of life that defined his generation's hopes and that set limitations upon the fulfillment of those hopes. Before his novels appeared, however, eighteenth century Englishmen were sufficiently aware of the fact that their vital social problem was the interpenetration of the emergent middle class and the surviving aristocracy. His contemporaries had read authors who sought to educate the middle class in the manners and decorum of the disappearing aristocracy; they had been amused by authors who pointed up the gaucherie of the new man and woman, the new peer.[4]

Richardson's particular dramatization of this social condition was the exposure of his middle-class heroine to seduction by a nobleman. The significance of the act lies, on the one hand, in the fact that—up to a point—the heroine does seek union with the aristocrat who threatens her integrity, and, on the other hand, in the fact that the marriage does not, after all, take place. If *Clarissa* may be read as a "parable on the antithesis of the aristocratic and middle-class codes," the parable contrives to demonstrate finally the superiority of the latter.[5] The aristocracy is put in its place (Lovelace, we presume, goes to hell) and Clarissa, on her way to heaven, bestows blessings that assuredly have

[4] *Ibid.*, p. 129. [See p. 41 in this volume.]
[5] Downs, *op. cit.*, p. 182.

magical virtue (like the blessings bestowed by Isaac and by Jacob) on her mother and father, her sister, her brother, her uncles, Miss Howe, Mrs. Norton, the nurse, the servants. That is, by her death, symbolically she makes great her class, gives supernatural sanction to its code, donates to it her mana, making of it an embodiment of the order of the universe.

Noticeably, the religious myth and the myth of class overlap in a good many places, for, whether by historical accident or inevitability, Puritanism became the moral code and the religious faith of the commercially prosperous middle class. Noticeably also, however, there are places where these two mythological aspects of the book seem to contradict each other. Lovelace's part in the religious myth is to represent evil; he is to be hated; above all, he is to be feared. But in the class myth he has an ambivalent status; he exerts powerful attraction; nevertheless, as the drama evolves, he is seen to be too vicious after all. Fear of what the aristocracy stands for (or what it stands for in Richardson's fantasy) overcomes the attraction of what it stands for. What has been indulged by this myth is the middle-class wish to be aristocratic, to be elegant and idle and uninhibited; for, like dreams, myths indulge the hopes and passions and impulses of men. But, also like dreams, they are subject to a "censor." The indulgence may be sidled up to, but it must not be carried too far. In actual dreams, the "censor" in the psyche acts by disguising the wish either under forms that can be morally approved, or under forms apparently so fantastic and incoherent that they seem morally irrelevant. In myths, on the other hand, where whole dramas are acted out with narrative coherence, the "censor" may offer a dramatic resolution which negates the indulged wish by substituting some other attraction—as, in *Clarissa*, the wish to be aristocratic is negated by a counterwish, the wish to embody in the middle class itself the universal order, both divine and social. The latter wish offers no moral difficulties; one has merely to look upon oneself and one's class as the highest product of the human race, the epitome of what God intended man to be; and, implicitly, what Richardson tells his readers is that the middle class, to see an image of what is socially and morally desirable, need not look beyond itself, but will find that image in what it already is. This is comforting doctrine, most particularly since the myth has already underhandedly indulged the desire for aristocratic pleasures.

Myth has its power and fertility not in singleness of meaning (like allegory) but in multiplicity of meaning—meaning that changes historically with social changes, and that changes at any one glance with the center one chooses to see in it. We shall have to add another center and another contour to the *Clarissa*-myth: namely, a dramatic vision of family life and its sanctions. If *Clarissa* were a "novel of manners" alone, we should find in it a description of how a family lived and sinned and suffered in the eighteenth century, all possibly psychologically fascinating and perhaps with some universal significance. But, being myth, its vision of family life is raised to intimacy with the supernatural. The Harlowes acquire their "bigness" from other equators and other ecliptics than those that would circumscribe family life in a novel of manners. For Richardson, the family was a microcosm of society. Families were, he said, "so many miniatures" of the community of the world. But the family was not only a miniature of the world; it was an expression of divine order. In a later book, *Sir Charles Grandison* (the hero of which is Lovelace's opposite and thus a moral therapy for readers too attracted to the aristocratic rake), Sir Charles expresses himself on the concerns of Deity: "Does He not," he asks, "interest Himself, if I may so express myself, in the performance of filial duty? May it not be justly said, that to obey your parents is to serve God?" The particular family relationship that is eminent in *Clarissa* is that of female child to male parent, and it is brought dramatically to bear on the affair of marriage. We may learn something enlightening about this relationship from eighteenth-century conduct books. A parent "can no more force a Child to marry against her Consent, than a Child is permitted to act contrary to the Parent." [6] This is a situation comparable to a modern highway situation in Florida, where a sign at a railroad crossing decrees that neither vehicle, car or train, can go ahead until the other one has started. Another conduct book (one which the printer Richardson himself probably printed) offers the possibility of reciprocal modulation and of decision of act. "There is one instance," this writer says,

> wherein obedience to parents is of more importance to children than any other in life, and yet where they too often fail to pay it; and that is in the article of marriage: for, as long as children continue a part of their parent's family . . . they are absolutely in their parent's power, and have no more right to dispose of themselves than they have to dispose of the parents' fortune, or inheritance, or any of their goods . . .

And then he takes up the parents' responsibility.

> Prudent parents well know, that such accomplishments as either arise from, or tend to establish true worth, can alone render any pair happy in an union that must last for life. This, I say, all prudent parents very well know; and therefore are best fitted to make a right choice for their

---

[6] This and the two following passages from conduct books are quoted by Alan D. McKillop, in *Samuel Richardson* (Chapel Hill: University of North Carolina Press, 1936), p. 135.

children; but still with this caution, that they do not offer violence to their inclinations, by forcing them to marry against their will. For the rest, it were infinitely better, that perverse children should actually die in the disappointment of their inclinations, than that they should make both themselves and their parents for ever miserable, by an unfortunate and undutiful marriage.

The critical and helplessly ambiguous situation with which Clarissa is faced is, as one critic has said, a "crisis that affects not merely the future of any imaginary individual but the social position of the eighteenth century unmarried woman." [7]

"To obey your parents is to serve God." But Clarissa, dangerously for this code, is economically independent. She could, practically speaking, do whatever her impulse led her to do. She could seek satisfaction anywhere that she chose. And she does "go off with a man." Richardson said, in correspondence, "Going off with a Man, is the thing I wanted most to make inexcusable." The "man," as we have seen, is an outlaw, a pariah, a threat, a social terror. But for this particular reading of *Clarissa* as a myth of family life, he is— in a word—the lover. Clarissa's "going off with" him is a symbolical alliance of daughter with lover against family, an alliance with the outlaw and criminal who represents enjoyments (in this context, enjoyments of love) which the financially consolidated bourgeois family cannot tolerate inasmuch as enjoyment of love would mean failure of sobriety, which is the moral pillar of family unity and financial security. The book begins with this rebellion. Actually, however, as the story progresses, it is not the daughter's rebellion that is thematically paramount, but the daughter's obedience; for her father's curse is far more effective emotionally upon her than the attraction of the lover, or than her desire to escape the sterile and brutal cash alliance with the suitor approved by the family. Furthermore, the father's curse is dramatically correlated with and confirmed by Lovelace's own viciousness; the lover who would take the daughter out of the family is exposed as the worst of all evildoers. From this point of view, the lover is indirectly a kind of moral employee of the father: he is the living scourge exercised by the father upon the rebellious daughter. The paramount motif is, then, not rebellion and escape, but acquiescence in parental values and return. Clarissa is the family's consoling symbol of the right-minded daughter. She has a great act to perform: her financial independence is not societally right; she voluntarily gives it up. And she returns to the parental nest. For Clarissa does make a symbolic return "to her Father's house" (her

---

[7] F. C. Green, *Minuet* (London: J. M. Dent & Sons, Ltd., 1935), p. 403.

last, punning, highly disingenuous letter to Lovelace tells him that she will meet him there). "Her Father's house" is, in this context, heaven, and here the Puritan myth and the myth of family life coincide. Mr. Harlowe is proxy for God, and Clarissa's return to her Father's house is a supernatural equivalent of the necessary "return" of all daughters to the parental authority. The values that are given final sanction here are the typical values of the right-thinking bourgeois family: the father's authority is supreme; the daughter must not wed for satisfaction of personal impulse, but, if she weds, must do so for the further consolidation and enrichment of the clan; the lover is condemned; there must, in a word, be no love, except insofar as love can serve the family economy.

Clarissa's whiteness, her debility, and her death are correlatives of the sterilization of instinct and the impotence that are suggested as the desirable qualities of family and social life. As we have said previously, Clarissa's death does not provide a tragic ending for the story, but a "happy ending," inasmuch as her death is equated with supernatural joys and rewards. The scene in the death room is an astonishing one. The room is crowded with people, all pressing around the dying woman to obtain her blessing. The mourning is as public as possible; every sigh, every groan, every tear is recorded. One is given to understand that nothing could be a greater social good than Clarissa's death, nothing could be more enjoyable than to watch her in her death throes (she performs them charmingly), nothing a greater privilege than to be present at this festival of death and to weep and sniffle in the common orgy. An instructive grace note to the scene is Mrs. Judith Norton's observation that to have her own eyes closed in death by her young friend Clarissa was a "pleasure" which she had often "promised" herself—a pleasure now, alas, not to be obtained. This macabre satisfaction crowns the value system of *Clarissa,* triumphantly capping a code of Puritanism in morals, parental authoritarianism in the family, and the cash nexus as the only binding tie for society at large—a cult, in short, of death.

Clarissa returns "to her Father's house" as the perfect daughter, the model of all daughters. The novel offers the symbolic formula for such perfection: Clarissa is the sexless daughter, the dead daughter. In reading *Clarissa* finally as a sexual myth, we are reading it as a construct of irrationals similar to a dream (although, in the case of myth, the mythmaker is "dreaming" not only his own dream, but society's dream as well), and, irrationally, the sexless daughter manages to have the most violent of sexual experiences. It has been said of Clarissa that, by setting such a price upon herself, she "represents that extreme of puritanism which desires to be raped. Like Lovelace's her sexuality is really violent, insatiable in its wish for destruction."[8] In a sense, she keeps her cake while eating it—a proverbial paradox that expresses aptly what happens in dreams, where the forbidden wish is indulged under a disguise of nonindulgence. The mythical potency of *Clarissa*, in this respect, is witnessed by the fascination held for generations of readers by the motif of the carnal assault on a virgin. Novel after novel repeated this motif, obviously feeding an immense appetite of the reading public for more of the same. The assault is sometimes frustrated, sometimes carried through (*Clarissa*, of course, allows both: Lovelace accomplishes his vile ends, but the lady, being drugged, is in a sense not there; moreover, her death and sainthood negate the whole affair). Abduction by a handsome nobleman, captivity in a house of ill fame, and the use of drugs on the virtuous heroine, are devices almost obligatory in these books.[9] Richard Chase, writing on the nature of myth, has suggested that "myth is the repository of repressed wishes" and that

> part of the magic power of myth stems from its ability to furnish "recognition scenes," in which we have the thrilling experience of coming face to face with a disinherited part of ourselves:[10]

The modern reader may be disinclined to find, in the captivity-and-assault sequences in *Clarissa*, "recognition scenes" of this kind, and indeed the device used by Lovelace appears extraordinarily crude; but the reader's disinclination may merely reflect the fact that Hollywood has elaborated subtler stratagems of wish fulfillment, under a more refined censorship. Lovelace's own frenzied fantasy was undoubtedly prophetic when he saw himself in the dock on trial for his life, and all the sympathies of the audience with the handsome criminal: "Even the judges, and the whole crowded bench will acquit us in their hearts! and every single man wish he had been me."

As for Clarissa's own perverted sexuality, we read it in the profusion of sexual images that, paradoxically, at the level of professed narrative intention are meant to illustrate her resistance to Lovelace and her protection of her virginity—for surely we must find ambiguous those contexts which illustrate the virtue of chastity and the wickedness of sex by an imagery making defloration attractive and exciting; but more

---

[8] V. S. Pritchett, *The Living Novel* (New York: Reynal & Hitchcock, 1947), p. 28.
[9] Cf. Mrs. Davys' *The Accomplish'd Rake* (1756), Jane Marishall's *History of Miss Clarinda Cathcart* (3d ed. 1767), Mrs. Sarah Scott's *Cornelia* (1750), Mrs. Woodfin's *Sally Sable* (before 1764), Diderot's *La Réligeuse* (1760). In the romances of Mrs. Radcliffe, as Mario Praz has pointed out, the motif of captivity manages to exploit the same set of sado-masochistic attractions.
[10] *Quest for Myth* (Baton Rouge: Louisiana State University Press, 1949), p. 101.

especially we find her sexual violence in the constant identification of sex and death, phallic images and images of assassination. The identification of love and death is one of the oldest puns and one of the oldest of myth motifs; it is found in the great love stories—in the stories of Tristan and Iseult, Phaedra and Hippolytus, Dido and Aeneas, Antony and Cleopatra (it is found also quite literally in the life histories of salmon, ephemerids, and some spiders, a fact which is perhaps of significance in deepening our appreciation of the literary instinct in this matter). The sexual myth in *Clarissa* is founded in the love-death identification, and acquires power from that ancient and universal perception; but as *Clarissa* formulates the love myth, it becomes perverse, inasmuch as "love" here is conceived so strangely and exclusively as physical violation, an act of stabbing or ripping, with no implication of any aspect of sexual passion except a passion to murder and be murdered. Indeed, it is impossible to think of either Clarissa's or Lovelace's attitudes as involving any sensuality; for the word "sensual" pertains to gratification of the senses, and we find it difficult to discover those senses which might be gratified by stabbing. Their passion symbolizes gratification, not of sensual life, but of a submerged portion of the emotional life whose tendency actually opposes gratification of the senses—the death wish, the desire for destruction. And it is here that the mythical representation of sexual relationships in *Clarissa* coincides with and deeply reinforces the mythical representation of social values and the values of family life. From each point of view, the book is a paean to death. Richardson is the great poet of the adolescence of our own acquisitive, aggressive culture—a culture that has elaborated the cognate political myth of a world divided between two powers, one "good," one "bad," each engrossed in the devising of magical weapons for the destruction of the other, each "censoring" the grand death wish with a diplomacy designed to bring about a marriage in all profit and decency.

Dr. Samuel Johnson said of Richardson's heroines that they all had "a kind of obliquity in their moral vision," and, commenting particularly upon the casuistry which he found in Clarissa, he complained, "You may observe there is always something which she prefers to truth." Clarissa's character has been read by certain critics as a study in the divided mind. We must certainly acquiesce in a reading of her story as a psychological study; but our own reading of the novel as myth finds the psychological study to be but one level in a multileveled construct whose depth and richness derive from vast social dreams in which the individual character, however interesting from the point of view of character study, is at the same time more than an individual character—is a fabulous creature of epic stature, clothed with the ideals of a culture and of a race. In this reading, Clarissa's moral "obliquity," her "divided mind," are a function of mysterious indulgences in the forbidden, through which a Puritan-capitalistic culture found its systematic inhibitions gratefully removed, while, at the same time, it had in Lovelace a whipping boy for the same indulgences. But through Clarissa also the systematic inhibitions of this culture must receive their supernatural sanction, their "higher authority"; for the race does demand "higher authority" for its mores, simply in order to face itself with equanimity and to perpetuate itself proudly. Having so much dependent on her, so many and such complex duties to perform for her readers, Clarissa may well appear as a moral casuist and a divided mind.

# Clarissa and Lovelace

## by Ian Watt

Clarissa is, among other things, the supreme embodiment of the new feminine stereotype, a very paragon of delicacy. This is a crucial factor in her relations with Lovelace, who carefully contrives not to propose marriage in such a way as would enable Clarissa to agree without compromising her delicacy, which she refuses to do: "Would he have me catch at his first, his *very* first word?" she asks on one occasion, and on another, when Lovelace cruelly asks if she has any objections to delaying a few days until Lord M. can attend the wedding, she is forced by her sense of "due decorum" to answer, "No, no, you cannot think that I should imagine there can be reasons for such a hurry." As a result, even Anna Howe thinks that Clarissa is "over-nice, over-delicate," and she strongly urges that Clarissa "condescend to clear up his doubts." Richardson, however, points out in a footnote that "it was not possible for a person of her true delicacy of mind to act otherwise than she did, to a man so cruelly and insolently artful": and in fact Lovelace understood this very well, as he explained to Belford: "Never, I believe, was there so true, so delicate a modesty in the human mind as in that of this lady . . . this has been my security all along." [1]

The reinforced taboo on women avowing their feelings in courtship is, therefore, primarily responsible for the way that the deadlock between Clarissa and Lovelace drags out so long, becoming uglier and more desperate in the process. Richardson, indeed, with remarkable objectivity, even makes Lovelace challenge the whole basis of the code. He wonders whether women should really be proud of having "wilful and *studied* delays, *imputed to them*" over marriage: "are they not," he

---

"Clarissa and Lovelace" (Editor's title). From *The Rise of the Novel* by Ian Watt (London: Chatto & Windus, Ltd.; Berkeley: University of California Press, 1957), pp. 225–38. Copyright © 1957 by Chatto & Windus. Reprinted by permission of the publishers. These pages are from Chapter VII, "Richardson as Novelist: *Clarissa*."

[1] II, 28, 312, 156; I, 500; II, 156, 475. [Page references are to Everyman's edition (1932).]

suggests, "indelicate in their affected delicacy; for do they not thereby tacitly confess that they expect to be the greatest gainers in wedlock; and that there is *self-denial* in the pride they take in delaying." [2]

Lovelace is himself a representative of the masculine stereotype against which the feminine code is a defence. He believes, for example, that the hypocritical bashfulness of the *"passive* sex" justifies his own in using forceful methods. "It is cruel to ask a modest woman for her consent," he writes, and finds a kind of support in the views of Anna Howe who believes that "our sex are best dealt with by boisterous and unruly spirits." Clarissa sees that a larger issue is at stake, and pleads that a "modest woman" should "distinguish and wish to consort with a modest man" such as the unexciting Hickman: but Lovelace knows better; women do not really desire such a lover—"a *male virgin*—I warrant!" For, as he rather wittily puts it, a virtuous woman can "expect . . . the confidence *she* wants" if she marries a rake, whereas she cannot but consider the virtuous male "and herself as two parallel lines; which, though they run side by side, can never meet." [3]

Lovelace himself, like the rakes and heroes of Restoration drama, gives his allegiance to a debased form of romantic love, thus underlining his historical role as the representative of the Cavalier attitude to sex, in conflict with the Puritan one represented by Clarissa. Sexual passion is placed upon a different and higher plane than the institutional arrangement of marriage, and so, although the divine Clarissa Harlowe can almost make him think of "foregoing the *life of honour* for the *life of shackles*," his darling hope is "to prevail upon her to live with [him] what [he] call[s] the life of honour," in which he will promise "never to marry any other woman," but in which their felicity will be uncontaminated by the rites of matrimony.[4]

That, at least, is his scheme: to win her on his own terms; with always the possibility that he can marry her afterwards, once his personality and his code have had their triumph. "Will not the generality of the world acquit me, if I *do* marry?" he asks. "And what is that injury which a *church rite* will not at any time repair? Is not the *catastrophe of every story that ends in wedlock accounted happy?*" [5]

As the world goes, Lovelace is perhaps as close to the average view as Clarissa, and his attitude finds some support in the story of *Pamela*. But Richardson was now in a much more serious mood, and, as he announced in the Preface, was now determined to challenge "that dangerous but too-commonly-received notion, *that a reformed rake*

---

[2] II, 457.
[3] III, 214; II, 147, 73, 126; III, 82.
[4] I, 147; II, 496.
[5] III, 281.

*makes the best husband."* So he introduced the rape when Clarissa is unconscious from opiates, which is perhaps the least convincing incident in the book, but which serves a number of important moral and literary purposes.

First, and most obviously for Richardson's didactic purpose, it puts Lovelace wholly beyond the pale of any conception of honour, and proclaims to all the barbarity which lies below the genteel veneer of rakery; this Lovelace himself comes to realise, and curses himself for having taken the advice of Mrs. Sinclair and her crew. Not, of course, out of moral compunction, but because it is an admission of complete defeat: in his own eyes, since, as he says, "there is no triumph in *force*. No conquest over the will":[6] and in the eyes of the world, since, as John Dennis cynically remarked, "A rape in tragedy is a panagyrick upon the sex . . . for . . . the woman . . . is supposed to remain innocent, and to be pleased without her consent; while the man, who is accounted a damned villain, proclaims the power of female charms, which have the force to drive him to so horrid a violence." [7]

Once Lovelace has found that, contrary to his expectation, it is not a case of *"once overcome . . . for ever overcome,"* Clarissa is able to demonstrate the falsity of his view of the feminine code, and defy him in the famous words, "That man who has been the villain to me that you have been shall never make me his wife." Clarissa's sense of her own honour is much more important than her reputation in the eyes of the world; the code, in fact, is not a hypocritical sham; Lovelace's assumption that "the for-better and for-worse legerdermain" would "hocus pocus . . . all the wrongs I have done Miss Harlowe into acts of kindness and benevolence to Mrs. Lovelace" is completely disproved, and he succumbs to such "irresistible proofs of the love of virtue for its own sake." [8]

If this were all, the conflict in *Clarissa* would still, perhaps, be too simple for a work of such length. Actually, however, the situation is much more complex and problematic.

Freud showed how the artificiality of the modern sexual code "must incline [the members of society] to concealment of the truth, to euphemism, to self-deception, and to the deception of others." [9] In *Pamela* this self-deception produces irony: the reader contrasts the heroine's pretended motives with her transparent but largely unconscious pur-

---
[6] II, 398.
[7] *Critical Works*, [ed. Hooker (Baltimore, 1939–43)], II, 166.
[8] III, 318, 222, 412, 222.
[9] " 'Civilised' Sexual Morality and Modern Nervousness," *Collected Papers* (London, 1924), II, 77.

pose. In *Clarissa,* however, a similar unawareness of sexual feeling on the heroine's part, which by others may be interpreted as gross lack of self-knowledge, if not actual dishonesty, becomes an important part of the dramatic development, deepening and amplifying the overt meaning of the story.

Johnson observes of Clarissa that "there is always something which she prefers to truth." [10] But Anna Howe justly points out that as far as women's communication with men is concerned, this duplicity is imposed by the sexual code: for, as she says, if a woman writes "her heart to a man practised in deceit, or even to a man of some character, what advantage does it give him over her!" [11] The real tragedy, however, is that the code also makes Clarissa withhold her sexual feelings from Anna Howe, and even from her own consciousness, and it is this which creates the main psychological tension in the early volumes, for which Johnson particularly admired Richardson.[12] The correspondence of Clarissa, and, to a lesser extent, of Lovelace, is an absorbing study because we can never assume that any statement should be taken as the complete and literal truth. Perhaps one of the reasons for Johnson's admiration was that, although . . . he believed that a man's "soul lies naked" in his letters, he also knew that "There is . . . no transaction which offers stronger temptations to fallacy and sophistication than epistolary intercourse." [13]

The counterpoint of these unconscious duplicities in the early volumes is built upon the fact that Anna believes that Clarissa is in love with Lovelace, and does not believe Clarissa's protestations that her elopement was entirely accidental and involuntary on her part. After the marriage has been long delayed, Anna Howe even thinks it necessary to write to Clarissa: "What then have you to do but to fly this house, this infernal house! Oh that your heart would let you fly the *man!*" Lovelace, it is true, seizes the letter, and Clarissa escapes on her own initiative. Nevertheless, until half the book is done, there is a genuine ambiguity about the situation in everyone's mind; we are fully entitled to suspect Clarissa herself of not knowing her own feelings: and Lovelace is not altogether wrong in suspecting her of the "female affectation of denying [her] love." [14]

As the story develops, Clarissa herself gradually makes this discovery. Very early she has cause to wonder "what turn my mind had taken to dictate so oddly to my pen" in the course of a letter about Lovelace;

---

[10] *Johnsonian Miscellanies* [ed., G. B. Hill (Oxford, 1897)], I, 297.
[11] III, 8.
[12] *Johnsonian Miscellanies*, I, 282.
[13] "Pope," *Lives of the Poets,* ed. [G. B.] Hill [(Oxford, 1905)], III, 207.
[14] III, 11; I, 515.

and her debates with Anna Howe about her real attitude to him eventually force her to question whether her original hope that she could reform Lovelace was not actually a mask for less creditable motives. "What strange imperfect beings!" she reflects. "But *self* here, which is at the bottom of all we do, and of all we wish, is the grand misleader." "Once you wrote," she confesses to Anna Howe, "that men of his cast are the men that our sex do not *naturally* dislike: while I held that such were not (however *that* might be) the men we *ought* to like." She cannot deny that she "could have liked Mr. Lovelace above all men," and that there may be some justice in the tenor of Anna's raillery that she did not "attend to the throbs" of her heart; her principle that we should "like and dislike as reason bids us" was not so easy to practise as she imagined; and she convicts herself "of a punishable fault" in having loved him, punishable because "what must be that love that has not some degree of purity for its object?" But, as she realises, "love and hatred" are not "voluntary passions," and so, although without any full clarification of her feelings, she admits "detection" by Anna of her passion for Lovelace: "*Detection*, must I call it?" she wonders, and adds defeatedly: "What can I call it?" [15]

Throughout the novel Clarissa is learning more about herself, but at the same time she is also learning more about the much blacker deceptions of Lovelace. The minor reticences and confusions revealed in the feminine correspondence are insignificant compared to the much grosser discrepancies between Lovelace's pretended attitude to Clarissa and the falsehoods and trickeries which his letters reveal. The masculine code allows him to practise, and even openly avow, his complete lack of truth and honour in his pursuit of the opposite sex. As Belford points out, "*our honour,* and *honour* in the *general acceptation* of the word are two things," and Lovelace's honour is such that he has "never lied to man, and hardly ever said truth to woman." As a result of these revelations we realise that the code which might seem to make Clarissa too prudent is not prudent enough when measured against the outrageous means which men allow themselves to gain their ends. But if Clarissa's code fosters the self-ignorance which helps to place her in Lovelace's power, it at least does not involve conscious deception; and so Lovelace is forced to see that since Clarissa cannot "stoop to deceit and falsehood, no, not to save herself," Belford was right when he asserted that "the trial is not a fair trial." [16]

The sophistries both conscious and unconscious produced by the sexual code, then, helped Richardson to produce a pattern of psycho-

[15] I, 47; II, 379, 438–439; I, 139; II, 439.
[16] II, 158; IV, 445; III, 407; II, 158.

logical surprise and discovery very similar in nature to that in *Pamela*, although the counterpoint between feminine self-deception and masculine trickery is of a much more extended and powerful kind. But Richardson's explorations of the unconscious forms taken by the sexual impulse also took him much further; and he added to the already complex series of dualities embodied in the relationship of Lovelace and Clarissa quite another range of meanings which may be regarded as the ultimate and no doubt pathological expression of the dichotomisation of the sexual roles in the realm of the unconscious.

The imagery in which the relation between the sexes is rendered indicates the basic tendency of Richardson's thought. Lovelace fancies himself as an eagle, flying only at the highest game; Belford calls him "cruel as a panther"; while Anna sees him as a hyena. The metaphor of the hunt, indeed, informs the whole of Lovelace's conception of sex: he writes to Belford, for example: "we begin when boys, with birds, and when grown up, go on with women; and both, perhaps, in turn, experience our sportive cruelty." Then he gloats as he pictures "the charming gradations" by which the bird yields to its captor as he hopes Clarissa will yield to him, and concludes, "By my soul, Jack, there is more of the savage in human nature than we are commonly aware of." But Jack is already aware of it, in Lovelace's case at least, and replies: "Thou ever delightedst to sport with and torment the animal, whether bird or beast, that thou lovedst and hadst a power over."

Sadism is, no doubt, the ultimate form which the eighteenth-century view of the masculine role involved: and it makes the female role one in which the woman is, and can only be, the prey: to use another of Lovelace's metaphors, man is a spider, and woman is the predestined fly. [17]

This conceptualisation of the sexual life has had an illustrious literary history since Richardson. Mario Praz has seen *Clarissa* as the beginning of what he calls "the theme of the persecuted maiden," a theme which was taken up by de Sade, and played an important part in Romantic literature.[18] Later, in a somewhat milder form, this picture of the sexual relationship established itself in England. The Victorian imagination was haunted by the perpetual imminence of attacks on pure womanhood by cruel and licentious males, while, in a Rochester or a Heathcliff, the feminine and Puritan imaginations of Charlotte and Emily Brontë produced a stereotype of the male as a combina-

[17] II, 253; IV, 269; II, 245-249, 483, 23.
[18] *The Romantic Agony*, trans. Davidson (London, 1951), pp. 95-107.

tion of terrifying animality and diabolic intellect which is equally pathological.

The complement of the sadistic and sexual male is the masochistic and asexual female; and in *Clarissa* this conception is present both in the imagery connected with the heroine and in the underlying implication of the central action. As regards imagery, Clarissa, significantly, is symbolised not by the rose but the lily: Lovelace sees her on one occasion as "a half-broken-stalked lily, top-heavy with the overcharging dews of morning," and Clarissa later arranges that her funeral urn be decorated with "the head of a white lily snapped short off, and just falling from the stalk." [19] In the realm of action, the rape itself, when Clarissa is unconscious from opiates, may be regarded as the ultimate development of the idea of the feminine sexual role as one of passive suffering: it suggests that the animality of the male can only achieve its purpose when the woman's spirit is absent.

Even so, Clarissa dies; sexual intercourse, apparently, means death for the woman. What Richardson intended here is not wholly clear, but it may be noted that he had already shown a remarkable awareness of the symbolism of the unconscious in *Pamela*. When the heroine is still terrified of Mr. B. she imagines him pursuing her in the shape of a bull with bloodshot eyes; later, when a happy resolution is in sight she dreams, appropriately enough, of Jacob's ladder.[20] It is significant, therefore, that just before her elopement, Clarissa should have a dream in which Lovelace stabs her to the heart; then, she reports, he "tumbled me into a deep grave ready dug, among two or three half-dissolved carcasses; throwing in the dirt and earth upon me with his hands, and trampling it down with his feet." [21] The dream is primarily a macabre expression of her actual fear of Lovelace; but it is also coloured by the idea that sexual intercourse is a kind of annihilation.

This connection haunts the later part of the story. Though afraid of Lovelace, she goes off with him; and later, when his intentions are becoming more evident, she several times offers him knives or scissors to kill her with. One of these occasions is thus reported by Lovelace: "baring, with a still more frantic violence, part of her enchanting neck, Here, here, said the soul-harrowing beauty, let thy pointed mercy enter." Unconsciously, no doubt, Clarissa courts sexual violation as well as death; and when the violation comes its equation with death is apparent to both parties. Lovelace announces, "The affair is over. Clarissa lives"—as though the contrary might have been expected; while

[19] III, 193; IV, 257.
[20] *Pamela*, I, 135, 274. [Everyman's edition (1914).]
[21] I, 433.

later Clarissa directs that if Lovelace insists "upon viewing *her dead* whom he ONCE before saw in a manner dead, let his gay curiosity be gratified." [22]

In a sense the coming death to which Clarissa here refers is a working out of her own initial masochistic fantasy: having equated sex and death, and having been violated by Lovelace, her self-respect requires that the expected consequence ensue: her decline is as the physician says, clearly not a bodily matter but "a love case." [23] Not much is said about the covert and implacable cause why her fate cannot be otherwise, but there is never any doubt about the fact itself: anything else would prove her deepest self to have been wrong.

This, of course, is not the only cause of her death, which has a very complex motivation. It is, for example, quite consistent with Richardson's beliefs that Clarissa should prefer death to the burden of her sexual desecration, even though it is, as Lovelace says, "a mere *notional violation*." [24] But there is also more than a hint that what Clarissa cannot face is not so much what Lovelace has done or what the world may think about it, but the idea that she herself is not wholly blameless.

This idea is most clearly expressed in one of the fragments which she writes in her delirium after the rape:

> A lady took a great fancy to a young lion, or a bear, I forget which—but of a bear, or a tiger, I believe it was. It was made her a present of when a whelp. She fed it with her own hand: she nursed up the wicked cub with great tenderness; and would play with it without fear or apprehension of danger . . . But mind what followed: at last, somehow, neglecting to satisfy its hungry maw, or having otherwise disobliged it on some occasion, it resumed its nature; and on a sudden fell upon her, and tore her in pieces, And who was most to blame, I pray? The brute, or the lady? The lady, surely! For what *she* did was *out* of nature, *out* of character, at least: what it did was *in* its own nature.[25]

Lovelace, being a man, had done only what was to be expected: but Clarissa had acted out of nature in toying with him. Looking back, she perhaps remembers that Anna Howe, mocking her own claim that "she would not be in love with him for the world," had ironically congratulated her on "being the first of our sex that ever I heard of who has been able to turn that lion, Love, at her own pleasure, into a lap-dog." And this bitter reminder that she was wrong may have caused her to look within and glimpse the truth that even she was not

[22] III, 238, 196; IV, 416.
[23] II, 468.
[24] III, 242.
[25] III, 206.

above what Lovelace calls the "disgraceful" weaknesses "of sex and nature." [26] With such a belief poisoning her mind, the need to be delivered from the body becomes imperative; she must act out in a very literal fashion the words of St. Paul in *Romans*: "I delight in the law of God after the inward man. But I see another law in my members, warring against the law of my mind . . . O wretched man that I am! Who shall deliver me from the body of this death?"

In a historical perspective, it seems clear, Clarissa's tragedy reflects the combined effects of Puritanism's spiritual inwardness and its fear of the flesh, effects which tend to prevent the development of the sexual impulse beyond the autistic and masochistic stages. Freud and Horace are agreed that *Naturam expellas furca, tamen usque recurret* —a sentiment, incidentally, which was familiar to Richardson since Lovelace quotes it—and it is not surprising, therefore, that Clarissa's *Liebestod* should suggest that the erotic impulse has been channelled in varied and divergent directions. The perverse sensuous pleasure which she takes in every detail of the preparations for her coming death is primarily due to the feeling that she is at last about to meet the heavenly bridegroom: "I am upon a *better preparation* than for an earthly husband," she proclaims. "Never bride was so ready as I am. My wedding garments are bought . . . the easiest, the *happiest* suit, that ever bridal maiden wore." But her pleasure in her own approaching demise also has a strong narcissistic quality. Belford reports that "the principal device" she chose for her coffin "is a crowned serpent, with its tail in its mouth, forming a ring, the emblem of eternity:" emblem of eternity, doubtless, but also emblem of an endlessly self-consuming sexual desire.[27]

Opinions may well vary over the details of the meaning of the psychopathological aspects of *Clarissa,* but there can at least be no doubt that this was one of the directions which Richardson's imagination took, and that he there demonstrated a remarkable insight into the by now notorious sophistries of the unconscious and subconscious mind. Further evidence of this is to be found in the scenes after the rape, and in Clarissa's incoherent letter to Lovelace: Fielding praised it as "beyond anything I have ever read." [28] Another great contemporary admirer, Diderot, specifically pointed to the exploration of the deeper recesses of the mind as Richardson's *forte*—a testimony which carries considerable authority in the light of his own treatment of

[26] I, 49; III, 476; see also II, 420.
[27] II, 99; IV, 2, 303, 256–257.
[28] [E. L. McAdam, Jr.], "A New Letter from Fielding" [*Yale Review*, XXXVIII (1948)], 305.

the theme in *Le Neveu de Rameau*. It was Richardson, Diderot said, "qui porte le flambeau au fond de la caverne; c'est lui qui apprend à discerner les motifs subtils et déshonnêtes qui se cachent et se dérobent sous d'autres motifs qui sont honnêtes et qui se hâtent de se montrer les premiers. Il souffle sur le phantôme sublime qui se présente à l'entrée de la caverne; et le More hideux qu'il masquait s'aperçoit." [29] Such certainly is the nature of the voyage of discovery which we take in *Clarissa*; and the hideous Moor is surely the frightening reality of the unconscious life which lies hidden in the most virtuous heart.

Such an interpretation would imply that Richardson's imagination was not always in touch with his didactic purpose; but this, of course, is in itself not unlikely. The decorous exterior, the ponderous voice of the lay bishop, expresses an important part of Richardson's mind, but not all of it; and, his subjects being what they were, it is likely that only a very safe ethical surface, combined with the anonymity of print, and a certain tendency to self-righteous sophistry, were able to pacify his inner censor and thus leave his imagination free to express its profound interest in other areas of experience.

Some such process seems to have occurred in Richardson's portrayal of Lovelace as well as of Clarissa. There was probably a much deeper identification with his rake than he knew, an identification which left traces in such a remark as this of Lovelace: "Were every rake, nay, were every man, to sit down, as I do, and write all that enters into his head or into his heart, and to accuse himself with equal freedom and truth, what an army of miscreants should I have to keep me in countenance!" Elsewhere, the prodigious fertility of Lovelace's sexual imagination surely suggests a willing co-operation on the part of his creator's far beyond the call of literary duty: Lovelace's plan, for instance, of wreaking his revenge on Anna Howe, not only by ravishing her, but in having her mother abducted for the same fell purpose is a monstrously gratuitous fancy which is quite unnecessary so far as the realisation of Richardson's didactic intentions are concerned.[30]

The ultimate effect of Richardson's unconscious identification, however, would seem to be wholly justified from an aesthetic point of view. The danger in the original scheme of the novel was that Lovelace would be so brutal and callow that the relationship with Clarissa would be incapable of supporting a developing and reciprocal psychological pattern. Richardson, however, diminished the disparity between his protagonists by supplying their personalities with psychological undertones which do something to qualify the apparently diametrical opposition between them. He mitigated Clarissa's perfec-

[29] *Œuvres*, ed. Billy [Paris, 1946], p. 1091.
[30] II, 492, 418-425.

tions by suggesting that her deeper self has its morbid aspects—a suggestion which actually increases the pathos of her story but which brings her closer in a sense to the world of Lovelace; and at the same time he led us to feel that, just as his heroine's virtue is not without its complications, so his villain's vices have their pitiable aspect.

Lovelace's name—in sound as in etymology—mean "loveless," [31] and his code—that of the rake—has, like Clarissa's, blinded him to his own deepest feelings. From the beginning one side of his character is continually struggling to express its love for Clarissa openly and honourably, and it often almost succeeds. Clarissa, indeed, is aware of this undercurrent in his nature: "What *sensibilities*," she tells him, "must thou have suppressed! What a dreadful, what a judicial hardness of heart must thine be; who canst be capable of such emotions as sometimes thou hast shown; and of such sentiments as sometimes have flown from thy lips; yet canst have so far overcome them all, as to be able to act as thou hast acted, and that from settled purpose and premeditation." [32]

This division in Lovelace between conscious villainy and stifled goodness provides yet another satisfying formal symmetry to the conduct of the narrative. For, just as Clarissa began by loving Lovelace unconsciously and then was forced to see that, in truth, he did not deserve it, so Lovelace begins with a feeling in which hate and love are mixed, but comes eventually to love her completely, although only after he himself has made it impossible for her to reciprocate. Clarissa could perhaps have married Lovelace, very much on her own terms, had she known her own feelings earlier, and not been at first so wholly unaware, and later so frightened, of her sexual component; so Lovelace need not have lost Clarissa, if he had known and been willing to recognize the gentler elements in his personality.

The ultimate reason why this was impossible is, indeed, the exact complement of that which causes Clarissa's virtual suicide: both their fates show the havoc brought about by two codes which doom their

[31] See Ernest Weekley, *Surnames* (London, 1936), p. 259. Names are often a guide to unconscious attitudes, and those of Richardson's protagonists tend to confirm the view that he secretly identified himself with his hero—Robert Lovelace is a pleasant enough name—and even unconsciously collaborated with Lovelace's purpose of abasing the heroine: "Clarissa" is very close to "Calista," Rowe's impure heroine; while Harlowe is very close to "harlot." This verbal association seems to be on the verge of consciousness in a letter of Arabella's to Clarissa: she tells her that James will treat her "like a common creature, if he ever sees you," and then, referring to her doubts as to whether Lovelace will ever marry her, adds in a frenzy of contempt: ". . . this is the celebrated, the blazing Clarissa—Clarissa *what? Harlowe,* no doubt!—And Harlowe it will be, to the disgrace of us all." (II, 170–171.)

[32] III, 152.

holders to a psychological attitude which makes human love impossible, since they set an impenetrable barrier between the flesh and the spirit. Clarissa dies rather than recognise the flesh; Lovelace makes it impossible for her to love him because he, too, makes an equally absolute, though opposite, division: if he wishes "to prove her to be either angel or woman," Clarissa has no alternative but to make the choice she does, reject her physical womanhood, and prove, in Lovelace's words, that "her frost is frost indeed." At the same time for him also the only possibility of salvation lies in the rejection of his own illusion of himself which, like Clarissa's, is ultimately a projection of false sexual ideology. "If I give up my contrivances," he writes in a moment of heart-searching, "I shall be but a common man." But, of course, he is, like Clarissa, so deeply attached to his own preconceptions of himself that he cannot change; the deadlock is complete, and, as he confesses, "what to do with her, or without her, I know not."[33]

For Lovelace also, therefore, death is the only way out. His end, it is true, is not a suicide, but it is like Clarissa's in the sense that he has in part provoked it, and that he has been forewarned in a dream, a dream where, thinking at last to embrace her, he sees the firmament open to receive her and then, left alone, the floor sinks under him and he falls into a bottomless Inferno. His unconscious premonition is confirmed by the event, but not before he has made expiation, admitting to his slayer Colonel Morden that he has provoked his destiny, and imploring Clarissa's Blessed Spirit to look down with pity and forgiveness.[34]

So ends a relationship that, in this at least like those of the great lovers of myth and legend, endures beyond death. Clarissa and Lovelace are as completely, and as fatally, dependent on each other as Tristan and Isolde or Romeo and Juliet; but, in keeping with the novel's subjective mode of vision, the ultimate barriers that prevent the union of Richardson's star-crossed lovers are subjective and in part unconscious; the stars operate on the individual through varied psychological forces, forces which are eventually, no doubt, public and social, since the differences between the protagonists represent larger conflicts of attitude and ethic in their society, but which are nevertheless so completely internalised that the conflict expresses itself as a struggle between personalities and even between different parts of the same personality.

This is Richardson's triumph. Even the most apparently implausible, didactic or period aspects of the plot and the characters, even the rape and Clarissa's unconscionable time a-dying, are brought into a larger

[33] II, 208; III, 190, 229.
[34] IV, 136, 529.

dramatic pattern of infinite formal and psychological complexity. It is this capacity for a continuous enrichment and complication of a simple situation which makes Richardson the great novelist he is; and it shows, too, that the novel had at last attained literary maturity, with formal resources capable not only of supporting the tremendous imaginative expansion which Richardson gave his theme, but also of leading him away from the flat didacticism of his critical preconceptions into so profound a penetration of his characters that their experience partakes of the terrifying ambiguity of human life itself.

# The Plan of *Clarissa*

## by Frederick W. Hilles

When Smyth Loftus wrote to Richardson from Ireland: "I am really astonished at the account you give of the manner of your writing," he was unconsciously echoing what another divine, John Stinstra, had written from Holland: "I am extremely astonished, Sir, by your telling me that you never write by a plan." [1] These were but two of Richardson's many correspondents who learned from him that he was an "irregular" writer. "I . . . can form no plan," he told Lady Bradshaigh, "nor write after what I have preconceived." And to Aaron Hill he spoke of following a "No-Plan" when composing *Clarissa*.[2]

If this were true of *Clarissa* it would indeed be astonishing. I suspect that Richardson has been misunderstood; and I suggest that this misunderstanding has led to some highly questionable literary criticism. At the end of the nineteenth century, for example, Clara Linklater Thomson could term Richardson's plots "loose and ill-constructed"; "he rambles on from one event to another, without troubling much about their coherence." Richardson "probably never gave a moment to the consideration of form." The epistolary method suited him because "he obviously composed without any preconceived plan." [3] Serious charges these, and perhaps they may be fairly brought against *Pamela II* or *Sir Charles Grandison*. But surely an author should be judged by his masterpiece, particularly when that masterpiece is a novel consisting of something like a million words.

His surviving correspondence throws a good deal of light on that No-Plan for *Clarissa*. First, it is clear, he wrote out what must have

---

"The Plan of *Clarissa*" by Frederick W. Hilles. From *Philological Quarterly*, XLV (1966), 236–48. Copyright © 1966 by the University of Iowa. Reprinted by permission of the University of Iowa.

[1] *The Correspondence of Samuel Richardson*, ed. A. L. Barbauld (London, 1804), v, 157, 258. Hereafter referred to as *Correspondence*.

[2] *Selected Letters of Samuel Richardson*, ed. John Carroll (Oxford: Clarendon Press, 1964), pp. 182, 71. Hereafter referred to as *Letters*.

[3] *Samuel Richardson* (1900), pp. 247, 248, 242.

## The Plan of Clarissa

been a very full sketch of the book, a sketch that he submitted to at least two of his mentors. In June 1744 Edward Young discussed the character of Lovelace and Clarissa's triumphant death. A few weeks later Aaron Hill commented on "that good and beautiful design I send you back the wide and arduous plan of." [4] By wide he means, I suppose, extensive—that is, detailed. It would have been uncharacteristic of Richardson to have prepared a plan that would have fitted on a page or two.

The author was a printer, a very busy printer at this time, but during the next four months he managed to make a beginning. Early in December, three years before the first volumes were to be published, he sent to Hill the letters that were designed to open the novel. A year later the book had not yet been finished, but it sounds as though Richardson was still following his original plan. Young's additions would adorn Clarissa's "last hours . . . they are entirely conformable to the frame *I have designed she shall then be in.*" [5] A few weeks later when sending Hill a greatly revised opening he could say that it had been so completely rewritten that those who had earlier read it would "think it a new Thing were they to see it." Some time after this, perhaps in the spring of 1746, he let Sophia Westcomb read his first volume. In October she wished to "reperuse" it.[6] Publication of that volume was still fourteen months away.

Just when he completed the first draft of the book it is not possible to say.[7] In October 1746 he wrote: "I once read to a young Lady Part of [Lovelace's] Character, and then his End; and upon her pitying him, and wishing he had been rather made a Penitent, than to be killed, I made him still more and more odious." This would indicate that the book had been completed some time earlier. Yet in that same letter he speaks of the work "as it now stands," and in January 1747 he has only "got into the 4th Century of Letters." [8] Since the first edition contained more than five hundred numbered letters, he still had some distance to go. Probably in spite of his declaration in the preface to the

---

[4] A. D. McKillop, *Samuel Richardson, Printer and Novelist* (University of North Carolina Press, 1936), pp. 120f.

[5] *Letters*, pp. 61, 62; italics mine.

[6] *Letters*, pp. 64, 69.

[7] According to W. M. Sale, Jr. (*Samuel Richardson, a Bibliographical Record* [Yale University Press, 1936] p. 49), "The original text, written or transcribed in vellum-bound note books, consisted of about 2,000 pages, with approximately 300 words to the page." This would be less than two-thirds the length of what was published in the first edition. Prof. Sale's source, I assume, is Richardson's letter to Hill dated 5 Jan. 1746/7.

[8] *Letters*, pp. 73f, 84.

first volume that "the whole Collection" was "ready for the Press," he had not really completed the book when the first two volumes appeared in December 1747. The reception of the initial volumes, he there said, would guide him as to the shaping of the rest of the book.

In any event the evidence that we have supports his statement that he was an irregular writer. That statement, however, must be qualified. He *had* a plan, a plan in writing, but what he wrote had to be licked into shape—was subjected to elaborate recension which presumably modified that plan. And yet the modifications were in matters of detail only. From the beginning Richardson had clearly in mind the "triumphant" ending, the deaths of Clarissa and Lovelace.

"What a happy genius," commented Stinstra, "that can thus prosecute his way through so many mazes and labyrinths, which perplex your common readers, and never deviate, without ever consulting a map." [9] Map is another word for plan, and a plan is something that shows the dimensions, relative positions, etc., of different parts of a designed or completed structure. So far we have been considering the designed structure of *Clarissa*. What does a map of the completed book reveal?

One way of mapping it is to plot it according to the calendar. Richardson confessed that he had taken some pains in the "fixing of Dates." [10] What he wished to avoid was making "the Writers do too much in the Time." But his decision to use the calendar year for structural purposes indicates that he was not above the consideration of form. The novel begins in January; it ends in December. Clarissa leaves home in the spring; the sordid climax occurs in June (actually on Midsummer night); she dies in September, shortly before the autumnal equinox; and Lovelace is killed in December, a few days before the winter solstice.

The principal device on the heroine's coffin is a serpent with its tail in its mouth, emblem (we are reminded) of eternity. It is also the emblem of fate. In my end is my beginning. This circular figure reflects the shape of the novel, which begins with a duel and ends with a duel. The whole is a cycle. When we have completed it, it is well an old age is out, and time to begin a new. A remark of Coleridge's (he was speaking of poetry) is here applicable.

> The common end of all *narrative* . . . is to convert a *series* into a *Whole*: to make those events, which in real or imagined History move on

[9] *Correspondence*, v, 258.
[10] *Letters*, p. 63. See Arthur Sherbo, "Time and Place in Richardson's *Clarissa*," *Boston Univ. Studies in English*, III (1957), 139–46.

in a *strait* Line, assume to our Understandings a *circular* motion—the snake with its Tail in its Mouth.[11]

Some such idea was in Hardy's mind when he wrote of that "beauty of shape" that is to be found in a literary masterpiece. "Herein," he goes on to say,

> lies Richardson's real if only claim to be placed on a level with Fielding: the artist spirit that he everywhere displays in the structural parts of his work. . . . No person who has a due perception of the constructive art shown in Greek tragic drama can be blind to the constructive art of Richardson.[12]

The constructive art in *Clarissa* is best observed by breaking it up into roughly equal parts, according to the eight volumes in which it was printed.[13] The scene at the beginning and throughout the first quarter is Harlowe Place. These two volumes are, in Richardson's words, "chiefly taken up with the Altercations between Clarissa and the several persons of her Family." And these altercations are "the Foundation of the whole" (VIII, 328).[14] We are introduced to the characters, note the hostility between Lovelace and the Harlowes, observe Clarissa as she is "pulled and pushed," "drawn and driven," forced to oppose her parents, and forced at the end of the second volume to run off with Lovelace.

Throughout the central section of the book Clarissa is a prisoner not of her family but of Lovelace. With the exception of four days in Hampstead she is living at "a vile House" kept by Mrs. "Sinclair." Her arrival there occurs near the end of volume III; her final escape takes place in the early part of volume VI. Between these two points are the two central volumes. The fourth works up from a relatively quiet beginning to the "nightly surprizes" (IV, 217), Lovelace's sickness and the fire; by the end of the fifth "the affair is over" (V, 314). Balancing the first two volumes are the last two which depict the contrasting "exits," to use one of Richardson's favorite words, of the heroine and her tormentor. Volume VII, which might have been entitled Holy Dying (Taylor's book is facetiously criticized by Lovelace in the previous volume [VI, 171f]), ends with Clarissa's death. The

---

[11] *Collected Letters of S. T. Coleridge*, ed. E. L. Griggs (Oxford: Clarendon Press, 1956), IV, 545, as quoted by M. H. Abrams in *From Sensibility to Romanticism*, ed. F. W. Hilles and H. Bloom (Oxford, 1965), p. 532.

[12] Thomas Hardy, *Life and Art* (New York, 1925), p. 70.

[13] The seven volumes of the first edition disguise the basic structure because Richardson had smaller type used in the last two volumes. The third and subsequent editions appeared in eight volumes. See Sale, pp. 49ff.

[14] References in brackets to volume and page are to the Shakespeare Head edition of *Clarissa* (Oxford: Blackwell, 1930).

story proper ends in the next volume when Lovelace is killed, but before that we have gone back to Harlowe Place (in my end is my beginning) as we accompany Clarissa to her final resting place, note in her will reflections of her early life, and hear about her in Anna's long letter to Belford. The greater part of the third and sixth volumes serve as bridges linking the *massif central* with the first and last quarters.

The first two volumes may be regarded as a unit, but each has its own organization. After an introduction of six letters the story gets under way. And the story in the first volume is of Clarissa slowly becoming entangled with Lovelace. At the start she does "not like him at all: He seemed to have too good an opinion both of his person and parts." Soon after, her "regards are not so much engaged . . . to another person as some of my friends suppose." When clear-eyed Anna Howe tells her she is falling in love, Clarissa can firmly reply: "THIS man is not THE man" (I, 15, 57, 69). A quarter of the way through the volume she is pleased to hear good of Lovelace; "yet, my dear, I had no *throbs*, no *glows* upon it! *Upon my word*, I had not." At the three-quarter mark she is pleased with what Lovelace has just said to her, but she can say this "without an imputed *glow* or *throb*" (I, 83, 261). Soon after, however, she sends her friend an extensive analysis of him, and as the volume nears the end she writes what is to me one of the few effective additions (or "restorations"), first printed in the third edition. A prisoner in her own home, terrified by her family's threats of sending her to Uncle Antony's moated grange, she suddenly bursts out (I, 334): "But what shall I do with this Lovelace? . . . such protestations of inviolable faith and honour; such vows of reformation; such pressing arguments to escape from this disgraceful confinement— O my Nancy, what shall I do with this Lovelace?" In spite of herself she is being attracted to him. "I intended," wrote Richardson, "the Flame should be inspired and grow, unknown to herself, and be more obvious, for a good while, to everybody than to herself." [15] At the conclusion of the first volume we know that she is in love, or at least strongly interested in "a man."

The second volume begins in a different key, with four letters from Anna Howe, including the delightful imaginary sketches of Solmes, Hickman, and Lovelace when schoolboys. When she imagines young Lovelace as "an orchard-robber, a wall-climber, a horse-rider without saddle or bridle, neck or nothing" (II, 8) we are being prepared for the end of this volume. Just before and just after the middle Clarissa (1) learns of the Rosebud affair, in which "Mr. Lovelace comes out

---

[15] *Letters*, p. 81.

# The Plan of Clarissa

with so much advantage," and (2) experiences the climactic interviews with Solmes, which are even more advantageous to Lovelace (II, 170, 200ff). As the volume nears the end the tempo steadily increases. Clarissa tells Lovelace she will leave home with him, records her frightful dream, changes her mind and writes the letter of revocation.

> *Sunday, Four in the Afternoon.* My Letter is not yet taken away—. . . *Seven o'Clock.* There remains my Letter still!—. . . *Monday Morn. April 10. Seven o'Clock.* O my dear! There yet lies the Letter, just as I left it! . . . *Eleven o'Clock.* He has not yet got my Letter . . .—But he is at the garden-door—* * I was mistaken! —How many noises *unlike,* be made *like* to what one fears!

And the next letter begins: "O my dearest friend! . . . your Clarissa Harlowe is gone off with a man!" (II, 280–339)

In the first edition the second volume ended with Anna's reply to this letter: "Good God of Heaven and Earth!—But what shall I say? —I am all impatience for particulars." And Anna was voicing the feelings of the reading public, which had to wait some five months before the next installment of two volumes appeared. Similarly, to digress for a moment, the fourth volume of the first edition ended at a tense moment, foreshadowing *The Perils of Pauline.* "O for a Curse to kill with!—Ruined! Undone! Outwitted! Tricked!—Zounds, man, the Lady is gone off!—Absolutely gone off!—Escaped!" We hear the lady's account of the escape, and then: *"Io Triumphe,* Io Clarissa, sing!" (V, 16, 58) Lovelace, dressed like a bridegroom, is at Hampstead, where she is hiding. What is to happen? Although readers were assured that the remainder of the work would be published "at once," they had to wait for more than seven months to satisfy their curiosity. Samuel Johnson thought, or at least told Richardson, that it was "a kind of tyrannical kindness to give only so much at a time as makes more longed for." [16] The author, of course, picked his breaking-off points astutely. To what extent his publishing the book in installments affected the structure of *Clarissa* we shall probably never know.

The plan of *Clarissa* reveals a plot that is highly symmetrical. As has been said, the foundations are carefully laid in the first quarter. During the greater part of the third volume Clarissa is full of questions as to her future (shall she marry? shall she go to London?), while Lovelace's behavior is soundly based on what he calls the Rake's creed. The central volumes are the keystone of the arch, so that volume VI balances III, VII and VIII balance I and II. In volume VI, after Clarissa has escaped and by letters from others has proved to herself

---

[16] *The Letters of Samuel Johnson,* ed. R. W. Chapman (Oxford: Clarendon Press, 1952), I, 50. He was here speaking not of *Clarissa* but of *Sir Charles Grandison.*

Lovelace's villainy, her behavior is soundly based: she knows exactly what lies ahead of her and approaches this with serenity. But Lovelace has lost much of his self-assurance, raises questions and with Belford expresses doubts as to the Rake's creed.[17] Up to the middle of the book it is conceivable that Clarissa will marry her lover; her behavior when she thinks he is sick is significant. But once the half-way point has been passed, marriage is out of the question. "I am already determined as to him" (v, 196). ". . . such an alliance can never *now* take place" (vi, 138). Only careless readers like Leslie Fiedler, if indeed he should be called a reader of the book, can say that Clarissa continues to love Lovelace after the rape.[18]

The symmetry of the plot suggests a highly stylized dance in which the two chief performers change places. Clarissa is a country girl. She possesses certain attributes that connote fresh air, healthy domesticity. She is interested in her bantams and pheasants, pleased with her dairy house. One thinks of Lady Teazle before Sir Peter married her: "My daily occupation to inspect the dairy, superintend the poultry," etc.[19] Unlike Lady Teazle Clarissa has no desire to go to London. She is unacquainted "with the ways of that great, wicked town" (II, 268). Yet at the end of her life, "by strange melancholy accidents," she finds herself lodged in the Parish of St. Paul Covent Garden (VIII, 106), the theatrical district and, as Hogarth shows us in "Morning," the haunt of revellers. The pattern is reversed for Lovelace. Early in the book we learn that "he lived a wild life in town . . . where, till he came acquainted with our family, he used chiefly to reside." The "country was always glad" when he and his companions went up again (I, 24f). When in London, according to Anna, he was "often at Plays, and at the Opera." Clarissa in reply thinks of him "accustomed, perhaps, to

---

[17] These questions and doubts are for the most part additions first printed in the third edition, VI, 311–16, 325f. They occur at the three-quarter point of the volume exactly balancing the three letters that present the Rake's Creed, which are a quarter of the way through Vol. III, [III, 76–95; VI, 339–44, 353–55]. These additions, driving home a point that some early readers missed, support the thesis of M. Kinkead-Weekes in *"Clarissa* Restored?" (*R.E.S.* New Series, x (1959), 156–71). For Richardson's insistence on the importance of the three letters in III see *Letters*, p. 143. The text of this letter [as originally printed in *N&Q*, 4th series, iii (1869), 375–78] is sadly garbled. The original is in my possession.

[18] Leslie A. Fiedler, *Love and Death in the American Novel* (New York, 1960), p. 30. Two pages later Fiedler writes: "The critic's ignorance of the novel itself is unpardonable." Yet he has just informed us that "at the end Lovelace is killed in a duel by his closest friend." I can't resist quoting another gem from the same source: "Practically everyone who knows the name of Richardson knows the meager plot of *Pamela:* how the virtuous governess resists the advances of her employer's son." Governess!

[19] *School for Scandal*, II, i.

town-women, and their confident ways" (II, 164, 167). In London he is in his element. Yet during the last five months of his life he lives almost entirely in the country.

In the early part of the story Clarissa is discomposed, "in *tumults*," incensed and terrified, "nettled and alarmed," apprehensive and miserable (I, 5, 68). As she suffers she changes. She becomes enrolled in the School of Affliction, "an excellent School . . . in which we are taught to know ourselves, to be able to compassionate and bear with one another, and to look up to a better hope" (VI, 420). And at the end of her life she is "chearful and serene." "My spirits," she says smiling, "will hold out purely." She is "perfectly serene," "serene and calm," "sweetly calm and serene" (VII, 223, 270, 271, 348, 450).

We are told at the outset, and this may surprise some readers, that Lovelace is "a sober man," whose behavior is "calm and gentlemanly" (I, 74, 28). He is, of course, "very gay." He himself tells us in his first letter that he possesses debonnaire (he uses the word as a noun) and assurance (I, 7, 214). He reveals energy, a zest for living, a love of acting. As she slowly gets the upper hand he changes. The bravado is still with him (notably in his "trial" at Lord M's and at Col. Ambrose's ball), but though he "puts on" "these lively airs" he confesses that he is sick at his soul. He is vexed and ailing, *inexpressibly miserable,* and at the end considers himself "the most miserable of beings" (VI, 395; VII, 125, 348; VIII, 265).

Throughout the book Lovelace refers to Clarissa as his "angel." At first we accept this term in a figurative sense. She is a beautiful and attractive young girl. But as she suffers she becomes angelic in a different sense. Belford discovers "a kind of holy Love for this Angel." Mrs. Smith and Mrs. Lovick know that they have an angel in their house, as does the clergyman who sees her there (VI, 328, 390; VII, 214). Even Mrs. Sinclair and young James Harlowe agree on this point (VIII, 59, 282). "In short, Ladies," declares Lovelace (VI, 243f), "in a word, my Lord, Miss Clarissa Harlowe is an Angel. . . . What, then, Lovelace, are you?—"

Early in the story Anna refers to him facetiously as the devil. Just before and just after the rape she calls him devil in all seriousness (I, 76; V, 267; VI, 158). The maid at Mrs. Moore's could not keep her eye from his foot, "expecting, no doubt, every minute to see it discover itself to be cloven" (V, 89). After the rape his best friend asks him if he be not the devil, while Clarissa writes: "O Lovelace, you are Satan himself" (V, 317, 335). When Lovelace compares himself to Milton's devil it is to Satan as he appears in the earlier parts of *Paradise Lost,* Satan the hero (V, 88). Just as Milton's Satan is degraded, metamorphosed into a reptile, so is Richardson's. It is not the gay and dashing hero who sees Clarissa after the rape. "Lips trembling, limbs quaking, voice inward, hesitating, broken—Never surely did miscreant look so *like* a miscreant!" "The Angel, as soon as she found her wings, flew from me. I, the reptile kneeler, the despicable slave, no more the proud victor, arose" (v, 348; vi, 27). And after he learns of her death he "sits grinning like a man in straw; curses and swears, and is confounded gloomy; and creeps into holes and corners, like an old hedgehog hunted for his grease" (vii, 468).

In various ways passages foreshadow what is to come or echo what has gone before. Midway in the first volume Clarissa is ordered to use the back stairs when going to or from her room so that her incensed family will not have to see her. Midway in the final volume Col. Morden reports that the conscience-stricken Harlowes make use "of less convenient back-stairs, that they may avoid passing by the doors of her apartment" (i, 167; viii, 180). When, early in the story, her mother tells her she must "think of being Mrs. Solmes," Clarissa writes: "*There* went the dagger to my heart," and in her Freudian dream Lovelace stabs her to the heart. Shortly before her death Belford likens her to "a harmless deer that has already a barbed shaft in her breast," and Lovelace declares that a letter bringing him the bad news he dreads would stab him "to the heart" (i, 104; ii, 283; vii, 170, 333). Before he takes Clarissa to Mrs. Sinclair's Lovelace asks: "Is not Calamity the test of Virtue?" After she has left Mrs. Sinclair's Clarissa says: "Calamity is the test of Integrity" (iii, 304; vii, 218). A list of such echoes would be a long one.

In a discussion of the structure of an epistolary novel something should be said of the letters themselves. Richardson is able to maintain the simplicity of plot at which he aimed by playing his characters off against each other as letter writers. Intelligent and attractive, with backgrounds that are similar, Clarissa and Anna Howe have much in common, but the differences between the two are obvious, and these differences are reflected in the way in which they express themselves. Likewise Lovelace and Belford share the same sort of background but differ as men. The resulting contrasts in style and in point of view, noted the author, "make Episodes useless." [20]

It may be instructive, in this connection, to observe the pattern

---

[20] "Hints of Prefaces for *Clarissa*," p. 4 in *Augustan Reprint Society Publications*, No. 103, ed. R. F. Brissenden (1964). For the beginnings of a study of such stylistic differences see Willian J. Farrell, "The Style and the Action in *Clarissa*," *Studies in English Literature*, iii (1963), 365–75. [See pp. 92–101 in this volume.] "Lovelace," remarks Farrell in the opening paragraph, "writes and even speaks in a style long associated with the courtly love letter, while his victim resists his advances in the pathetic language of contemporary 'she-tragedy.'"

## The Plan of Clarissa

made by the groupings of letters. In the first quarter of the book, while we are in Harlowe Place, there are ninety-six letters printed.[21] Of these Clarissa writes sixty-nine and Anna twenty. What goes on here is seen almost entirely from the point of view of the two girls. Lovelace writes but four of the letters. The shift when we reach the central section is significant. Nine weeks elapse from the time Clarissa arrives at Mrs. Sinclair's until she finally escapes. During the first three weeks Lovelace is relatively well-behaved. The next three weeks culminate in the fire episode, which convinces the lady of his designs on her. The rape and her madness and her impressive recovery occur in the final period. In the first three weeks Clarissa writes sixteen, almost half, and Anna six of the thirty-four letters. At the same time Lovelace writes seven and Belford two. But in the second of the three periods the two girls account for only six of the thirty-eight letters, three apiece. Lovelace writes twenty-seven, well over two-thirds of the total. And in the last of the three periods Clarissa writes but one, Belford two, and Lovelace all the rest, sixty-two. Belford takes over after Clarissa's "vile arrest." From that time until her death we are given thirty of her letters and thirty of Lovelace's. Anna writes fourteen, but Belford forty-seven. And Belford's is the predominant point of view in the final volume as well. Broadly speaking, during the first third of the book we see through Clarissa's eyes, during the central part through Lovelace's, and end by viewing the two chief characters through the eyes of a man who is Lovelace's confidant but becomes Clarissa's devoted servant. The contrasting points of view account for the texture of the book.

This element of contrast is basic to the general plan. It is revealed in the juxtaposition of scenes that are sentimental and scenes that are comic, of passages consisting of moral reflections and passages of dramatic dialogue. The fact that Clarissa's death is sandwiched in between those of Belton and Mrs. Sinclair hardly needs to be mentioned, though it is ironic that all three deaths are described by Belford, who earlier had written: "I cannot say, that I at all love these scenes of Death and the Doctor so near me" (IV, 26). What Richardson hoped would be "very striking" [22] is, of course, the contrast between Lovelace's "dreadful exit" and "the triumphant one" of the divine Clarissa.

When Clarissa unbolted the garden door and admitted Lovelace, he trod air and hardly thought himself a mortal. Borrowing an idea

---

[21] Actually many more than that are enclosed, quoted, or paraphrased in the numbered letters. My calculations are based on those letters that Richardson himself numbered.

[22] *Letters,* p. 122.

of Horace, he took off his hat as he walked, "to see if the Lace were not scorched, supposing it had brushed down a star" (III, 27, 33).[23] Offsetting this, after the tide has turned, he reports that Clarissa is above, where she can "look down upon me, while her exalted head is hid from me among the Stars" (VII, 90). " 'But indeed, Sir, I have long been greatly above you.' Long, my blessed Charmer!—Long indeed—For you have been *ever* greatly above Me, and above your Sex, and above all the World" (VIII, 141). Earlier she was "soaring upward to her native Skies. She was got above earth, by means, too, of the *Earth-born:* And something extraordinary was to be done to keep her with us Sublunaries" (III, 302).

Lovelace is the blackest of villains, Clarissa the brightest of innocents. "Darkness, light; Light, darkness; by my Soul! . . .—I am all error, all crime. . . . I find all just, all right, on your side; and all impatience, all inconsideration, on mine" (III, 151, 155). The contrasts are extreme: night vs. day, fire vs. water, loathsome animal vs. delicate flower; most often they suggest height and depth. She is an "angel sent down to save" but charges her tormentor to dig a hole deep enough to conceal her unhappy body (III, 140; V, 371). We are bombarded with words like haughty, deep, raise, subside, exaltation, stooping, aspiring, sinking, her altitudes, his baseness.

> Her whole person was informed by her sentiments. She seemed to be taller than before. How the God within her exalted her, not only above me, but above herself! . . . I acknowledged the superiority of her mind; and was proceeding—But she interrupted me—. . . My Mind, I believe, is indeed superior to yours, debased as yours is by evil habits: But I had not known it to be so, if you had not *taken pains* to convince me of the inferiority of yours" (V, 252).

Although Lovelace is nominally a Christian, he constantly swears by pagan gods, by Jupiter, "by all the *Dii Majores,* as well as *Minores*" (V, 50). Belford (IV, 363) thinks both gods and men should be concerned about Clarissa's fate. After a while such phrases take on Manichean overtones. The whole universe is concentrating on what is happening to our heroine. "God's eye is upon us!—. . . the women looked up to the ceiling, as if *afraid* of God's eye, and trembled. And well they might; and *I* too, who so very lately had each of us the devil in our hearts" (VI, 70).

All of this is caught up in Lovelace's last dream.

---

[23] Compare last line of Horace's *Odes,* I, i. Also, from Herrick's "The bad season makes the Poet sad,"

>    And once more yet (ere I am laid out dead)
>    *Knock at a Starre with my exalted Head.*

## The Plan of Clarissa

... I thought I would have clasped her in my arms: When immediately the most angelic form I had ever beheld, all clad in transparent white, descended in a cloud, which, opening, discovered a firmament above it, crouded with golden Cherubs and glittering Seraphs, all addressing her with, Welcome, welcome, welcome! and, encircling my charmer, ascended with her to the region of Seraphims; and instantly, the opened cloud closing, I lost sight of *her*, and of the *bright form* together, and found wrapt in my arms her azure robe (all stuck thick with stars of embossed silver) which I had caught hold of in hopes of detaining her; but was all that was left me of my beloved Clarissa. And then (horrid to relate!) the floor sinking under *me*, as the firmament had opened for *her*, I dropt into a hole more frightful than that of Elden; and, tumbling over and over down it, without view of a bottom, I awakened in a panic; and was as effectually disordered for half an hour, as if my dream had been a reality" (VII, 159f).

As if—? In the novel it *is* a reality. We move from above the firmament to the lowest depths.

*Clarissa* is a powerful book. In it is a "sustained intensity, that sense of emotional and mental urgency which infuses human affairs, no matter how trivial, and gives them an added measure of meaning."[24] Those words were written not of *Clarissa* but of the modern novel. Parts of *Clarissa* are dated, but there is much that is modern in the artistry of Samuel Richardson. The world of *Clarissa* is made to seem vast. The way the story slowly unfolds results in a density, a complexity, that calls to mind the mazes and labyrinths mentioned by Stinstra. But mazes and labyrinths in the plural fail to bring out the unity of the book. *Clarissa* is not a number of mazes. It is one large one—a mighty maze, but not without a plan.

[24] John McCormick, *Catastrophe and Imagination* (London, 1957), p. 26.

# The Style and the Action in *Clarissa*

## by William J. Farrell

In recent years, much emphasis has been placed on the realism of Richardson's style. Perhaps the most persuasive advocate of this emphasis is Ian Watt, who argues that the master-printer's rhetoric breaks with "the traditional decorums of prose," avoids the polished eloquence of earlier fiction, and adopts the artless but authentic accents of the familiar letter.[1] There is a great deal of truth in such a position, of course, but as a description of Richardson's stylistic achievement, it is somewhat oversimplified. Bold and independent as his work is, this novelist did not discard the conventions of previous prose but used them wherever and whenever they suited his artistic purpose. In *Clarissa*, for example, Lovelace writes and even speaks in a style long associated with the courtly love letter, while his victim resists his advances in the pathetic language of contemporary "she-tragedy." Although these rhetorical patterns are not always present, they follow the movement of the narrative, appearing or disappearing as the situation demands. Much of the novel's artistic complexity depends upon this relationship between style and action, in fact, and requires not only the reader's recognition of such rhetorical modes but also his understanding of their correspondence to the over-all structure.

Undoubtedly one of the reasons for accepting Richardson's prose as untraditional stems from his own condemnation of elaborate styles. But an author's criticism of a certain kind of writing does not rule out his use of it. Even though Richardson assigns a courtly rhetoric to Lovelace's correspondence, for instance, he expressly condemns the "empty flourishes" and "incoherent rhapsodies" of the conventional love letter. "Shallow heads and designing hearts," he argues in his

---

"The Style and the Action in *Clarissa*" by William J. Farrell. From *Studies in English Literature, 1500–1900*, III (1963), 365–75. Copyright © 1963 by Rice University. Reprinted by permission of the author and Rice University.

[1] *The Rise of the Novel* (Berkeley and Los Angeles, 1959), pp. 193–196.

familiar letterbook, "endeavor to exalt their mistresses into goddesses, in hopes of having it in their power to sink them into the characters of the most credulous and foolish of their sex."[2] Richardson probably had in mind the numerous *Academies of Compliments* that offered models of eloquence and catalogues of praises for the inarticulate lover. From their first appearance in 1640 to their last version in 1784, these and similar handbooks furnished their readers with hackneyed metaphors, trite personifications, and stock allusions to myths and literature, usually strung together in a hyperbolical description of the lady or an exaggerated account of the devotee's suffering.[3] Normally, the woman is a "saint to whose shrine I daily offer up my scalding sighs" or at least "a heavenly creature in mortal carcass." If her beauty is compared to Venus's or her comeliness to Pallas's, then her lips are invariably "more red than coral," "her neck more white than aged swans," and her voice so pleasant that it "strikes music's sweetest harmony." The lover, on the other hand, apologizes for his mad boldness, laments his mistress's cruelty, but always assures her that he is "unto my last gasp yours." Such eloquent missives were not confined to letter collections, of course, but as Professor Kany points out in his study of the epistolary novel, they also flourished in many contemporary French and Spanish romances.[4] And if Afra Behn's or Eliza Haywood's narratives are in any way typical, this kind of letter was as popular in English fiction as it was in continental narratives.[5]

Apparently the author of *Clarissa* knew or at least knew of this stylistic tradition in both forms. His parody of such prose in the fa-

[2] *Familiar Letters on Important Occasions*, ed. B. Downs, The English Library (New York, 1928), p. xxviii.

[3] For most of my information about these précieuse letter-books, I am especially indebted to Katherine G. Hornbeak's *The Complete Letter-Writer in English: 1568–1800. Smith College Studies in Modern Languages*, XV, Nos. 3–4 (Northampton, 1934), pp. 50–76.

[4] Charles E. Kany, *The Beginnings of the Epistolary Novel in France, Italy, and Spain. University of California Publications in Modern Philology*, XXI, No. 1 (Berkeley, 1937), p. 111.

[5] Afra Behn's *The Lucky Mistake* (1689) and her *Love Letters to a Gentleman* (1671) contain many examples of the courtly love letter. These billet-doux are even more common in Eliza Haywood's narratives, where they punctuate the action of such novels as *Love in Excess* (1719), *The British Recluse* (1722), *The Injured Husband* (1723), *Idalia* (1723), and *The Rash Resolve* (1724). They also appear in many anonymous pieces, such as *The Adventures of Lindamira* (1702) and *The Brothers* (1730), as well as in numerous translations, like *Passionate Love-Letters Between a Polish Princess and a Certain Chevalier* (1719) or *Letters from a Lady of Quality to a Chevalier* (1721). So frequent is their appearance, in fact, that they became a standard object of parody. See, for example, Fielding's satire on academy eloquence in Bk. III, Chapter VI of *Jonathan Wild*.

miliar letterbook seems to be directed at models like those in the *Academy of Compliments,* while Pamela's criticism of the same style definitely attributes it to "French" romances.[6] No matter what the source, however, Richardson's heroines always describe this mode of writing as rakish and seductive. Pamela warns Miss Stapylton of the moral danger of any lover who uses "the flowers of rhetoric," Clarissa labels Mr. Tourville's eloquent praises as "gross affronts," and Harriet Byron says of one admirer that she "both despises and fears a very high complimenter."[7] Nor are these ladies unjustified in associating this style with a designing heart. Roderigo in *The Wife's Resentment* (1720), Lysander in *The British Recluse* (1722), and Don Ferdinand in *The Unfortunate Mistress* (1723) are only a few of the many villains who seduce the heroines of romance with their "academy" eloquence.[8] So common are these ill-intentioned rhetoricians in the early novel that even pre-Richardson women distrusted any proposal couched in the courtly style. Noting that her lover's billet-doux "have more gallantry than sincerity," for instance, the author of *The Letters from a Lady of Quality* (1721) comes out and asks her devotee: "What is your design?—What will be the consequence of . . . that submissive, yet prevailing eloquence?"[9] The academy note became such a formalized device for seduction, in fact, that when Mrs. Haywood translated this letter collection, she could describe in her appended essay the step-by-step influence which a précieuse style supposedly had on a lady.

> Though we know each line is an arrow aimed at our virtue . . . our curiosity . . . seldom fails engaging us to peruse them: from that we fall to examining the happy turn of thought, . . . discover unnumbered beauties in every sentence,—and admire the author's love, or wit, or both, which have inspired him with so uncommon a delicacy: thence we reflect on meanings there, to which perhaps he is a stranger—and

[6] *Pamela,* Everyman's Library (London and New York, 1914), II, 448ff.

[7] *Pamela,* II, 448; *The History of Clarissa Harlowe,* in *The Works of Samuel Richardson* (London, 1888), II, 456; *Sir Charles Grandison,* in *The Novels of Samuel Richardson* (New York, 1901), I, 11. All subsequent page references to these novels will be from the above-mentioned texts.

[8] *The Wife's Resentment* was written by Della Riviere Manley and appears in her collection of novels, *The Power of Love* (London, 1720), pp. 175-228. Both *The British Recluse* and *The Unfortunate Mistress* were composed by Eliza Haywood and can be found in *The Works of Mrs. Eliza Haywood,* I-IV (London, 1724). The first appears in vol. II, 1-138; the second, in vol. III, 1-135.

[9] This letter collection was originally published by Edmé Boursalt under the title *Lettres nouvelles, avec treize lettres amoureuses d'une Dame à un cavalier* (Paris, 1699). I quote from Eliza Haywood's translation, *Letters from a Lady of Quality to a Chevalier,* in *The Works of Mrs. Eliza Haywood,* III, 7.

prepossessed by this time, construe everything to the advantage of his passion.[10]

This declension was acted out time and time again in the plays, novels, and letter collections of the day, and although it sometimes led to a happy love affair, the result was usually a disappointed young lady and a triumphant seducer. Little wonder, then, that Richardson assigned a précieuse style to Lovelace.

In his very first letter to Belford, the rake confesses: "Those confounded poets, with their terrenely-celestial descriptions, did as much with me as the lady; they fired my imagination, and set me upon a desire to become a goddess-maker." [11] And indeed, Lovelace is a goddess-maker. Describing Clarissa to his friend Belford, he virtually heaps one academy image on another as he exults in her recent abduction:

> If you love to see features that glow, though the heart is frozen and never yet was thawed; if you love fine sense, and adages flowing through teeth of ivory and lip of coral; an eye that penetrates all things; a voice that is harmony itself; an air of grandeur, mingled with a sweetness that cannot be described; a politeness that, if ever equaled, was never excelled —you'll see all these excellences, and ten times more, in this my Gloriana.[12]

The hyperbolical praises, the conventional poetic metaphors, the allusion to Gloriana, and certainly the lady's frozen heart place this passage in the tradition of courtly rhetoric. But Lovelace is much more sophisticated than the seducers in conventional romances. Although his letters to Belford are filled with "empty flourishes" and "incoherent rhapsodies," he carefully avoids such a style in his early correspondence with Clarissa. Writing to her friend Miss Howe, she naively observes: "Yet Mr. Lovelace, the least of any man whose letters I have seen, runs into these elevated absurdities"—and then ironically adds: "I should be one to despise him for it if he did. Such language looks always to me, as if the flatterer thought to find a woman a fool, or hoped to make her one." [13] Knowing that Clarissa will be put off rather than captivated by flowery compliments, Lovelace assumes a plain, sober, even hesitant manner of speech with her. Notice, for example, how he persuades her to pretend that she is his wife:

---

[10] "A Discourse concerning Writings of this Nature, by way of Essay," *The Works of Mrs. Eliza Haywood,* III, 7. (The page numbers in this volume begin over again with each individual work.)
[11] *Clarissa,* I, 184.
[12] *Clarissa,* I, 450–451.
[13] *Clarissa,* I, 459.

> Why, my dearest life, if you will hear me with patience—yet I am half afraid that I have been too forward, as I have not consulted you upon it—but as my friends in town, according to what Mr. Doleman has written, in the letter you have seen, conclude us to be married—Surely, sir, you have not presumed—Hear me out, dearest creature, [etc].[14]

Once Lovelace has achieved his objective, of course, he dashes off a triumphant letter to Belford, filled with the usual courtly eloquence. The sentence structure is far from disjointed, the language is anything but bare, and his "dearest life" quickly becomes "my goddess," "my empress," and "my angel."

The plain style is a mask for Lovelace, then, but it is not always a successful one. Although Clarissa regards "the hesitating voice" as one of the signs of "true respect," she quickly notices what she calls the "contradictory bashfulness" of his speech.[15] Her suspicions are further confirmed by Lovelace himself, who cannot maintain this mask for any length of time. Whenever he gains some triumph—or whenever he is pushed to the point of desperation—the sober pose is forgotten, and all the florid exclamations of academy rhetoric push into his conversation. As Clarissa remarks at one point: "He says too many fine things of me and to me . . . the man indeed at times is all upon the ecstatic." [16] Nor is she any less perceptive in interpreting the meaning of this stylistic shift: "But to my shame and confusion, I know too well to what to attribute his transports. In one word, it is to his triumph." And, to be sure, this is the case. Within less than a month after Clarissa's abduction, Lovelace has set aside his plain speech and, asserting that "true politeness and sincerity are reconcilable," he tells his love that she has "the most delicate mind in the world," that he long admired her "superior talents and wisdom," and that unless she should indulge him with her company, he could not live any longer.[17] When the lady sharply rejects these effusive compliments, the rake is taken aback and secretly complains to Belford:

> What can be done with a woman who is above flattery, and despises all praise but that which flows from the approbation of her own heart? Well, Jack, thou seest it is high time to change my measures. I must run into the pious a little sooner than I had designed.[18]

But such resolutions last only for a short time. Although his moralizing speeches, delivered in a plain and sober style, convince Clarissa

---

[14] *Clarissa*, II, 416.
[15] *Clarissa*, II, 210.
[16] *Clarissa*, II, 166.
[17] *Clarissa*, II, 207.
[18] *Clarissa*, II, 212.

"that the man must be in earnest," he soon tires of his role and reverts to his old familiar courtly language.[19] This is especially true in his quarrels with the lady, when sheer desperation forces him to drop his stylistic pose. After one of their very violent arguments, for instance, Lovelace seizes her hand and cries out: "Darkness, light: light, darkness; by my soul; just as you please to have it. Oh, charmer of my heart! take me, take me to yourself: mould me as you please: I am wax in your hands; give me your own impression." [20]

Although Richardson associates this kind of language with a designing heart, he also takes such "incoherent rhapsodies" as symptomatic of uncontrolled passion. At least this is the way that Clarissa views these figurative outbursts, and—in this case—the way Lovelace himself interprets the speech. But whether it reveals triumph or desperation, cunning or genuine emotion, academy rhetoric always signifies the emergence of the villain's rakish nature. As a result, Lovelace's shift from the plain to the flamboyant style—or from the flamboyant to the plain—reflects a parallel change in his relationship to Clarissa. Although his hesitating speech eventually and ironically becomes a genuine expression of his awe for the lady, his unadorned style is usually a mask, while the courtly compliments and exclamations are, strangely enough, a manifestation of his true self. By associating his villain with a well-known stylistic tradition, then, the author is able to distinguish the "real" Lovelace from any of his poses.

Now if this were the only way in which Richardson ever used a conventional style, his prose could still be described as anti-traditional. After all, the mere fact that he assigns a style he dislikes to his degenerate hero hardly puts this author's work in the same tradition with those novels and romances that use it as a matter of course. But Richardson does not condemn all artificial styles so harshly—and, in fact, shows great fondness for at least one of them. This is the theatrical, declamatory mode in which Clarissa berates her lover, laments her misfortunes, and pleads for her chastity. Although it functions somewhat differently from Lovelace's courtly rhetoric, it too follows the movement of the action and underlines the dramatic progress of the narrative. Just as Lovelace's plain, sober speech gives way to romantic rhapsodies in moments of triumph or desperation, so too Clarissa's language loses its conversational idiom to the pathetic accents of formal stage-rhetoric as she nears her tragic fate. Her first arguments with her lover may be as heated as the later ones, but they lack the sublimity and elevation of her final denunciations. Notice

---

[19] *Clarissa*, II, 247.
[20] *Clarissa*, II, 273.

her pert, even petulant tone in this early quarrel over a legacy. The original subject has been forgotten, and both characters are giving vent to general grievances.

> Can't you go on, sir? You see I have patience to hear you. Can't you go on, sir? I can, Madam, with my sufferings. . . . Your sufferings, then, if you please sir? [21]

Lovelace then complains of how Clarissa's brother provoked a quarrel, how he dogged Lovelace, who avoided him only for Clarissa's sake.

> Your generosity this, sir; not your sufferings; a little more of your sufferings, if you please—I hope you do not repent that you did not murder my brother!
> My private life hunted into! My morals decried! Some of the accusers perhaps not unfaulty! . . .
> Facts, Mr. Lovelace!—Do you want facts in the display of your sufferings?—None of your perhapses. . . .[22]

This is not the divine Clarissa, but a very human young lady who knows all the tricks and tactics of the petty, domestic argument. Now contrast the above dialogue and its realistic diction with a much later passage, where the heroine berates Lovelace for describing his attempted rape as slight and accidental.

> Now, said she, that thou darest to call the occasion slight and accidental, and that I am happily out of thy vile hands, and out of a house I have reason to believe as vile, traitor and wretch that thou art, I will venture to cast an eye upon thee—and oh! that it were in my power, in mercy to my sex, to look thee first into shame and remorse, and then into death.[23]

The formal "thou," the archaic verb forms, the complex syntax, the balanced repetition of words, the oblique allusion to the basilisk myth —all combine in creating a style that is far more regal and far more oratorical than the accents of real-life. Instead of the short elliptical units that characterize the first passage, Clarissa prefers a long, sonorous periodic sentence as well as an elaborate contrary-to-fact exclamation. The pert "sir" is replaced by the more solemn "villain" in addressing Lovelace, while a commonplace clause such as "I have patience to hear you" becomes the more pompous expression "I will venture to cast an eye upon thee." Although this passage expresses the same general emotion that the dialogue does, there is no similarity whatever in either language or tone. Certainly Lovelace was right

---

[21] *Clarissa*, II, 271.
[22] *Clarissa*, II, 272.
[23] *Clarissa*, III, 369–370.

when he described it as a "violent tragedy speech," for like most of Clarissa's later denunciations, it certainly suggests the rhetoric of the stage.[24]

This comment is even more true of those passages in which she pleads for her chastity or laments the loss of it. Like the pathetic heroines of Otway and Rowe, she avoids the heavily metaphorical style so characteristic of academy prose, but prefers instead the equally artificial device of repeating words and syntactical structures. "See, Mr. Lovelace!," she will cry, "See at your feet a poor creature, imploring your pity; who for your sake, is abandoned of all the world. Let not my father's curse thus dreadfully operate! Be not you the inflictor, who have been the cause of it! but spare me, I beseech you, spare me!"[25] Not only the repetition of words and syntactical units but even the direct expressions of misery and melancholy suggest the style of a Calista, a Monimia, or a Belvidera. When the heroine of *Venice Preserved* pleads forgiveness from her father, for example, she begins:

> Oh, there's but this short moment 'Twixt me and fate: yet send me not with curses down to my grave; afford me one kind blessing before we part; just take me in your arms, and recommend me with a prayer to Heaven, that I may die in peace; and when I'm dead—lay me, I beg you, lay me by the dear ashes of my tender mother: she would have pitied me, had fate yet spared her.[26]

In both cases, the lady chooses an imperative sentence structure and repeats it over and over again, increasing her emotional intensity with each reiteration. Nor is this kind of repetition confined to the syntax; even the content of the passages is nothing more than an amplification of what was said in the first two or three lines. Just as Belvidera's commands—"afford me one kind blessing," "take me in your arms," "recommend me with a prayer,"—are simply varied repetitions on the theme "send me not with curses," so too Clarissa's pleas—"let not my father's curse thus operate" and "Be not you the inflictor"—are only other ways of saying "spare me." In addition to using reiteration as a structural device, both speakers describe their misery in direct and rather bald terms. Richardson's heroine, for example, uses such tear-

---

[24] This style also appears in the novels of the day. Take, for example, Violenta's pathetic tirade in Manley's *The Wife's Resentment* (1720), Cleomira's moving pleas in Haywood's *The British Recluse* (1722), or Alvarez's mournful laments in *The Brothers* (1730). But as we shall see, Richardson seems to have associated this manner of speaking with the drama rather than the romance.

[25] *Clarissa*, III, 287.

[26] *Venice Preserved*, V. v. 64–72. I quote from *The Works of Thomas Otway*, ed. J. C. Ghosh (Oxford, 1932), II, 271.

evoking expressions as "poor," "pity," and "abandoned" much in the same way that Belvidera employs the words "fate," "grave," and "die." Often such language will create sad little vignettes of the victim, either as she is or as she imagines herself. Thus Clarissa will ask Lovelace to *see* her at his feet, imploring his honor, or she may dream that she laid her head "down on cold earth" to die. Not only does this parallel Belvidera's picture of her own death, but it also echoes Calista's vision of herself, "dying in my cave on that cold earth I mean to be my grave." [27] The particular heroine or the particular play doesn't matter, of course. Such rhetorical devices as these were common to all the pathetic women that wept and implored on the eighteenth-century stage, and if Clarissa's style resembles Belvidera's or Calista's, it is only because they all share a common language with the other tragic heroines of the day.

Richardson does more, however, than just assign a theatrical style to Clarissa's declamations; he continually and explicitly calls attention to their higher-than-life qualities. If such a passage is not simply labeled as a "tragedy speech," some comment will usually be made about its stage-like delivery. Thus Lovelace describes the heroine on one of these occasions as "waving her snowy hand, with all the grace of moving oratory," or he will mention at another time "that emphatical propriety which distinguishes this admirable creature in her elocution from all the women I ever heard speak." [28] Then, when a reader hears Clarissa cry out: "Consider me, dear Lovelace—on my knees I beg you to consider me as a poor creature who has no protection; who has no defense but your honor," he will expect and thus accept those elevated and dramatic accents, knowing that it is the "divine" Clarissa who speaks.[29]

Now the lady does not use this style all the time, not even in the latter part of the novel.[30] But when Lovelace makes his first intrusion into her room, when he tries to bring her back to Mrs. Sinclair's, or when he confronts her after the rape, Clarissa does respond to his villainy in the pathetic rhetoric of the stage. As the tragic denouement approaches and as the heroine grows in nobility and stature, these

---

[27] *The Fair Penitent,* IV. i. I quote from *Nicholas Rowe: Three Plays,* ed. J. R. Sutherland (London, 1929), p. 221.

[28] *Clarissa,* IV, 76; III, 286.

[29] *Clarissa,* III, 286.

[30] Unfortunately, Richardson did not practice such restraint in *Sir Charles Grandison,* where he assigns the style to Clementina della Poretta. Whenever this heroine appears on the scene, she invariably breaks forth in the pathetic accents of the stage, no matter what the subject or issue. The continual presence of this style naturally destroys all its dramatic effectiveness, annoying rather than moving the reader.

elevated speeches become more frequent, but they never become commonplace. Richardson reserves his high style, in other words, for the most serious, the most significant scenes. He uses it to distinguish the pert, petulant girl in the legacy argument from the tragic heroine on the verge of suicide. Just as the appearance and disappearance of Lovelace's courtly style suggests the pattern of his triumphs and failures, so too the emergence of Clarissa's dramatic rhetoric parallels and thus emphasizes her role as the pathetic but noble victim. In the eyes of the author, her sublimity of character requires a mode of expression that surpasses rather than imitates the accents of ordinary speech. What then could be more appropriate than a style long associated with the weeping women of "she-tragedy"? Far more than mere fustian, such language clearly places Clarissa in a long line of noble and usually virtuous heroines who suffered equally unfortunate fates. In the light of this, it is hard to see how anyone can say that Richardson broke with all previous stylistic traditions. Although the author's attention to minute detail anticipates the realism of later novels, Clarissa's speeches and Lovelace's letters certainly show that he did not ignore the conventions of literary prose but rather adapted them to the artistic needs of his work.

# Clarissa Harlowe and Her Times

## by Christopher Hill

I disagree with the view that the interest of *Clarissa Harlowe* is "almost entirely historical" (Q. D. Leavis, *Fiction and the Reading Public*, p. 99). On the contrary, it seems to me one of the greatest of the unread novels. Its greatness derives in part from what it says, by implication, about society and about the relations of individuals with social institutions, notably marriage. But it is a paradoxical book in that its achievement is more profound than the author himself seems to have been aware. A historical approach may help us to appreciate in their social context the moral problems that Richardson presents. I propose in these notes to consider the novel in the light of eighteenth-century economic developments and evolving Puritan attitudes towards society, marriage and the individual.

## I

In a recent article, Professor Habakkuk argued that the early eighteenth century saw "an increasing subordination of marriage to the increase of landed wealth, at the expense of other motives for marriage." "Political power was becoming more dependent on the possession of landed wealth" than it had been in the sixteenth and early seventeenth centuries, when it owed more to royal favour; and so among the upper classes marriage was bent "more systematically to the accumulation of landed wealth" ("Marriage Settlements in the 18th century," *Trans. Royal Hist. Soc.*, 1950, pp. 24–5). Professor Habakkuk sees this as a cumulative tendency dating from the mid-seventeenth century, the result of technical legal changes by which the father became in effect life tenant of the estate. The eldest son came to occupy a unique position of authority; and the estate, the

---

"Clarissa Harlowe and her Times" by Christopher Hill. From *Essays in Criticism*, V (1955), 315–40. Copyright © 1955 by Basil Blackwell, Ltd. Reprinted by permission of F. W. Bateson.

family property, acquired greater importance than the individual owner.

The new legal devices themselves sprang from "profound changes . . . in the attitude to the family and to land." These changes were related to the necessity of adapting landownership to a society in which standards of expenditure were set by those whose wealth derived from sources other than land, and in which taxation fell heavily on landowners ("English Landownership, 1680–1740," *Economic History Review*, 1940, pp. 6–10). They were the consequence of the political compromises of 1660 and 1688, by which the landed class had been left in possession of its property but deprived of power to check the development of capitalism. Professor Habakkuk draws especial attention to the staying power of the greater gentry, to the importance of the concentration of estates for their survival, and to marriage as a means of increasing the size of estates (ibid., pp. 3–5; "Marriage Settlements," pp. 18, 27, 29). Pamela's Mr. B. noted that "We have so many of our fine titled families who have allied themselves to trade (whose inducements were money only) that it ceases to be either a wonder as to the fact, or a disgrace to the honour" (*The Works of Samuel Richardson*, ed. E. Mangin, 1811, III, 175).

The relevance of this to *Clarissa Harlowe* will become clear if we recall its elaborately described point of departure. The Harlowe family, Clarissa told Miss Howe, was "no inconsiderable or upstart one, on either side." Its wealth had already been increased by judicious marriages. But some families "having great substance, cannot be satisfied without rank and title." Among the Harlowes "some of us" held "the darling view . . . of *raising a family*." The whole family strategy was planned with this end in mind. The uncles, one enriched by the discovery of minerals on his property, the other by the East India trade, intended not to marry. The eldest (and only) son, James, the real power in the family, thought that his two sisters might be provided for with £10–15,000 apiece; and then all the real estate—their grandfather's, father's, uncles'—and the remainder of their personal estates would descend on him. This, together with James's expectations of a great estate from his godmother, "would make such a noble fortune, and give him such an interest, as might entitle him to hope for a peerage. Nothing less would satisfy his ambition." He regarded his grandfather and uncles as his stewards, and daughters as encumbrances on a family: "to induce people to take them off their hands, the family stock must be impaired" (*Works*, V, 80–1, 30–1). "In order to give his daughter a dowry," wrote Professor Habakkuk, "a landowner raised money by a mortgage on his lands" ("English Landownership," 7; cf. "Marriage Settlements," 15, 23–7).

But the grandfather's will "lopped off one branch of my brother's expectations." To the indignation of the whole family the old man passed over his sons and elder grandchildren in favour of Clarissa. The other members of the family, he thought, were adequately provided for; and he had been very fond of Clarissa. But this seemed to the rest of the family insufficient reason for disregarding the interests and ambitions of the family unit. To obviate jealousy, Clarissa gave up to her father's management everything she had inherited from her grandfather, contenting herself with what her father allowed her (V, 81, 90–2). After she had left home, he still retained possession of her property.

The family had been in favour of Lovelace's proposals to the elder sister, because they hoped that this connection might help to gain a peerage. But when he switched his attentions to Clarissa, the design to concentrate the estates and aggrandize the family was seriously endangered. There was always the possibility that the uncles might follow their father's example and their own inclinations. Lovelace had a good clear estate, and prospects of a peerage; if he married Clarissa, why should not the family property be concentrated on them, since James could no longer have it all? "This little syren is in a fair way to out-uncle, as she has already out-grandfather'd us both!" said James anxiously to Arabella. He and Arabella both had good reason to wish to "disgrace and keep down" Clarissa quite apart from Arabella's jealousy of her sister, arising from Lovelace's transfer of his addresses (V, 79, 85–7).

So it was proposed to marry Clarissa to the deplorable Mr. Solmes, and to tie the marriage up with conditions whose object was to keep her estates in the family if possible. Richardson describes Solmes as an upstart, "not born to the immense riches he is possessed of: riches left by one niggard to another, in injury to the next heir, because that other is a niggard." Solmes was "very illiterate: knows nothing but the value of estates, and how to improve them, and what belongs to land-jobbing and husbandry." "His courtship indeed is *to them*"— to James and Arabella. Mr. Solmes was ideal for their purposes. He had no relations whom he valued, and so was prepared to bid high for the honour of union with the Harlowes. He was "mean enough," Clarissa said, ". . . and wicked enough to propose to *rob* of their just expectations his own family . . . in order to settle all he is worth on me; and if I die without children and he has none by any other marriage, upon a family which already abounds." "Now a *possibility* is discovered (which such a grasping mind as my brother's can easily turn into a *probability*) that my grandfather's estate will revert to it [the Harlowe family] with a much more considerable one of the man's own." So Clarissa's marriage to Solmes would positively contribute to "family aggrandizement." Mr. Solmes, Clarissa's mother assured her,

> has even given hopes to your brother that he will make exchanges of estates, or at least that he will purchase the northern one; for you know it must be entirely consistent with the family-views, that we increase our interest in this county . . . A family so rich in all its branches, and that has its views to honour, must be pleased to see a very great probability of taking rank among the principal of the kingdom.

To this Clarissa replied: "for the sake of this plan of my brother's am I, Madam, to be given in marriage to a man I never can endure?" (V, 48–9, 87–90, 130).

The grandfather's will from the start sets personal affection in conflict with family ambition. Richardson originally intended to call the novel *The Lady's Legacy,* as though to emphasize this setting. He stressed it again in his Postscript, when defending the slow start of the novel. The altercations in the Harlowe family, he said, are "the foundation of the whole" (XII, 432). It was because she would "rather be buried" than marry Mr. Solmes that Clarissa first contemplated throwing herself on Lovelace's protection, and later became a halfwilling accomplice in his abduction of her. Then her family utterly cast her off, and she was left in the complete isolation which was so important for the development of Richardson's plot.

Critics have sometimes suggested that Richardson's picture of the Harlowes was overdrawn. Professor Habakkuk's conclusions suggest that he was depicting, even if in a heightened form, a typical attitude among the bigger landowners. Lady Bradshaigh, who at one time "thought it scarcely possible that there could be such a father as old Harlowe" came across a similar real-life story in March 1751 (*The Correspondence of Samuel Richardson,* ed. A. L. Barbauld, 1804, VI, 100). So, although the alternatives of love or money in marriage were old ones, they were especially topical in Richardson's day; and with them the related problems of parental authority, of the daughter's right of choice.

It was Miss Howe who drew the moral, and it is not clear whether Richardson intended us to agree, or to regard it as an example of her warm-hearted impetuosity: "You are all too rich to be happy, child. For must not each of you, by the constitutions of your family, marry to be *still* richer? . . . Is true happiness any part of your family view? So far from it, that none of your family but yourself could be happy were they *not* rich." But Clarissa came very near to the same moral in a moment of bitterness about the family schemes. "And yet, in my opinion, the world is but one great family. Originally it was so.

What then is this narrow selfishness that reigns in us, but relationship remembered against relationship forgot?" Soon afterwards Clarissa, in her isolation and loneliness, now longing for death, cried out with tragic intensity: "What a world is this!—What is there in it desirable? The good we hope for, so strangely mixed, that one does not know what to wish for! And one half of mankind tormenting the other, and being tormented themselves in tormenting" (V, 61, 50; VI, 39).

II

Where did Richardson obtain these insights, in his apparently uneventful rise from industrious apprentice to successful printer holding court to middle-class ladies in his Hammersmith grotto? He can only, I think, have learnt them from his society, the society which produced *The Fable of the Bees, Gulliver's Travels, The Beggars' Opera* and *Jonathan Wild*; the society in which another great artist preoccupied with the relation of the sexes was advancing from "The Harlot's Progress" *via* "The Rake's Progress" to "Marriage à la Mode."

The novel as a literary form arose with the bourgeoisie: and it was Richardson's bourgeois characteristics that were his main appeal. Polite circles were offended by his style and his morality. It was especially in sexual behaviour that the standards of the bourgeoisie differed from those of the aristocracy. In the years just before Richardson wrote, the word "prude" made its first appearance as "a courtly word for a female Hypocrite": it was a word of the anti-Puritans. "Indelicate" and "indelicacy," which arose at the same time, represent the middle-class contribution to the vocabulary of feeling (see R. P. Utter and G. B. Needham, *Pamela's Daughters*, 1937, 63, 44). It was Pamela's bashfulness that revealed that she was "not of quality" (III, 171–2).

Nor should we ignore Clarissa's bourgeois characteristics, which are part of her no less than of Richardson, however unattractive we may find them. The diary which she kept in order to avoid waste of time is very much in the Puritan and bourgeois tradition. Her charity at 10 per cent, with its prim restriction to "the lame, the blind, the sick and the industrious poor, and those whom accident has made so, or sudden distress reduced" is in the same tradition. "The common or bred beggars I leave to others, and to the public provision" (XII, 344–7; VIII, 238). Pamela's programme of philanthropy reads rather like the prospectus of a Quaker firm which has discovered that charity pays (III, 151). Richardson's own habit of hiding half-crowns among the types in his printing-office to reward the earliest riser is illuminating in its condescending kindness towards those workmen with whom their employer did not care to communicate except in writing.

The social background to *Clarissa*, then, is this developing bourgeois society, of which Richardson was part and parcel, and which was the main novel-reading public. The aristocracy owed its continuing predominance in part to its concentration of family property by entail and marriages for money. Political compromise between aristocracy and bourgeoisie had been arrived at in the seventeenth century; but compromise in the realm of ideas was still being worked out. Richardson's novels, Mrs. Leavis tells us, are "bourgeois art" (op. cit., 122).

## III

Dr. Arnold Kettle, in the most illuminating pages on Richardson known to me, remarked on "the solidity of his scene," and suggested that it is the social situation that gives *Clarissa* its strength, even despite Richardson. "Though Richardson is sentimental, *Clarissa*, by and large, is not." Richardson "stumbled on a situation fully tragic" (*An Introduction to the English Novel*, I, 68–71). Most other critics have been misled by the way in which Richardson defended his novel against contemporary attacks. His object, he then alleged, was the defence of Christianity against scepticism; and he claimed that poetic justice triumphed in *Clarissa*, even if only in the next world (XII, 410–35). But we should take more seriously what the novel says than what its author thought it necessary to say in rebuttal of criticism on the moral plane. Richardson resolutely refused to let poetic justice triumph on earth by allowing a penitent Lovelace to be happily married to Clarissa. "The man who has been the villain to me that you have been shall never make me his wife" (IX, 357). Clarissa had advanced beyond the conventional "marriage-covers-all" morality which makes Pamela so nauseating.

What the novel does is to examine the effect on individuals of property marriage and all that goes with it. How do individuals react to this monstrous perversion, which we must take as given? How does it affect their relations with other human beings? These are the questions Richardson seems to ask: and the novel is his answer. It is difficult to tell how far his criticisms are conscious: it all seems as natural and unpremeditated as Shakespeare. Richardson wished his public to believe that he worked without a plan (see *Correspondence*, V, 258; VI, 117–18). But a synopsis of *Clarissa*, substantially as we know it, had been written before mid-1744, over two and a half years before the book was completed (A. D. McKillop, *Samuel Richardson*, Chapel Hill, 1936, 120). The structure at least was carefully thought out.

There is also evidence within the novel itself that the economics of marriage was a conscious target. Indeed the attitude of the Harlowes seems at times to be used to explain, if not to justify, Lovelace's conduct. One of the stories told to his discredit was of his seduction of Miss Betterton. Here is Lovelace's version:

> Miss Betterton was but a tradesman's daughter. The family, indeed, were grown rich, and aimed at a new line of gentry; and were unreasonable enough to expect a man of my family would marry her. I was honest. I gave the young lady no hope of that; for she put it to me . . . Indeed, when I got her to the issue, I asked her no question. It is cruel to ask a modest woman for her consent. It is creating difficulties for both. Had not her friends been officious, I had been constant and faithful to her to this day, as far as I know (VII, 256).

An element in the high comedy of that passage is the parallel between the Harlowes and this family, slightly lower down the social ladder, which "aimed at a new line of gentry." The sub-implication that all is fair when such schemes are afoot might extend to the original Harlowe plan to marry him to Arabella. Lovelace often speaks of his hatred for the whole Harlowe family, Clarissa excepted, and of his desire to be avenged on them. Schemes for property marriage lead to breakdown of respect for the institution; that is the conclusion. Marriage by purchase stimulates sex-war, as in restoration comedy.

"Are we not devils to each other?—They tempt us—we tempt them. Because we *men* cannot resist temptation, is that a reason that *women* ought not, when the whole of their education is caution and warning against our attempts? Do not their grandmothers give them one easy rule—Men are to ask—Women are to deny?" It is good social comment, even though it is unplausibly introduced in a rebuke from Lovelace to Belford for invalidating "the force which a virtuous education ought to have in the sex, by endeavouring to find excuses for *their* frailty from the frailty of ours" (VII, 313).

> Do not the mothers, the aunts, the grandmothers, the governesses of the pretty innocents, always, from their very cradles to riper years, preach to them the deceitfulness of man?—That they are not to regard their oaths, vows, promises?—What a parcel of fibbers would all these reverend matrons be, if there were not now and then a pretty credulous rogue taken in for a justification of their preachments, and to serve as a beacon lighted up for the benefit of the rest? Do we not then see, that an honest prowling fellow is a necessary evil on many accounts? . . . At worst, I

am entirely within my worthy friend Mandeville's assertion, that *private vices are public benefits* (IX, 242-3).

Lovelace's own offer to Clarissa, the only time he came near to making one, was sordidly financial. "All will be my own," he wrote shortly afterwards, "by deed of purchase and settlement." It was because she was holding out for favourable terms, he supposed, that Clarissa "makes every inch of her person . . . sacred." *"MARRIAGE, with these women . . ."* wrote Lovelace with heavy emphasis, "is an atonement for all we can do to them. A true dramatic recompense" (VIII, 106-7, 360; X, 252). Lovelace might have learnt the sentiment from *Pamela, or Virtue Rewarded*. His sneer was justified, but it was aimed not at Clarissa but at his own female relatives, who were still trying to arrange a marriage.

Lovelace's own morality was "to marry off a former mistress, if possible, before I took to a new one: to maintain a lady handsomely in her lying-in; to provide for the little one, if he lived, according to the degree of the mother, if she died. And the promise of this was a great comfort to the pretty dears, as they grew near their times" (VII, 256). His more constructive proposal was for marriage on an annual lease, terminable at will by either party. He made it flippantly, yet also produced some rational arguments: such an arrangement would work in certain respects to woman's advantage: all "married tyrants" must be "upon good behaviour from year to year." Some might prefer Lovelace's attitude to Richardson's own platonic leanings towards polygamy (IX, 296-300; *Correspondence*, VI, 179-218; see p. 120 below).

Lovelace, then, is clear enough. As the name suggests, he descends from the heroes of restoration comedy, who were also much obsessed by the relation of the sexes in a world of property marriages and post-Puritan hypocrisy. Lovelace came of an aristocratic family with long traditions. He looked down on the Harlowes as a family "not known to the county a century ago." Clarissa's uncle approved of Lovelace's feudal attitude to his tenants. "It was a maxim with his family, from which he would by no means depart, never to rack-rent old tenants, or their descendants." He liked to see all his tenants look fat, sleek and contented, even if his rent-roll was £300 or even £400 the worse for it (VIII, 49; V, 83). That was a very old-fashioned attitude in 1748.

Lovelace is intelligent, witty, unscrupulous. We are meant to think his attitude towards women deplorable; but Richardson seems almost to suggest (e.g. in the Miss Betterton affair) that society is partly to blame for it. Faced by the fact that marriage is a matter of money, not affection; that society trains women to trap men into matrimony,

Lovelace hits back at the sex indiscriminately and without mercy. He is in the tradition which leads from restoration comedy through Mandeville (whom we have just seen him quoting) on to Jack Wilkes, with whom we are in the world of modern politics.

For Lovelace is more than a stock stage profligate. Richardson gives him another dimension. He sets him firmly in the social context by putting some curiously radical political views into his mouth. It is difficult to be sure how Richardson meant us to take them. Are we to disapprove, as is suggested by his condemnation of "Revellers as well as Levellers" in a letter to one of his young lady friends? *(Notes and Queries,* 4th series, iii, 376.) Or did he use Lovelace as a mouthpiece for ideas for which he wished to take no responsibility? Or was he merely building up a complex, witty and intelligent character? I suspect Dr. Kettle is right in suggesting that Richardson was more attracted to Lovelace than he himself realized (op. cit., I, 69–70). We recall his friendship for the disreputable Colley Cibber; his kindness to Mrs. Laetitia Pilkington, who truthfully said of herself and Cibber "neither of us set up for immaculate chastity." *(Correspondence,* II, p. 130. Mrs. Pilkington was trying to persuade Richardson to spare Clarissa. Cf. J. Nichols, *Literary Anecdotes of the 18th century,* 1812, IV, 583.)

Richardson's political flirtation in the seventeen-twenties with the "witty and wicked" Duke of Wharton, "a kind of Lovelace," is also relevant. Wharton may indeed have been the former patron from whom Lovelace is believed to have been drawn, and who also served as model for Mr. B. in *Pamela* (Nichols, IV, 580; McKillop, 11, 108–20, 133–4). Richardson's naive surprise that ladies found Lovelace attractive, and his anxiety to blacken his character in his correspondence, suggest an uneasiness about his creation. The standard comparison with Satan in *Paradise Lost* is just.

Whatever the explanation, there Lovelace's views are. He was in favour of annual Parliaments, as well as of annual marriages. He attacked lawyers, though far less vigorously than did Fielding (IX, 300; X, 7). He pilloried war and military glory, not once but many times. Moreover, on almost every occasion Lovelace went out of his way to attribute the responsibility for wars to "royal butchers."

> I have not the art of the least artful of any of our Christian princes, who every day are guilty of ten times worse breaches of faith; and yet, issuing out a manifesto, they wipe their mouths, and go on from infraction to infraction, from robbery to robbery; commit devastation upon devastation; and destroy—for their glory! And are rewarded with the names of *conquerors,* and are dubbed *Le Grand;* praised, and even deified, by orators and poets, for their butcheries and depredations. While

I, a poor, single, harmless prowler; at least *comparatively* harmless; in order to satisfy my hunger, steal but one poor lamb; and every mouth is opened, every hand is lifted up, against me (VIII, 141, 281; X, 7; XII, 261).

The tone is almost that of *Jonathan Wild*. And again it is society that is at fault. Lovelace, if not justified, at least felt his guilt extenuated by the crimes committed in society's name.

Nor, it seems, were princes for Lovelace simply personifications of the state. More specifically, they stood for the money power, the power that bedevilled the relation of the sexes, that drove Clarissa to her doom.

The pretty simpleton knows nothing in the world; nor that people who have money never want assistants in their views, be they what they will. How else could the princes of the earth be so implicitly served as they are, *change they hands ever so often,* and be their purposes *ever so wicked?*

In the last resort, indeed, as the platitudinous Lord M. reminds us, the King of England was subordinate to the money power represented in the House of Commons. "That house has the giving of money: and *money makes the mare to go;* ay, and queens and kings, too, sometimes; to go in a manner very different from what they might otherwise choose to go" (X, 14; VIII, 263).

There are in fact two moralities in Lovelace's world: the morality of the rich and of the poor. The two nations are quite distinct. "Poverty is generally susceptible," Lovelace noted: Clarissa was less likely to believe she was being taken to a brothel if the madame was well dressed and proposed handsome marriage arrangements for her "nieces" (VII, 358). Here is "family aggrandizement" again in a bitterly ironical context.

The poor have morality thrust upon them. Lovelace observed that Miss Howe's messenger

seems to be one *used to poverty,* one who can sit down satisfied with it, and enjoy it; contented with hand-to-mouth conveniences, and not aiming to live better tomorrow than he does today, and than he did yesterday. Such a one is above temptation, unless it should come clothed in the guise of *truth* and *trust*. What likelihood of corrupting a man who has no hope, no ambition? Yet the rascal has but *half* life, and groans under that,

Lovelace added, dispelling the illusion of poverty as an idyllic state. He was trying to screw himself up to get rid of the "half-alive" man by killing him, but decided against it. "Were I a king, or a minister of state . . . it were another thing" (VII, 181. Cf. Pamela's cry: "For,

O! what can the abject poor do against the mighty rich, when they are determined to oppress?"—I, 127).

Lovelace is too often shown conscious of the contrast between his light-hearted wickedness and the honesty of the poor for it not to be intentional.

> Were it not for the poor and middling, the world would probably, long ago, have been destroyed by fire from Heaven. Ungrateful wretches the rest, thou wilt be apt to say, to make such sorry returns, as they generally do make, to the poor and middling! (VII, 361).

Even Clarissa thought that "the low and the illiterate are the most useful people in the common-wealth," and therefore it would be a pity to educate them unless they wish it very much or are exceptionally talented, "as a lettered education but too generally sets people above those servile offices by which the business of the world is carried on," and certainly makes them no happier (VIII, 160–1; cf. 298, III, 363).

The lower classes have hard work and morality thrust upon them. In contradistinction to this theme of morality shaped by society, Richardson introduces the counterpoint of "free" individuals shaping their own morality. Clarissa, criticized for being too considerate to servants, replied "I have my choice, *who* can wish for more? Why should I oppress others to gratify myself? You see what free-will enables one to do; while imposition would make a light burden heavy" (XII, 343–4). Wealth and connections make Clarissa free, and Lovelace too. But, unlike Lovelace, Clarissa is virtuous because she freely (under the guidance of divine grace) chooses what is right. The contrast between bourgeois morality and that of their betters was put even more clearly by Pamela, who told Mr. B. that he should above all boast that "brought up to an affluent fortune, uncontrolled in your will, your passions uncurbed; you have, nevertheless, permitted the divine grace to operate upon your truly noble heart, and have seen your error," and married Pamela. Richardson's attitude is much less robustly attractive than Fielding's sneers at the nobility from whom he descended (e.g. *Joseph Andrews*, Everyman, 19, 117–19, 145–6); but it is also a social criticism.

Lovelace, like Clarissa and Mr. B., is "free" by his wealth and connections. Others, including Pamela herself, have conventional morality ground into them by social pressures, have no freedom of choice. The truly virtuous are those of the "free" who "permit" divine grace to operate upon their hearts: and so voluntarily, not of social necessity, take virtue upon them. (Historically, predestination was always a middle- and lower-class theology; the conception of free-will was then possible only above a certain income level.)

One of the morals of Clarissa, then, was that expressed, in large type, in her dying words "God Almighty would not let me depend for comfort on any but himself" (XII, 92). Clarissa was one of the "free"; yet by divine grace she managed, even in the totally isolated state in which she found herself, to be as virtuous as Pamela, even if not so rewarded. Her isolation is important. The family's insane desire to raise itself leads to her being cut off from it, and she is left entirely alone, with no one she can trust. The isolated individual, and a woman at that, has to fight single-handed—not, like Robinson Crusoe, against nature, but against all the resources of "free" man, she who had believed that all humanity was one family.

Yet this "freedom" is an illusion, as Richardson involuntarily shows. The individual cannot escape from his society. Lovelace sawed off the branch on which he sat. His "freedom" was the result of his inherited wealth, of the property-marriage system: so his refusal to play the property-marriage game meant the end, so far as his family was concerned—unless he abandoned this part of his freedom on which he most prided himself, his sexual irresponsibility. Clarissa, by refusing to marry Solmes, separated herself from her family. Though she won a greater freedom of moral choice by her isolation, yet nevertheless this did not save her from finally being cut off from all possibility of living in her society. Freedom in each case turned out to be merely ignorance of necessity. Therefore Richardson was reduced, in defending the only conscious positive morality he depicts, to call in the next world to redress the balance of this.

## IV

Richardson very carefully created the Robinson Crusoe situation: one suspects he had some difficulty in stopping Miss Howe from rushing to Clarissa's side. This abstraction of the individual from society is, of course, not peculiar to Richardson. It was an essential part of the Puritan tradition. The Puritan heroes wrestled alone with their God. In *Paradise Lost* the drama which decided the fate of humanity, but which also prefigured the struggle within every man and woman, was enacted in a garden, in the pre-social state. Adam and Eve's unity in isolation before the rest of creation was emphasized in the closing lines of the poem:

> They hand in hand with wandring steps and slow,
> Through *Eden* took thir solitarie way.

The same tradition set Samson alone to work out his reconciliation with God, led Christian to desert wife and children in the quest for salvation. *Robinson Crusoe* was preceded by Henry Nevill's *The Isle of Pines,* published the year after *Paradise Lost;* and Gulliver was no less isolated from the societies in which he found himself. The Hobbist and the Lockean individuals both existed before society: society is artificial, not natural. At the same time the Noble Savage was coming into fashion, beginning with *Oroonoko* (1688, but probably written 25 years earlier).

This is a complex subject on which it is easy to over-simplify, but at least one common factor in these various examples of a literary and philosophical fashion is a desire to cut the individual free from the inherited traditions, customs and laws of society, to set him alone to work out his personal salvation in the sight of God only, in a state of "freedom." It is of a piece with that individualism which the new bourgeois society created, in reaction against the corporate loyalties and customs of subordination which had united feudal society. The individual must decide for himself how to behave: the Puritan conduct books had tried to help individuals to solve their own moral problems which had previously been dealt with by the priest at the confessional.

We can, I think, see the same trend in the contemporary popularity of literature about criminals and social outcasts (*The Beggar's Opera, Jonathan Wild,* later *The Newgate Calendar*). Again we contemplate the actions of men and women, if not in the state of nature, at least in a social state which is not bound by the traditional inherited conventions: and this criminal society is regularly used to satirize the conventions of existing society, just as Rousseau was to use the state of nature to criticize the laws and institutions of states in his day. Society would keep breaking in, and the desire to create a Robinson Crusoe situation is no more than a tendency. But I believe it helps us to see the links connecting the Puritan individualism of Milton, Bunyan and their successors with the romanticism of the French revolutionary epoch, which posed the individual *against* society, no longer merely separated him from it.

## V

The property family confronted Clarissa in the form of parental authority, which had its economic basis in the father's ability to grant or withhold marriage portions to his daughters. (Richardson made this point in his *Letters written for Particular Friends,* 7th edition, 98.) Many passages in the novel discuss this necessary accompaniment of "family aggrandizement"—necessary even where, as with the Harlowes, the father's authority was only a fiction, the reality usurped by the son (V, 298; VI, 152–4; VII, 215–16, 220–3, 234; VIII, 76, 85–6).

In putting the problem of marriage and property relations in the centre of his novel, Richardson was following a well-worn track. Dialogue III of Defoe's *Religious Courtship* has a plot similar to that of *Clarissa,* turning on the alternatives of marrying for money or for religion. *Moll Flanders* and *Roxana* explore the position of women in the society of Defoe's day. Passages like Mr. Badman's courtship of a rich young lady are perhaps more direct antecedents of the eighteenth-century novel than *Pilgrim's Progress.* Such works show the Puritan conduct books and sermons leading straight on to the novel, and cast a retrospective light on the social importance of the former in forming and expressing public opinion, as well as on the moral functions which early novels had to perform or pretend to perform. When we recall Richardson's own *Letters written for Particular Friends,* which immediately preceded *Pamela,* the links become clear and direct. What is remarkable is the extent to which in *Clarissa* Richardson has thrown off the bonds of the religious treatise.

*Clarissa* represents the supreme criticism of property marriage. But in this it is a culmination of the Puritan tradition. In medieval society, aristocratic marriage had been a property transaction pure and simple: courtly love was sought (in literature at all events) outside marriage. But matrimonial fidelity was less highly valued, in either sex, before or after marriage, than later. It was a common form for the noble dame of the Middle Ages to have a lover; and the father who announced that the lady was his wife when he heard that she had borne him a son was not unique.

The rise of capitalism and protestantism brought a new conception of marriage, of which Milton's is the highest: a companionship based on mutual affection. The social basis for this view of marriage was the small workshop or farm in which the wife was in fact a help-meet to her husband: there was no such practical co-operation between the rentier landlord and his lady. In the Puritan conception fidelity in the wife, and pre-marital chastity, begin to be insisted on with a new vehemence. Since love was ideally the basis of marriage, then the marriage must be inviolate. In practice in most marriages property was still the main consideration: and in the world of capitalist production expensive goods must not be shop-soiled or tarnished. The first lesson Shamela's mother taught her was that "a Married

Woman injures only her Husband, but a Single Woman herself" (*An Apology for the Life of Mrs. Shamela Andrews*, 1741, 35). Insistence on absolute premarital chastity goes hand-in-hand with the bourgeois conception of absolute property, immune alike from the king's right to arbitrary taxation and the church's divine right to tithes. Dr. Johnson noted that the chastity of women was "of the utmost importance, as all property depends upon it"; and, in contradistinction to the elder Mrs. Andrews, he thought a wife who broke her marriage vows more criminal than a husband who did the same—because of the doubts that would be cast on the succession of property (Boswell, *Life of Johnson*, Everyman, I, 347–8, 623–4; II, 287–8).

Richardson's challenge to conventional assumptions seems almost to have been deliberate. He rejected the appeals of his friends to save Clarissa. He refused to allow a happy ending in which, in Lovelace's words, "marriage covers all" (X, 252). Having put Clarissa to the supreme test, in isolation, and she having come through with her virginity triumphantly preserved, Richardson pressed the logic of the situation (and of the Puritan conception of virtue) a stage further than most of his contemporaries would have dared. Apparently determined to establish the principle that chastity of the mind is more important than chastity of the body, he allowed Lovelace to rape Clarissa under the influence of drugs. The goods, from the point of view of the market, were irreparably damaged.

Clarissa's standards, however, are those of the Puritan ideal, not those of conventional market morality. (Cf. L. L. Schücking, *Die Familie in Puritanismus*, Leipzig, 1929, 184.) From the beginning she had consoled herself in her desperate situation by the purity of her motives. "Let me wrap myself about in the mantle of my own integrity, and take comfort in my unfaulty intention!"—"As to my reputation, if I leave him—that is already too much wounded for me, now, to be careful about any thing, but how to act so that my own heart shall not reproach me. As to the world's censure, I must be content to suffer that" (VII, 287; VIII, 212–13).

Clarissa's attitude is a logical application of the protestant theory of justification by faith, with its emphasis on the inner intention of the believer rather than on his external actions. Purity of motive, chastity of mind, is more important than formal rectitude of behaviour. (Contrast, as so often, Fielding's resolute defence of justification by works in the dispute between Parson Adams and Parson Trulliber.—*Joseph Andrews*, 126–7.) That is why Clarissa's fate appealed so desperately to eighteenth-century Englishmen, brought up in the protestant tradition. Her dishonour was outward, formal only: internally she remained spotless. So Miss Howe: "Comfort yourself

... in the triumphs of a virtue unsullied; a will wholly faultless" (X, 213). Virtue has its own aristocrats, superior to the aristocracy of birth: that was an old Puritan theme.

But society was too strong, as Clarissa had already realized. She had no sense of guilt: her conscience was clear. But she knew what society's verdict would be. Its standards are those of the market: justification by faith was for Sundays only. Society judges by events, not by motives. Clarissa knew it, and it was this that made her death inevitable. How could she have lived? There was no room in a commercial society for flawed goods. She regarded death, in fact, as a release, for "she has no *wilful* errors to look back upon with self-reproach." So Belford explained to Lovelace, adding that "the reason is evident" why Lovelace could not view death with equal fortitude (XI, 388). Clarissa's standards, high Puritan standards, were not of this world: they could only be realized in the after-life. They are a *criticism* of this world's standards. That, surely, is the damning indictment of his society that Richardson drew up, even if he was not fully aware of all its implications.

## VI

There had, we can now see, been a fundamental flaw in Puritan morality, upon which Richardson, however unconsciously, laid his finger. Historically Calvinism made for equality against feudal privilege or arbitrary royal rule: but in Calvinist theory some men were more equal than others. The Calvinist conception of the church was a dual one: in one sense the church was the whole community, in another sense it was the elect only. So a minority had special rights in the government of the church, the election of ministers, the administration of discipline. And in practice the minority of the godly was all too easily equated with the minority of the propertied. Locke transferred this dualism to political theory, as Professor Macpherson has brilliantly shown: his society in one sense includes every inhabitant, but in another excludes those who have no property ("The Social Bearings of Locke's Political Theory," *The Western Political Quarterly*, 1954, 1–22). At an earlier stage Calvinist political theory had obtained the same consequences more crudely by saying that revolt was justified when led by the lesser magistrate—J.P.s, House of Commons—but not when it was a spontaneous outburst of the many-headed monster.

Now if some men were more equal than others, *à fortiori* men were more equal than women. From the earliest days of protestantism the position of women had presented difficulties. On the one hand the wife's status was elevated: she became her husband's helpmeet. If all believers are priests, do not women have the same direct relation to God as men? In some sects they were admitted to full church membership. In the most radical congregations women were even allowed to preach.

Yet the protestant sects attributed divine inspiration to the letter of the Bible, newly translated into the vernacular for all to read; and the Bible is explicit on the subordination of women. Woman is made for man, not man for woman, said St. Paul. The economic environment of early capitalism helped to prevent women rising to full equality with men. It was a patriarchal society. In the family farm or small business, although there was partnership between man and wife, the husband was still the senior partner. He for the market only, she for the market through him. And even this precarious economic balance of the heroic age of Puritanism was breaking down in the late seventeenth and eighteenth centuries, as the domestic stage of industry began to be superseded. The workshop was separated from the home. In factories, however atrociously female labour was sweated, women began to enjoy an equality in exploitation with men. But the wife in the lower middle-class family became less a helpmeet in the business and more tied to domestic duties: among the new upper middle class she became a sentimentalized angel of the home excluded from all other interests, a lady of leisure—and a novel-reader (Utter and Needham, chapter 2). Economic, legal and religious developments combined to depress the status of these women. Nunneries no longer offered what Milton had ungallantly called "convenient stowage for their withered daughters" (*Prose Works*, Bohn, III, 80); the Virgin was no longer at the right hand of her Son to intercede for her sex. In her place stood St. Paul and the Patriarchs.

The difficulties are apparent in the greatest Puritan and post-Puritan literature. Milton's noble hymn to wedded love nearly burst through the theological bonds of "he for God only, she for God in him" when Adam decided that Paradise would be well lost for Eve. Defoe in many of his novels was concerned with the conditions on which women might attain freedom, and concluded, coolly enough, that money was the necessary basis. Women who did not inherit wealth had been left with no marketable commodity but their sex, which they could trade either in the open marriage market, as Pamela taught them, or on the black market like Roxana and Moll Flanders. Marriage remained the more desirable state: Moll Flanders "kept true to this notion, that a woman should never be kept for a mistress that had the money to make herself a wife." (Shakespeare Head edition, 1927, I, 60.) For the freedom even of a Roxana was limited by the ultimate sanctions of a society in which the laws are made by men, as Clarissa and Lady Bradshaigh both pointed out.

Yet in this world of male economic dominance, the small Puritan voice still whispered that women have souls, that salvation is a matter of direct personal relationship to God. Women should by co-operation with the divine purpose be as capable as men of receiving the grace that makes free; even if their attainment of this freedom would shatter the standards taken over by patriarchal bourgeois society from an earlier age.

It is Richardson's greatness, it seems to me, that his respect for Clarissa's integrity led him to push the Puritan code forward to the point at which its flaw was completely revealed, at which it broke down as a standard of conduct for this world. His *conscious* desire in writing the novel was to assert the bourgeois and Puritan conception of marriage against the feudal-cavalier standards of Lovelace and the Harlowe emphasis on concentration of property. But the contradictions of subordination in equality which were inherent in the Puritan view of women were too strong for him. Hence the inadequacy of his own later explanations of the moral of *Clarissa,* his uneasy reassertion of defences whose weakness he must have suspected. He appealed to other-worldly sanctions. He insisted, ludicrously, that after all Lovelace was no atheist. He quoted all the best authorities, from Aristotle to Addison, to buttress his claim that poetic justice triumphed. "In all reciprocal Duties the Non-Performance of the Duty on one Part is not an excuse for the Failure of the Other." That, he told Miss G. in January 1750, was the "Great Rule, inculcated throughout the History of Clarissa." The Harlowes would be punished, and Clarissa rewarded, in the next world *(Notes and Queries,* 4th series, iii, 376). It is the morality of *Familiar Letters written for Particular Friends,* and of *Pamela,* which *Clarissa* had in fact left behind.

Most revealing was Richardson's long discussion with Lady Bradshaigh. That sensible woman used the logic of *Clarissa* against its author. (This fact, and the vogue of *Clarissa,* suggests that the problems with which Richardson fumbled were set by society, were problems of which others were conscious once Richardson had formulated them. We may compare Mrs. Knowles's discussion with Boswell, who thought that she was too ambitious in hoping that women could ever be the equals of men, even in heaven.—*Life of Johnson,* II, 207.) Lady Bradshaigh (without acknowledgment) used Clarissa's point that the laws of society were made by men, adding provocatively that men had made them "to justify their tyranny" (*Correspondence,* VI,

193-4, 205-6). Lady Bradshaigh argued for equality in sex relationships, since "perfect love casteth out fear." Richardson was reduced to differentiating between divine and human love, to quoting the authority of St. Paul and of Milton on Divorce. But he also launched into a theoretical defence of polygamy, citing the patriarchs of the Old Testament. ("What do I care for the patriarchs!" Lady Bradshaigh retorted boldly. "If they took it into their heads to be tyrants, why should we allow them to be worthy examples to imitate?")

The possibility of polygamy seems always to have lurked behind the protestant conception of equality-inequality of the sexes. Luther was prepared to authorize it in certain circumstances. Milton, in his defence of the analogous right of the husband to put away his wife, was able to cite an impressively long list of protestant theologians on his side. We may also recall Henry Nevill's *The Isle of Pines,* that early example of the Robinson Crusoe situation, which showed a reversion to the state of nature that included a happy polygamy. Richardson too thought that "the law of nature does more than allow of polygamy." It was to be eschewed only because forbidden by the law of England. "I am extremely well satisfied with the laws of my country. Were polygamy to be allowed by them, I know not my own heart, if I would give into the allowance" (*Correspondence,* VI, 190-4, 205-9, 218 and *passim*). Parson Williams's defence of polyandry in *Shamela* (one husband for money, another for sexual satisfaction) was a shrewder thrust at Richardson than its author knew (p. 49).

So, though Richardson came near to breaking through the dualism of bourgeois and Puritan modes of thought in *Clarissa,* he could not escape from it in his own convictions. Emotionally, the author of *Clarissa* was of Lady Bradshaigh's party without knowing it. Intellectually, the husband of a lady who had "high and Harlowean ideals of parental authority" succumbed in part to her outlook. He was as unsuccessful in establishing a human relationship with his own daughters as Milton had been, and had to defend himself on this score from those who thought he was not living up to his own ideals (*Correspondence,* I, clxxxix, VI, 282). The pace was going rather fast: one wonders how the master printer would have reacted if his daughters *had* behaved like Clarissa.

Yet the novel remains. Clarissa did break through the social conventions of her time by pressing to its ultimate implications the religious orthodoxy of her society. Dr. Kettle again puts it well:

> Tragedy occurs when a situation arises which men, at the particular point in development that they have reached, are unable to solve. Such a situation in the eighteenth and nineteenth centuries—and the problem is not yet answered—was the growing consciousness of women of

the necessity of their emancipation (by which is not meant mere formal emancipation, parliamentary votes, etc.) and the inability of class society to admit such freedom without destroying something essential to itself. Clarissa *has* to fight her family and Lovelace; they for their part *cannot* let her win without undermining all that is to them necessary and even sacred (Op. cit., I, 70–1.)

I am not sure that, in practice, women before Mary Wollstonecraft were *conscious* of the need for emancipation. Some may have resisted the pressures that degraded and humiliated them, but resistance was as yet hardly more than passive in face of an irreversible trend. This, then, was the tragic situation that forced itself upon the attention of the artist and writer. It is Richardson's achievement that he encompassed this situation and depicted it in such a way as to bring it to general consciousness. So he helped, more, certainly, than he would have wished, and in spite of the limitations of his creed and outlook, to prepare women for an awareness of "the necessity of their emancipation."

## VII

Seen in this perspective, the moral issues raised by *Clarissa* have their place in the evolution of ideas from Luther's doctrine of the priesthood of all believers, through the Puritan conception of the infallible conscience, on to the romantic individualist revolt. Clarissa's behaviour, she explained to Miss Howe, arose

> principally from what offers to my own heart; respecting, as I may say, its own rectitude, its own judgment of the *fit* and the *unfit;* as I would, without study, answer *for* myself *to* myself, in the *first* place; to *him* [Lovelace] and to the *world,* in the *second* only. Principles that *are* in my mind; that I *found* there; implanted, no doubt, by the first gracious Planter: which therefore *impel* me, as I may say, to act up to them . . . let others act as they will by *me* (VIII, 105; cf. X, 213, quoted on pp. 116–17 above).

The philosophical implications of that heavily emphasized explanation are worth pondering. It contains the spirit that had enabled the seventeenth-century Puritans to withstand persecutions and to win revolutionary wars; but it also looks forward to the not very Puritan Mary Wollstonecraft and Shelley.

"For myself," Clarissa told Lovelace,

> if I shall be enabled, on due reflection, to look back upon my own conduct, without the great reproach of having wilfully, and against the light

of my own judgment, erred, I shall be more happy than if I had all the world accounts desirable (IX, 254).

So the regicides had spoken in 1660, knowing that they would be condemned in earthly courts. Clarissa was not yet a romantic rebel; and the heroic age of Puritan individualism was over when its doctrines were applied to the matrimonial problems of a middle-class young lady. Clarissa's age was no longer revolutionary: "everybody" knew what was right; the light of nature told them. The tyranny of the static society was too powerful. And yet Clarissa knew that society could not refute her, even if it would not forgive her. The fact that she could be justified only in heaven witnesses to the breakdown of the noblest aspirations of Puritanism in face of the realities of bourgeois society. In seventeenth-century England the Puritan revolution had failed: the bourgeois revolution had succeeded. Professor Perry Miller has traced a similar decline and fall in New England from the City on a Hill of the Pilgrim Fathers to the eighteenth-century acceptance of religion as good for business and social subordination (Perry Miller, *The New England Mind: from Colony to Province*, Cambridge, Mass., 1953, *passim*).

It is instructive to compare *The Atheist's Tragedy* (1611) with *Clarissa Harlowe*. The plot of Tourneur's play turns on D'Amville's scheme to arrange marriages and set aside rival heirs in order to focus the descent of wealth on his sons. In Tourneur's day such schemes were absolutely evil: worship of the money power was specifically related to atheism. But D'Amville thought his mere murders insignificant when compared with economic oppression by landlords in decaying feudal society, in just the same way as Lovelace set his theft of "but one poor lamb" against the robberies and devastations of "royal butchers." Either passage might have inspired Chaplin's M. Verdoux.

Tourneur's Atheist anticipates Hobbist man in desiring power after power infinitely, in fearing death above all. His cowardice enabled the God-fearing Charlemont to get the better of him. Puritanism tamed this absolute Marlovian individualism, adapted it to existence in a competitive society. By setting men free from the fear of death it gave them the courage which the atheist lacked. By Richardson's day, thanks to the courage of the religious revolutionaries, a society had been established in which the money power ruled. Accumulation for heirs was socially accepted and blessed by the church. And Lovelace regarded jests on sacred subjects as a mark of ill-breeding (XII, 426–7).

Diderot's and Rousseau's enthusiasm for *Clarissa*, then, was not fortuitous; though Richardson, who was "disgusted" by the *Nouvelle Heloise* (Nichols, IV, 598) would have appreciated it as little as Luther did the German peasants' appeal to his authority. For under a new revolutionary impulse in the later eighteenth century, the same inner voice to which Clarissa listened led more flamboyant spirits on to a *deliberate* flouting of the conventions which the old-maidish Richardson could not have conceived without horror. The advice which inner voices give tends to change as society changes, and to change more quickly than the official philosophies of society.

Anna Howe felt no pity for Mrs. Harlowe because she had deprived herself of the power to show maternal love and *humanity*. The stress on the duty to mankind is a good Puritan sentiment; but the word *humanity* again links Richardson with the ideologues of the French Revolution. Belford, in his supreme appeal to Lovelace, urged him "to be prevailed upon—to be—to be *humane,* that's all—only that thou wouldst not disgrace our common humanity" (VII, 76, 375). Only! It was a very large only. For it was not merely the individual wickedness of Lovelace that disgraced "our common humanity." It was also the greed of the Harlowes, it was property marriage, it was society and its institutions. I quote again, because I think they have an added significance if my analysis is at all correct, Clarissa's bewildered words at the beginning of the novel: "And yet, in my opinion, the world is but one great family. Originally it was so. What then is this narrow selfishness that reigns in us, but relationship remembered against relationship forgot?" (V, 250). "Owing to Richardson," wrote Diderot, ". . . I feel more love for my fellow creatures" (quoted in I, xv).

Clarissa travelled, if this is not too fanciful, through the whole history of humanity. She looked back to days when mankind was all one family—legendary days which had been vividly imagined realities to the seventeenth-century democrats whom Richardson's Monmouthite father must have known; she passed through and revolted against the feudal-patriarchal family and the tyranny of money; she looked forward to a society in which women shall have attained full equality of status. She died with words on her lips which were a verbal expression of the purest protestant and bourgeois individualism, and yet which in the context ("one half of mankind tormenting the other and being tormented themselves in tormenting") had their fullest meaning only for the outcasts and the "unfree" of eighteenth-century society, and transcended that society's possibilities: "God Almighty would not let me depend for comfort upon any but Himself" (VI, 39; XII, 92).

# On *Sir Charles Grandison*

## by A. D. McKillop

One of Richardson's purposes in portraying an ideal gentleman in *Sir Charles Grandison* (1753-54) was to present an antitype to Lovelace and Tom Jones. The complacent assumption that polite society can stand, when properly purged of vice and error, was easily made by Richardson and his public; the novelist could be shaken loose from such an assumption only by an exceptionally intense situation such as develops in *Clarissa*. The ideal of the "gentleman," though fortified by the prestige of the ruling classes and the whole Western tradition, hampered the novelist in so far as it substituted a carefully defined type or standard for an ultimately unclassifiable human being. The name suggests the aristocracy, and Richardson may have remembered a work which he had helped to print, the English translation of Giannone's *History of Naples* (1729-31), which was dedicated to the Earl of Grandison and his son Viscount Falkland: "I have at hand the noble Historian, who, in his Catalogue of Heroes (great as any *Greece* or *Rome* ever produc'd) has not two more beautiful Characters, than those of *Falkland* and *Grandison*." Richardson's Grandison is a baronet, not a peer; the ideals of reason and nature must be realized within the fixed system imposed by his status. He is invariably courteous, rational, and benevolent, but his attitudes toward much of the world are formal and somewhat remote —toward the lower classes and the trading classes, toward politics and public life. He executes a virtuous and rational retreat or semi-retreat to private life, which, as noted above in the discussion of *Clarissa*, could be opposed alike to the evils of new wealth, the arrogance and licence of the old aristocracy, and the follies of fashion. His accomplishments are social rather than cultural; he is not a poet like his libertine and extravagant father. He is the center of a large

"On *Sir Charles Grandison*" (Editor's title). From *The Early Masters of English Fiction* by A. D. McKillop (Lawrence: University of Kansas Press, 1956), pp. 81-97. Copyright © 1956 by the University of Kansas Press. Reprinted by permission of the University of Kansas Press. These pages are from Chapter II, section iii, "Samuel Richardson."

group of kinsmen, friends, and dependents, and above all he dominates a circle of refined and admiring women.[1] These relationships are conceived of as an extension of the family.[2] It is within such a circle that the virtuous man will naturally find a wife; this is preëminently true of Sir Charles Grandison and Harriet Byron, and the important principle of the domestic and socially approved setting for the love affair, the exact opposite of *mésalliance*, passes into later fiction.

Sir Charles's ideals are within reach for his time and place, so that he can never go to war with his world or be involved in the quixotic clash of ideal and real. On the other hand, he is too composed and complacent to succumb to the ennui that security and success might bring, like M. Pococurante. Though he is more disposed than Fielding's Mr. Allworthy to give authoritative moral judgments, both good men avoid mortal struggle with society and with themselves, and illustrate Fielding's dictum that "the wisest man is the likeliest to possess all worldly blessings in an eminent degree."[3] As a conduct-book *Grandison* builds on the program of Steele, thus briefly described in an ideal play to be written by one of his disciples:

> There are, I find, to be in [his drama] all the reverend Offices of Life, such as Regard to Parents, Husbands, and honourable Lovers, preserved with the utmost Care; and at the same Time that Agreeableness of Behaviour, with the Intermixture of pleasing Passions as arise from Innocence and Virtue, interspersed in such a Manner, as that to be charming and agreeable, shall appear the natural Consequence of being virtuous.[4]

Behind Sir Charles stands the figure of Bevil in Steele's *Conscious Lovers*, pointing the way to a program of benevolism in which the ideal of the gentleman is identified with an extension of "the reverend Offices of Life" to include an entire society. In practice, as has been remarked, benevolism as dramatized must be limited by personal experience and interest, but in theory it is all-embracing. The good man's benevolence is "diffusive," to use a favorite term of the moralists, and seeks out occasions.

---

[1] The best and most thorough analysis of Sir Charles in the light of his social background is that of Phyllis Patricia Smith, "The Eighteenth-Century Gentleman: Contributing Themes and Their Realization in Sir Charles Grandison," MS Dissertation in Radcliffe College Library.

[2] See Brian W. Downs, *Richardson* (1928), p. 191.

[3] *Tom Jones*, VI, iii.

[4] *Tatler*, No. 182. For the probable connection of this passage with early plans for *The Conscious Lovers*, see John Loftis, "The Genesis of Steele's 'The Conscious Lovers,'" *Essays Dedicated to Lily B. Campbell* (Berkeley and Los Angeles, 1950), pp. 176–77.

The communicating advice and comfort, assistance and support, according to the various exigencies of those with whom he converses, is his constant endeavour, and most pleasing entertainment. . . . [He] seeks for opportunities to be useful; 'tis part of the stated employment and business of his life. . . . You can't lay a greater obligation upon him than by proposing ways in which he may be useful, or enlarge his sphere of usefulness: For this is the point in which all his views, all his desires, all his satisfaction, center.[5]

*Grandison* was written with more regard to the presence of Richardson's friends and advisers than its two predecessors. It reflects their views to some extent, but it also shows the novelist at work as a self-conscious artist. Of the many references to *Grandison* among Richardson's correspondents, a brief report by Dr. Thomas Birch will suffice to show us the situation:

Mr. Richardson, the Printer, is employing himself in a Work, for which the Men will be as much oblig'd to him, as the Ladies have hitherto been, having, as he own'd to me some days ago, resum'd the Subject, which you heard him mention at your own House, of the virtuous & generous Gentleman. He complains to me of the Difficulty of enlivening it with proper Incidents: But we may safely trust to his Invention, which is inexhaustible upon all Occasions. He has desir'd me to give him an Hour or two's Attention on the reading of his Plan.[6]

Historically *Grandison* opened the way for the later Richardsonian novel of manners; here characters are brought from the isolated and sinister house in town or country into a cheerful society that frequents drawing rooms rather than the public haunts of fashion. Richardson had now served a long apprenticeship in fiction, and could skilfully vary setting and characterization, though he does not now seem to be markedly eager for experiments in technique. The interest is spread over a wider area than in the earlier books. The prefixed "Names of the Principal Persons" number fifty, "Men, Women, and Italians," and the elaborate Index includes about three times that number. We begin with the heroine Harriet Byron and her circle of friends in Northamptonshire at a time when she is about to go up to London—a kind of beginning which becomes almost standardized for this type of novel. She is twenty years old—it is time for her to be married. Lucy Selby's opening sentence, "Your resolution to accompany Mrs. Reeves to London has greatly alarmed your three lovers," suggests a direct narrative

[5] James Foster, *Sermons* (3rd ed.; 1736), I, 29–31.
[6] British Museum Addit. MS. 35,397, f. 299$^v$. Dr. Thomas Birch to Philip Yorke, later Lord Hardwicke, September 29, 1750.

which does not develop. The letters begin by giving us an elaborate and lightly touched social record. Harriet herself feels that she is virtually on the point of creating an epistolary novel:

> Shall I tell you what I imagine each person of the company I am writing about (writing in character) would say of me to *their* correspondents?— It would be digressing too much, or I would (I, 66).[7] What a length have I run! How does this narrative Letter-writing, if one is to enter into minute and characteristic descriptions and conversations, draw one on! (I, 86) What a great deal of writing does the reciting of half an hour or an hour's conversation make, when there are three or four speakers in company; and one attempts to write what each says in the *first* person! I am amazed at the quantity, on looking back. But it *will* be so in narrative Letter-writing (II, 414).

The scale and method of some of these performances suggest the structure of the Boswellian record. Continued attention is paid to details of gesture: "Once, indeed, he tried to speak: His mouth actually opened, to give passage to his words; as sometimes seems to be his way before the words are quite ready: But he sat down satisfied with the effort" (I, 60). This we may call the late Richardsonian treatment of mannerism, approaching Sterne.

As to the plot, Harriet is beset with lovers. The libertine Sir Hargrave Pollexfen plans a forced marriage and abducts Harriet, who is rescued by Sir Charles. Thus the hero makes an impressive delayed entrance, and we are introduced to the Grandison circle, dominated by Sir Charles and his sister Charlotte. The history of the Grandison family is given by Harriet, who is provided with documents and information for the purpose. But Richardson's letter-writing narratists are also interested participants, and Harriet is of course destined to fall in love with Sir Charles. The hero himself is not an important letter-writer. As far as the reader is concerned, he comes ready-made; we do not really see him developing or changing. There is of course elaborate illustration of his virtues—his numerous benefactions, his lofty intervention in the tangled affairs of kinsmen, friends, or even strangers, and his notoriously effective way of placating and disarming men who want to fight duels with him. All this has counted heavily against him with readers of later times. As Mark Twain says somewhere, "Few things are harder to put up with than the annoyance of a good example."

The plot is complicated by Sir Charles's Italian involvements, his conditional betrothal to Clementina della Porretta. Despite the

[7] [Page references are to the Shakespeare Head Edition.]

plan or outline which Richardson had, he hesitated as to how much emphasis to give to the Italian story. On October 22, 1751, he wrote to William Duncombe:

> Clementina's Fate is not yet come to my Knowledge. I have been hinder'd from enquiring after her; in other words, from pursuing her story. But I think she rises upon me. And as I know not what to offer next, being too irregular a scribbler to be able to write by a plan, I seem to be at a loss, to know what to do with her, or to fetch up Harriet again, and make her the principal Female character. . . .
>
> I want more time than my Business will allow me, now her story is become arduous, to adjust, reconcile, retrospect, connect, etc. I have half a Mind to lay by the Work for ever. A very little inducement will make me resolve to do so. Do you think it right at my time of life, and shook by maladies, that affect me mentally as well as corporally, to write Love Stories, and fill my head with Nugatories of Boys and Girls.[8]

Richardson ends by duplicating effects rather extensively. Clarissa, Harriet, and Clementina all meet social and moral obstacles as they are drawn into unavowed or imperfectly avowed attachments; all undergo various degrees of compulsion; all are confronted with the argument, "If you aren't really in love with A, why should you refuse to marry B?" The Porrettas persecute Clementina as the Harlowes persecute Clarissa, though of course Clementina never becomes a Richardsonian heroine in the full sense because she never becomes a major correspondent. Richardson here tries to repeat the gigantesque effect of *Clarissa* in a relatively facile and theatrical way, to execute a romantic variation of the novel of manners. It is significant that when John Scott of Amwell discusses the possibility of striking illustrations for Richardson's novels he notes that *Grandison* "abounds with fine situations" and refers particularly to the Italian heroines, Clementina herself and the jealous and passionate Olivia, who actually draws a dagger on Sir Charles:

> Now from the page of Richardson bestow
> On Clementina's face the lines of woe;
> Or let sweet Harriet's livelier beauty wear
> The soul-fraught eye and apprehensive air;
> Or draw the proud Olivia's rage-flush'd charms,
> When the calm hero seiz'd her deadly arms;
> And paint that hero, firm in trial prov'd,
> Unaw'd by danger, and by vice unmov'd.[9]

---

[8] Maggs Brothers, Catalogue 411 (1921), No. 2215.
[9] John Scott, "An Essay on Painting," in Robert Anderson, *The Works of the British Poets*, XI, 767.

Though admired by contemporaries, the Italian story seems to us to be at the same time colorless and theatrical, and Sir Charles's toplofty embarrassment, with the ideally eligible Harriet in England and the tragic Clementina in Italy, does not command our full interest and sympathy. After protracted negotiations which do not "engage the heart" like the deadlock in *Clarissa* or even the predicament of Pamela, Sir Charles is made free to marry Harriet by Clementina's scruples about marrying a heretic. It is interesting to mark Richardson's preference between the two heroines:

> "Will I give you Leave to think, that Harriet is superior to Clementina?" Indeed I will. I have owned the Superiority to our dear Lady B. And have reflected upon the Judgment of those who are struck with the Glare of a great Action, which was owing principally to a raised Imagination. Your beloved Sister is of Opinion with you, Madam, in preferring Harriet: And I will not choose for my Judges of the Work, any of those, who are of a contrary one.[10]

This verdict, like others pronounced in that period on the characters in the novels, appears to be based on the moral qualities of the character rather than on the success of the characterization; yet Richardson probably had enough power of self-criticism to realize that his Italian story, when compared with his best work, represented a failure of the imagination.

Next to Anna Howe, Charlotte Grandison is the most important of Richardson's lively ladies, and does much to sustain the level of the comedy of manners. She was a more important character for contemporary readers than she has been for later generations; her good and bad qualities were much discussed, and many agreed with the more sedate Harriet in blaming her for her perverse treatment of her husband, her "froppishness," to use one of Richardson's words. The Lord G.-Charlotte and Harriet-Charlotte contrasts . . . come from the cross-pattern of grave and lively characters in current comedy. The plan of *Grandison* permits the expansion of such roles. The duplication of themes from *Clarissa* is not confined to the Italian story, though most of the situations are toned down. Even the unscrupulous Sir Hargrave aims at enforced marriage, not seduction, and is far from being a complex egotist like Lovelace; other rakes and men of pleasure, like Sir Everard Grandison, are silly and futile rather than dangerous. Sir Thomas Grandison, the libertine father of Sir Charles, domineers over his daughters, but shows himself to be more sprightly and less

---

[10] *Boston Public Library Quarterly*, IV (1952), 219–20. To Lady Echlin, May 17, 1754. The "beloved Sister" is Lady Bradshaigh, one of Richardson's most important correspondents.

sullen than Clarissa's father. The approved social circles in *Grandison* contrast on the one hand with the domestic tyranny of the Harlowes and on the other hand with the folly and frivolity of fashionable life. Didacticism persists, but finer distinctions are being made, and the promptings of the comic spirit are beginning to make it easier to distinguish folly from wickedness. Within the groups presented the discriminated characteristics of the various ages of man count for much; the old, the middle-aged, and the young are all depicted, and we are expected to remember that Sir Charles's father is a middle-aged cynic, Harriet herself a girl of twenty (a year or two older than one would expect an unmarried beauty to be), the naïve Emily Jervois fourteen, and so on.

Impulse may be evil in the arrogant or wicked, but delightful, admirable, even playful in the virtuous, though untrustworthy in a whimsical person like Charlotte; on the other hand, mere impulse is so completely controlled in a moral paragon like Sir Charles that his actions often seem pompous and formal, whatever we are told about his feelings. This may be called sentimentalism if we mean by that term a harmonizing of the true, the good, and the beautiful, which is at the same time a harmonizing of self-love or self-approval with benevolence; but it is not sentimentalism in the sense that it exalts a mere release of feeling which carries with it the guarantee of its own virtue. Richardson's ethical position is well stated in one of Henry Grove's papers in the *Spectator:* "The Desire of doing Good . . . though antecedent to Reason, may yet be improved and regulated by it, and, I will add, is no otherwise a Virtue than as it is so." [11] Or, as Grove later put it, "the *virtue* of benevolence" is not to be identified "with the *instinct* called by that name"—an identification erroneously made, he says, by Hutcheson in his *Inquiry into the Original of Our Ideas of Beauty and Virtue.* For Richardson and Sir Charles the natural goodness of human nature is not a fixed dogma, but a working assumption convenient for the didactic novelist and the philanthropist.

> Surely, Dr. Bartlett, human nature is not so bad a thing, as some disgracers of their own species have imagined. I have, on many occasions, found, that it is but applying properly to the passions of persons, who, tho' they have not been very remarkable for benevolence, may yet be induced to do right things in *some* manner, if not always in the *most graceful.* . . . We should not too soon, and without making *proper* applications, give up persons of ability or power, upon conceptions of their general characters; and then, with the herd, set our faces against them, as if we knew them to be invincible. How many ways are there to over-

[11] *Spectator*, No. 588.

come persons, who may not, however, be naturally beneficent! Policy, a regard for outward appearances, ostentation, love of praise, will sometimes have great influences (IV, 156-57).

Richardson is at great pains to show that the good man's feelings and opinions must issue in deeds, and to avoid the common objection that sentimentalism substitutes feeling for action. The novelist's Concluding Note points out that such deeds are within the power of any man so situated, and that the purpose of the story is "to shew, by a series of facts in common life, what a degree of excellence may be attained and preserved amidst all the infection of fashionable vice and folly" (VI, 329). "The Chevalier Grandison, said the kind Jeronymo, speaks by *action:* It is his way. His head, his heart, his lips, his hands, are governed by one motion, and directed by one spring" (IV, 227-28). This is a restatement of the ideal of harmony that underlies sentimental ethics.

Love between the sexes of course poses the supreme problem in the harmonizing of passion with rational esteem and moral approval. The theme is always present in Richardson's novels from the first clumsy advances of Mr. B—to the concluding tableaux at Grandison Hall, though it reaches tragic heights only in *Clarissa*. Through much of *Grandison* this engrossing issue is discussed as in a long-drawn-out session of a bourgeois or genteel court of love. When Charlotte writes in anti-romantic vein, "Love-matches, my dear, are foolish things," Harriet replies:

> I remember, you once said, It was well that Love is not a passion absolutely invincible: But, however, I do not, my dear, agree with you in your notions of all Love-matches. Love merely *personal,* that sort of Love which commences between the years of fifteen and twenty; and when the extraordinary *merit* of the object is not the foundation of it; may, I believe, and perhaps generally *ought* to, be subdued. But Love that is founded on a merit that every-body acknowledges—I don't know what to say to the vincibility of *such* a Love (V, 70, 72).

This moral seriousness in a settled system, expressed in socially acceptable forms and in detailed illustrations and nice distinctions, imparts a sense of security and encourages lightness of touch. The feminine point of view prevails. As Clarissa herself had remarked,

> Who sees not that those women who take delight in writing, excel the men in all the graces of the familiar style? The gentleness of their minds, the delicacy of their sentiments (improved by the manner of their education) and the liveliness of their imaginations, qualify them to a high degree of preference for this employment (VIII, 224).

The tone of the later Richardsonian letter, abundantly illustrated in *Grandison* and in the novelist's own correspondence, is thus suggested in a letter to Miss Westcomb:

> And shall the modest Lady have nothing but her Silence to commend her? Silence indeed to me is a Commendation, when worthy Subjects offer not, and nothing but Goose-like Gabble-Gabble-Gabble (Begging their Flippancies' Pardon) is going forward; For Air, and Attention, and Non-Attention, as Occasions require, will show *Meaning* beyond what Words can; to the Observing: But the Pen will show *Soul*, and *Meaning* too!—Retired, the modest Lady, happy in her self; happy in the Choice she makes of the dear Correspondent of her own Sex (for ours are too generally Designers) Uninterrupted; her Closet her Paradise: Her Company, her self, and ideally the Beloved absent; there she can distinguish her self! By this Means she can assert and vindicate her Claim to Sense and Meaning—And shall a modest Lady then refuse to write? Shall she, in other Words, refuse to set down her Thoughts, as if they were unworthy of her self, of her Friend, of her Paper?—A Virtuous and innocent Heart to be afraid of having its Impulses *embodied* as I may say!—Tell it not in Gath—Lest the Daughters of the Philistines (the Illiteratae, if you please) rejoice!—Shall she refuse to give herself, by Use, a Facility, in so commendable an Employment; which on so many Occasions may be no less *useful* than commendable?—Shall she deny her self a Style, and, as I may say, an Ability to judge of the Style or Sense of others; or even of what she reads?—Hard, very hard, would she think it, if our Sex were to make a Law to deny hers, the Opportunities she denies her self.[12]

We enjoy the new style better when it gives us not the sentimental and didactic meditations of the "closet" but the notation and analysis of social detail. Amid the festivities and self-congratulations of the wedding day, Charlotte can write:

> The coach-way was lined with spectators. Mr. Selby, it seems, bowed all the way, in return to the salutes of his acquaintance. Have you never, Lady L., called for the attention of your company in your coach, to something that has passed in the streets, or on the road, and at the same time thrust your head thro' the window, so that nobody could see but yourself? So it was with Mr. Selby, I doubt not. He wanted every one to look in at the Happy Pair; but took care that hardly any-body but himself should be seen (V, 374).

One interesting result is the *ingénue* type of letter, written, but not at great length, by Emily Jervois, and afterwards further developed by Fanny Burney. There are even hints that the lighter letters could be

---

[12] To Miss Westcomb, no date. From the original in the Huntington Library. See *Correspondence*, ed. Mrs. Barbauld (1804), III, 252-53.

made a delicate instrument for high comedy, that is, for criticism of the basic assumptions made by the characters in the book. Harriet is not always excessively solemn about her troop of suitors: "Bless me, my dear, how am I to be distressed on all sides! by *good* men too; as Sir Charles could say he was, by good women" (IV, 41). And when it appears that Harriet is magnanimously giving up all hope of Sir Charles, and preferring the happiness of Clementina to her own, the facetious Uncle Selby contributes one of the subtlest comments in the whole work:

> My Uncle, in particular, says, the very pretension is flight and nonsense: But, however, if the girl, added he, can *parade* away her passion for an object so worthy; with all my heart: It will be but just, that the romancing elevations, which so often drive headstrong girls into difficulties, should now-and-then help a more discreet one out of them (IV, 56).

Charlotte's picture of the eternal friendship struck up between Harriet and Clementina, heroines both, "each admiring herself *in* the other," raises large issues and opens an important page in Meredith's Book of Egoism.[13] Charlotte and Harriet can speak of Sir Charles with salutary irreverence; the inevitable critic of the Egoist is an intelligent woman, as Fitzwilliam Darcy, Sir Austin Feverel, and Sir Willoughby Patterne were to discover. "After all, he ill brooks to be laughed at," says Charlotte (V, 5). There is a minor strain of uneasiness after the hero's return from Italy, a hint of impatience or dissatisfaction with his very virtues. Should he come unannounced to Selby House to claim, as all expect, the hand of Harriet? Should he send word in advance? "Or does he think," asks Harriet, "we should not be able to outlive our joyous surprize, if he gave us not notice of his arrival in these parts before he saw us?" (V, 88) Harriet had already hit the target with a remarkable bit of analysis:

> Do you think, my dear, that had he been the first man, he would have been so complaisant to his Eve, as *Milton makes Adam* [So contrary to that part of his character, which made him accuse the woman to the Almighty]—To taste the forbidden fruit, because he would not be separated from her, in her punishment, tho' all *posterity* were to suffer by it?—No; it is my opinion, that your brother would have had gallantry enough to his fallen spouse, to have made him extremely regret her lapse; but that he would have done *his own duty,* were it but for the

---

[13] VI, 255–56. For Meredith's interest in *Grandison*, see the original version of *The Ordeal of Richerd Feverel*, and consider the significant parallels between *Grandison* and *The Egoist*. For a comparison of the feminism of the two writers, see an anonymous article, "Samuel Richardson and George Meredith," *Macmillan's Magazine*, LXXXV (1902), 356–61.

sake of posterity, and left it to the Almighty, if such had been his pleasure, to have annihilated his first Eve, and given him a second (IV, 362).

At times Richardson taxes the letter form beyond the limits of his own scrupulousness and propriety. Once he goes so far as to record at length a troubled dream of Harriet's, recapitulating with broken imagery the principal events of the story (V, 257–59). "Incoherencies of incoherence!" she cries, and her "resveries" are not greatly extended, as they might be in modern stream-of-consciousness fiction, but even here Richardson is experimenting with his forms and testing their possibilities to the last.

*Grandison* furnishes the most striking illustration of the tendency of Richardson's novels to impart to the reader a feeling of close acquaintanceship or intimacy with a group of characters set in the framework of a familiar society. There is always a disposition to project the characters of fiction into the plane of actuality: quixotism in this sense has a long history, from the time when women might weep because "Amadis is dead," down to the days when the country folk, according to the story, rang the bells of the parish church to celebrate Pamela's marriage, to the famous leader in the *Times* beginning, "Soames Forsyte is dead," and to the state of mind of innumerable listeners who cannot be kept from sending in wedding presents if a character in a radio serial is getting married. Readers of *Grandison* thought of the characters as actual members of contemporary society; some of Richardson's circle took nicknames from the novel, and Continental readers enjoined their friends who were traveling to England to visit their favorite characters. "Je vous prie," says a Frenchman in Diderot's *Éloge de Richardson*, "de voir de ma part Miss Emilie, M. Belford, et surtout Miss Howe, si elle vit encore." It was this new intimacy, as well as the mere multiplication of novels, that set the moralistic critics of fiction to evaluating the works in terms of their overt teaching as supported by their social and psychological plausibility. More subtly, this extrapolation from books into life had a marked effect on literary criticism in general, notably in the new criticism of Shakespeare's characters which treated them as "real people" existing in a moral, social, and psychological system independent of the plays. This subject deserves further exploration.

Richardson's influence on the later eighteenth century novel has often been considered in contrast to that of Fielding, but such an opposition is oversimple or exaggerated. His position has likewise been defined in terms of sentimentalism. But Richardson's influence on later sentimentalism is hard to isolate; when it can be identified it works for artistic rigor and for minute and consistent analysis of detail. A full-scale Richardsonian imitation must be serious (with tragic possibilities), and at the same time finely analytical of manners and morals. The danger was that the serious would go into violence and sensationalism, that the analytical would run into triviality. The innumerable stories which give us a sprightly-serious correspondence between a heroine and her friend, a daring libertine, an abduction, and a seduction, are only superficially Richardsonian. It is unhistorical to see Richardson in every bourgeois seduction story—in the story of Faust and Gretchen, for example, as has been done by an able scholar.[14] Moreover, the story of Clarissa did not lend itself completely to the uses of the conduct-book. When the heroine of a novel of 1764 leaves her home to avoid a loveless marriage, her friend carefully explains to her angry father:

> Your child, sir, only desires a bare negative in a point whereon all her peace and felicity is dependent; she sets up no will of her own against you, nor has she presumed to make a clandestine, indiscreet choice. She has, indeed, flown from your house, but her flight was single, no giddy lover to assist, no unworthy confident [sic] to impel her to the commission of an action, that would have blasted your every hope and expectation.[15]

When Maria Susannah Cooper revised one of her novels, she explained that she had originally erred in making her heroine too independent of "the earliest duty of life":

> Emilia's heart was devoted to an object worthy of its attachment, but she engaged herself by a promise which abridged the right of parental authority. This defect in example lessened the influence of her precepts. The writer has now endeavoured to draw a perfect pattern of filial obedience, and female delicacy.[16]

Lovelace was endlessly imitated, not without moral misgivings and serious doubts about the probability of his elaborate plots, as in the utterances of one would-be seducer who happens to be named Lord Lovell:

> With your noble way of thinking you will probably wonder that I have not recourse to some stratagem, or even violence, to get her person into my possession, and so take the shortest way with my fair dissenter. But those schemes of rapes, or running away with women, are, in the first

[14] S. B. Liljegren, *The English Sources of Goethe's Gretchen Tragedy* (Lund, 1937).
[15] *Each Sex in Their Humour* (1764), II, 145–46.
[16] Dedication to *The Daughter: or the History of Miss Emilia Royston, and Miss Harriet Ayres* (Dublin, 1775), a revision of *Letters between Emilia and Harriet* (1762).

place, what I have always detested and despised: besides, they rarely or ever answer the end, and, in this country especially, are next to impracticable. But as to Clara, for many reasons that I could give you, the probability of succeeding in such an attempt would hardly be less than that of a Sallee rover's cruizing above bridge, and making prize of a Thames-wherry carrying a company to Vauxhall.[17]

The ineffectual imitations and modifications of the *Clarissa* plot force us to the conclusion that *Grandison* was imitated to more purpose than *Clarissa*. Yet, if it was only too easy to substitute commonplace melodrama and didacticism for the tragic issues of personality in *Clarissa*, it was also easy to reduce *Grandison* to conventional standards:

> Then asking, what book she had in her hand, Miss Spendlove told her, It was Sir Charles Grandison. And are you not charmed, my dear, resumed my sister, with Richardson's manner of writing? In my opinion, his works are better calculated for public utility, than any of his contemporaries—What justness, and delicacy of sentiment! What fine rules of morality! What a thorough knowledge of nature!—But are you not particularly pleased with the artless simplicity of Emily? How noble an effort was hers, to conquer a passion, that stole into her breast beneath the veil of gratitude, and which she indulged, as a generous sentiment.
>
> Miss Spendlove's embarrassment betrayed her. After a pause, she answered, with frequent hesitation, "Certainly, Madam, she was a noble girl—Yes—'twas a proper resolution—And to be sure—But don't you think Lady Grandison had a tincture of jealousy in her composition?—Lady Grandison's concern, my dear, reply'd my sister, with a sigh she could not suppress, seems rather to proceed from affection, and apprehension, for a fair friend, than a jealous suspicion. Indeed, whilst she suffered the pain of uncertainty, we cannot wonder at her fears; but after having received Sir Charles's addresses, she had such perfect confidence in his love and honour, that friendship only could give rise to her solicitude. Emily's resolution was highly praise-worthy, and she pursued the only method which could restore her heart, unwarily entangled in an illaudable passion.[18]

This is not contemptible, though perhaps it is drawn too fine for us. A discerning reader can still easily understand why *Grandison* was one of Jane Austen's favorite novels. Richardson handed on to Jane Austen the tradition of a judgment of society by the intelligent feminine mind, secured by an accepted social and moral system. The individual within the system is under close surveillance by the critic, and the questions raised are those of the interplay of personality and convention, the correction of one's judgments of people and situations, the adjust-

---

[17] *The Woman of Honour* (1768), I, 139-40.
[18] *The School for Wives* (1763), pp. 35-36.

ment of "candor" to the facts of life, the reconciliation of spontaneity and good manners, the art of being not too pliable and not too stubborn, the art of saving oneself from one's friends, the art of living with bores, stuffed shirts, and egoists, including members of one's own family. Jane Austen's titles denote these topics without any attempt to be ornamental or oblique—*First Impressions, Sense and Sensibility, Pride and Prejudice, Persuasion;* her themes represent the exquisite distillation of the social comedy of the *Grandison* tradition combined with a serious though not tragic treatment of family relationships which derives from *Clarissa.* On the "vincibility" of love and liking, and the place of "merit" in matchmaking, Jane Austen occupied common ground with Harriet and Charlotte. From *Grandison* also stems the treatment of the libertine as fool rather than villain; his position is often reduced to absurdity, and we get Willoughby in *Sense and Sensibility,* Wickham in *Pride and Prejudice,* and Sir Edward Denham in *Sanditon.* In this tradition the social comedy can never be separated from a basic system of moral judgments; the release of free and humorous criticism or irony, as it is now fashionable to call it, is never irresponsible though it may well be lighthearted; as an aspect of the art of the novelist it stands in vital relationship to a plot structure which embodies a social structure.

For convenience the modern tendency to revise our estimate of Richardson may be illustrated by Professor E. A. Baker's significant statement:

> He gave our literature the first example of that novel of personality, that history of the struggle for self-realization, which was to wait a century, for the recognition of a more enlightened scale of values, before other novelists could take it up and develop it. But of this, which was the real greatness of his achievement, Richardson was unaware, or aware very obscurely; nor did his contemporaries see what he was doing. To them and to himself he was simply the novelist of sensibility, and it was the value and interest of human feeling, as exhibited in his three novels, that riveted attention. No one observed that this was necessarily bound up with a new sense of the value and inexhaustible interest of the individual man or woman.[19]

Professor Baker later adds, "The study of feeling leads directly to the study of motive; the whole system of volitions and actions is opened up" (p. 71). In accepting in essentials this estimate of Richardson's position one may possibly give the novelist more credit for his own achievement, doubting whether long complex works can be created in utter ignorance of their real significance; there is some

---

[19] E. A. Baker, *The History of the English Novel,* IV (1930), pp. 18–19.

ground for considering *Pamela* an accident, but we can hardly dispose of *Clarissa* and *Grandison* in the same way. The critical formulas of Richardson and his age are not ours, and it is also true that many readers in the eighteenth century admired him for what we should consider the wrong reasons, and that many writers of the next generation, if they imitated him, imitated him in the wrong way. Despite his immense prestige in Western Europe, the exact extent of his influence in fiction of high value and significance, notably *La Nouvelle Héloïse* and *Werther,* remains questionable. Actual imitation is often insignificant, on a minor or secondary level. The history of Richardson's reputation, which cannot be reviewed here, shows that his special qualities were not completely submerged in the tide of sentiment, and in particular that the generation of Jane Austen and Lady Louisa Stuart, Coleridge and Hazlitt and Lamb, read him with greater intelligence and discrimination than it has been his fortune to meet with since, unless indeed the balance is being redressed at the present time. He remains the novelist of introversion and introspection, of scrutinized motives and attitudes, of the interplay of impulse and interest with code and convention that constantly ripples the surface of society and sometimes subjects the individual to an ordeal of crucial importance.

# Epistolary Technique in Richardson's Novels

## by A. D. McKillop

In passing from Samuel Richardson's little volume of familiar letters to *Pamela* we find, in place of a collection of brief letters touching on various situations, a massive collection of long letters developing a single situation.* Richardson calls his new method "writing to the moment"; he uses a letter-writer who records the passing thought, gesture, and incident in great detail while moving toward the novelist's foreordained end.[1] But the story told in this way is not merely a series of direct communications from the correspondent. Richardson, as an experienced printer, knew every step in the making of a book, and saw the completed and published novel as the result of a long and intricate process; he extended "writing to the moment" to include every step in the history of a published correspondence. The writing of the letters is only the beginning; they are copied, sent, received, shown about, discussed, answered, even perhaps hidden, intercepted, stolen, altered, or forged. The relation of the earlier letters in an epistolary novel to the later may thus be quite different from the relation of the earlier chapters of a novel to the later. It may seem obvious to say that the writing of the letters is an important part of the action of an epistolary novel, but this is not always so; the letters may be just sec-

"Epistolary Technique in Richardson's Novels" by A. D. McKillop. From *Rice Institute Pamphlet*, XXXVIII (1951), 36–54. Reprinted by permission of the author. Some points in this essay are echoed in Professor McKillop's commentary on *Sir Charles Grandison* (pp. 124–38). With the exception of the penultimate paragraph this essay has not been cut in order that the unity of the discussion be preserved.

* References to Richardson's novels are to the Shakespeare Head Edition, 18 vols., Oxford: Blackwell, 1929–31. The three novels, *Pamela*, *Clarissa*, and *Grandison*, are designated by the abbreviations *P.*, *Cl.*, and *Gr.* Small Roman numerals refer to the numbering of the letters in the Shakespeare Head Edition; Arabic numerals refer to pages.

[1] For an excellent brief statement of what "writing to the moment" means in keeping a journal or writing a novel, see Frederick A. Pottle's Introduction to *Boswell's London Journal 1762–1763* (New York, 1950), pp. 12–13.

tions of a narrative told in the first person, or may otherwise be submerged in the story. In a scholarly and well documented study of the subject, Professor Frank Gees Black makes the significant comment: "Though skill in particular cases qualifies the statement, it would seem that in letter fiction the epistle should be kept as a means of presenting the story and not be unduly obtruded as an agent in the narrative." [2] But in Richardson's work the emphasis on the letter is almost incessant and highly characteristic. And his putting the writing of the novel into the novel itself is far from artless. One would have to go no farther than Cervantes to find an author who puts the discovery of documents conveying the story into the story, and who represents the characters thinking of themselves as in a book. But the device of writing, editing, and even reading the novel within the novel is, I think, essentially new in Richardson—it has even been taken to be new and ingenious as recently as Gide's *Les Faux-Monnayeurs* (1925). A brief survey of the ways in which letter-writing, or, as we may say more pompously and accurately, the provision and transmission of documents, figures in Richardson's novels, may help to dispel the idea that Richardson simply cut up his moralizing narrative into long lengths which he called letters.

It is appropriate that Mr. B. should find Pamela in the first letter writing a letter, and that he should soon order her not to spend so much time in correspondence.[3] The first complication appears when the servant John regularly shows what she writes to Mr. B. before he carries her messages to her parents, as he later confesses in a surreptitious note. Then Pamela's pen gains momentum, and she begins to keep a continuous record which is relatively independent of the receipt and delivery of letters: "I will write as I have Time, and as Matters happen, and send the Scribble to you as I have Opportunity." [4] She even writes a letter when she expects to see her parents within twenty-four hours: "I will continue my Writing still, because, may-be, I shall like to read it, when I am with you, to see what Dangers I have been enabled to escape; and tho' I bring it along with me." [5] There is an underlying compulsion to explain that Richardson's major correspondents love writing in the epistolary way for its own sake.

When Pamela is removed to Lincolnshire and kept a prisoner there,

---

[2] Frank Gees Black, *The Epistolary Novel in the Late Eighteenth Century* (Eugene, Ore., 1940), p. 58. (University of Oregon Monographs: Studies in Literature and Philology, No. 2.) See also, for good comments on the dramatic function of letters in Richardson's novels, with special reference to *Pamela*, Ernest A. Baker, *The History of the English Novel* (10 vols.; London, 1924–39), IV, 22–24.
[3] *P.*, I, 3, 23–24.
[4] *P.*, I, 49.
[5] *P.*, I, 111.

the novelist himself has to intervene for several pages to tell the incidents leading to the visit of her father to Mr. B., since he has no one on hand to make the record—something that would never happen in Richardson's fully developed work. Pamela is now forbidden to carry on correspondence, and Richardson extends the principle of continuous record and has her keep a journal. Since she is expected to show all that she has written to her keeper Mrs. Jewkes, she has to conceal writing materials and smuggle out letters, as to the friendly Parson Williams. These letters are included in the journal; the process includes not only the writing but the copying of letters—one's own and those lent one to read. It is sobering to reflect that unless we remember this duplication of copies, we underestimate the paperwork done by Richardson's characters. Richardson, at least after 1740, kept copies of letters sent and sometimes of letters received, and his characters follow the same plan after they have hit their epistolary stride. This begins in Pamela's journal, and develops enormously. She becomes to a large extent her own compiler and editor. Much of this may seem mere *paperasserie,* such as the formal set of proposals for keeping her as his mistress which Mr. B. submits in writing: "I took a Copy of this for your Perusal, my dear Parents." [6] Richardson also begins in a small way the device of the fabricated or falsified letter when he has Mr. B. prescribe a short letter to be sent to her parents.[7] There is occasional dramatic use of letters, such as the misdelivery and interchange of letters from Mr. B. to Pamela and Mrs. Jewkes, so that Pamela discovers his plot against Parson Williams, and later the anonymous note warning her that Mr. B. intends to use the device of a mock-marriage— both important in raising and prolonging Pamela's suspicions.[8] Even more important is the impact of the journal on the later action. Pamela had managed to send the early part of the record to her parents by way of Williams; the second part she hid under a rosebush in the garden, and Mrs. Jewkes seized it. Thereafter the prudent girl kept the rest of the journal "sew'd in my Under-coat, about my Hips." [9] The part seized by Jewkes is turned over to Mr. B. Just as Pamela is represented as the author and editor of her own story, so Mr. B. is represented as the first reader.

> You have so beautiful a Manner, that it is partly that, and partly my Love for you, that has made me desirous of reading all you write; tho' a great deal of it is against myself: for which you must expect to suffer a little. And as I have furnish'd you with a Subject, I have a Title to

[6] *P.,* I, 263.
[7] *P.,* I, 127, 154–55.
[8] *P.,* I, 218–21, 307.
[9] *P.,* I, 311.

see the Fruits of your Pen.—Besides, said he, there is such a pretty Air of Romance, as you relate them, in *your* Plots, and *my* Plots, that I shall be better directed in what manner to wind up the Catastrophe of the pretty Novel.[10]

At his demand Pamela gives him the later part, including the account of her attempted escape. His comments and reactions are at this point a delayed response to the journal, though not of course an epistolary response; assuming that the reader has been interested in the original narrative, Mr. B.'s responses reënforce this original appeal and at the same time advance the action. Even if we do not agree that Richardson is completely successful in putting over this device, we should recognize the novelist's ingenuity.

Mr. B. is now in melting mood, and finds Pamela's insistence on returning to her parents perverse. The action moves quickly here; Richardson is not always tedious, and letters may precipitate as well as suspend the action. After the parting, as Pamela stops for the night, she sees in advance a letter which was to have been delivered to her at noon the next day, a letter which tells her that Mr. B. had been about to make honourable addresses to her when she expressed the preference for a return to her parents.[11] A record of Mr. B.'s underlying intentions is thus put before Pamela in time to dispose her to accept another letter the next day imploring her to return, the result of Mr. B.'s reading the rest of the journal. Perhaps, as the moralists tell us, she should not have gone back, but at least the premature opening of the first letter, with its touch of feminine curiosity, is ingeniously timed, and the climactic action produced by the reading of the journal is skillfully presented.

This climax is the most effective use of documentation in *Pamela*. The rest of the two-volume novel published in November 1740, which we may call *Pamela I,* is of less interest for epistolary technique, though Mr. B.'s sister Lady Davers, the strongest opponent of the marriage, is well presented in some vigorous quarrel scenes. The epistolary methods used in the two-volume sequel *Pamela II* of December 1741 do not show successful experimentation. The device of repeating and commenting on the earlier action is ineffectively extended, as when Mr. B. tardily supplements Pamela's original report of the early situation.[12] One of the most effective episodes in *Pamela II,* the showdown with Mr. B. about his incipient affair with a beautiful countess, is told by Pamela to Lady Davers in letters which are then read and supplemented by Mr. B., but without heightening the dramatic effect.[13] The

[10] *P.*, I, 317.
[11] *P.*, II, 6–7.
[12] *P.*, III, xxx.
[13] *P.*, IV, xxxi–xxxvi.

new social perspectives of *Pamela II* make the early story seem crude and awkward in retrospect: Pamela comments on the elevation of her own style, is ashamed to have strangers read her account of Mr. B.'s clumsy attempts at seduction, and remarks regretfully that she knew no "polite Courtship." [14] Some comparatively light social notation on the new level is developed in the letters of Polly Darnford, Pamela herself, and Lady Davers, and points forward to the later novels. The novelist at times tries to keep up an evenly balanced two-way correspondence. But the decline of dramatic interest invites digression and interpolation, always a threatening possibility in the epistolary novel.[15]

In line with the social setting, the action, and the psychology, *Clarissa* shows a more elaborate epistolary structure. Pamela is the only major correspondent in her story; whereas all readers of *Clarissa* are likely to remember the enormous narrative in terms of parallel series of two-way communications between Clarissa Harlowe and Anna Howe on the one hand, Robert Lovelace and John Belford on the other. Yet this is not the scheme as actually worked out; for a considerable span we are likely to find that one correspondent dominates, often writing long letters journal-wise, in which other letters or documents may be included or absorbed. The early action centers with morbid intensity on Harlowe Place, and Clarissa reports the crisis in the family circle in practically continuous narrative. The correspondence is carried on under difficulties; Clarissa is imprisoned by her family, and has to smuggle out letters to Anna Howe with the aid of trusted servants. There is also a carefully motivated secret correspondence with Lovelace: she wishes to pacify him so that he will not take violent action; she seeks a line of retreat in case her family forces the repulsive Solmes upon her; and, more vaguely, it is intimated that Lovelace appears as a possible lover and husband. But Lovelace's letters are not immediately pushed to the fore; as summarized and reported by Clarissa to Anna, they at first fall into the predominant line. We are told that Clarissa keeps complete files—"I have promised to lay before you all his Letters and my Answers." [16] Her task of copying is even more laborious than Pamela's. The arrangement seems clumsy, but the total effect is impressive: the elaborate documents connect Clarissa with the world and at the same time emphasize her tragic isolation. She carries on written negotiations with her family, even though they are under the same roof; Lovelace's world of pride and passion threatens in this se-

---

[14] *P.*, III, 14, 35–36, 159–60.
[15] For further comment on Richardson's methods in *Pamela II*, see Alan D. McKillop, *Samuel Richardson, Printer and Novelist* (Chapel Hill, N.C., 1936), pp. 57–61.
[16] *Cl.*, I, 180.

quence, but is kept at a distance; Anna Howe's world of normal social relationships, in which girls can innocently indulge their whims and quarrel harmlessly with parents and suitors, comes tantalizingly close, but Clarissa can never reach it. Anna's is sometimes a light epistolary comedy with Richardson's characteristic devices; thus in the long communication containing her sketch of Solmes, the earlier part of the letter is the theme of a discussion with her mother reported in the later part.[17]

Richardson does not go about his work simply by having everybody in the story write letters. No protracted correspondence ever takes place between Lovelace and Clarissa; their ambiguous relationship is described, always imperfectly, in letters to and by others, and does not allow the sharp commitments of direct written communication between principals. The novelist uses his secondary correspondents with great skill. Anna, like Belford later in the other series, gains for a time in importance; the crescendo of her letters presents the happy normal world denied to Clarissa and the shrewd yet inadequate judgments of that world; she sides against the Harlowes more sharply than the heroine herself, and points out that Clarissa is in love with Lovelace, and that if she takes flight with him, marriage is her only choice. After the actual flight, we come closer to parallel series, Clarissa to Anna and Lovelace to Belford, but the scheme does not become mechanical. Where there would be excessive duplication, Richardson continues to abridge and summarize Lovelace's letters, and sometimes to omit letters which the formal scheme of the novel would require. The originals of such letters may have existed, in some part, in the novelist's writing desk. He "restored" letters and passages to *Clarissa* in the third edition, and later made additions on a smaller scale to *Grandison;* no doubt other letters produced in the working out of the plans for the novels remained unpublished.

With the advance of Lovelace to the foreground of the correspondence, about the time of the removal of Clarissa from Hertfordshire to London, he enters on an elaborate series of forged and garbled letters, beginning with the faked letter from "Doleman" which tricks Clarissa into thinking that the lodging with the infamous widow Sinclair is eligible and respectable. Clarissa is plied with forged letters purporting to come from Lovelace's relatives, and is cruelly duped by an agent of Lovelace's, "Tomlinson," who pretends to be negotiating on behalf of her uncle. Lovelace also gets access to the Anna-Clarissa letters, and of course sends copious extracts to Belford. Thus one of the two main lines of letters is presented as impacted in the other. As the crisis ap-

---

[17] *Cl.*, I, xxvii.

proaches, Lovelace intercepts a letter in which Anna tells Clarissa the truth about the plots against her; since he knows Clarissa would expect a letter, he imitates Anna's hand and garbles the text. His *libido dominandi* does not adequately motivate these cumbersome devices, yet Clarissa's tragic isolation can still evoke an imaginative response. While, with mingled credulity and pride, she thinks that marriage negotiations are under way and that the situation is still largely within her control, a veil of deceptive documentation cuts her off from normal and rational humanity. Outrage follows deception. Clarissa escapes to Hampstead, is traced thither and confronted by Lovelace, lured back to London, and there drugged and violated. Lovelace's reports still enlarge upon his tricks and stratagems, but the curtain drops temporarily at the curt sentence, "The affair is over. Clarissa lives." [18] After Clarissa's later escape to Covent Garden she again becomes principal correspondent for a time and resumes connections with the outer world. She unravels the web of Lovelace's deceptions, and in unimpeded letters to Anna tells for the first time the details of the tragic return from Hampstead.[19] This is a masterly piece of narrative, surcharged with almost intolerable apprehension and agony; its power is partly due to the skill with which Richardson has held it back until Clarissa could tell the story with the tremendous weight of deliberate recollection. It is after all the complex letter mechanism that produces this powerful delayed effect, this merciless iteration of doom.

With the false arrest of Clarissa at the suit of the bawd Sinclair, her temporary imprisonment at Rowland's, and her final asylum at Smith's in Covent Garden, Belford intervenes and becomes for the first time the reporter of important matters; indeed for a considerable time he gains what we may call epistolary dominance not only in the Lovelace-Belford series but in the whole system of the book. His is the pen of a ready writer; both he and Lovelace use shorthand for their confidential correspondence with each other and for other records.[20] He begins his new role as an intermediary between Lovelace and Clarissa. Clarissa would be ready to tell her story herself, if she could; but after seeing specimens of Lovelace's letters and finding that Belford is worthy to be "the protector of her memory," she makes him her executor and the editor of the letters that tell her story.[21] As a reformed rake, he offers too much edifying comment to suit our taste; he divagates, for example, into the warning tale of the sad end of his fellow-rake Belton, and into a comparison between Rowe's *Fair Penitent* and Clarissa's

[18] *Cl.*, V, xxxii.
[19] *Cl.*, VI, xliv–xlvi.
[20] *Cl.*, VI, 113, 315.
[21] *Cl.*, VII, xix, xx.

story, yet he is by no means superfluous. In the reprisals and regrets of the latter part of the story the correspondence is more widely scattered; various members of the family have their say, including Colonel Morden, Clarissa's one true friend among her kinfolk, and it is Belford's part to keep the story from running into excessive fragmentation. Though Anna Howe is directed to collaborate with him, he remains in control. Anna's wit and spirit become irrelevant, and she naturally drops into the background, though Richardson goes too far when he sends her on a trip to the Isle of Wight during the last days of Clarissa's life.[22] Yet Belford is never dramatically central, like Clarissa and Lovelace, and Richardson slackens his grip at the end when he says that the Conclusion is "supposed to be written by Mr. Belford." [23]

The story runs its course to a foreseen conclusion, yet the shock of surprise can still be felt. The inept letters of the pedant Brand almost at the hour of Clarissa's death may remind us that Richardson had sought comic relief even in this tragedy; and now that Anna Howe and Lovelace can no longer write with gusto, he offers this heavy and heartless humor, with its remarkable burlesque of formal and didactic letter-writing. Finally, in contrast to the protracted reports and discussions connected with Clarissa's death, we have the swift denouement in which Lovelace goes to the Continent and falls in a duel with Morden—a short span in which Lovelace uses epistolary dominance only for a few curt words.

In summing up the use of letters in *Clarissa*, we may say that the correspondents report conflict and offer commentary. The conflict is not typically a head-on collision between one correspondent and another, assertion and reply; rather it is presented largely within the letters of a dominant correspondent, who may report dialogue in great detail, sometimes with dramatic notation, interpreting all signs and considerations in their bearing upon motives, intentions, and future action. A report of conflict thus becomes an elaborate assertion of personality, and here Richardson often dramatizes "the divided mind." This is preëminently true of the principal characters, Clarissa and Lovelace. For Miss Howe and Belford, the provision of comment outweighs the report of conflict, but when Richardson is at his best there is an organic connection. Secondary characters may be given over to one aspect or another; thus the Harlowe family represent conflict in its most brutal and sullen form, and are not enlightened enough to provide a significant commentary. Other secondary characters show a considerable variety of function.

[22] *Cl.*, VII, 109, 247.
[23] *Cl.*, VIII, 278.

In *Pamela* and *Clarissa* Richardson experiments with and extends epistolary technique. There is less innovation in *Grandison,* though some new effects and values appear. Instead of the isolated and distressed heroine writing her own history almost single-handed, as in *Pamela,* or with the aid of other correspondents who are primarily concerned with her affair, as in *Clarissa,* we now have an enormous expansion of social correspondence carried on without serious obstruction or threat, and usually intended to be shown about to a circle of friends. It has been noted that such work had already been done in *Pamela II* and in Anna Howe's part of *Clarissa.* The story and the letters go by groups—the Selby group in Northamptonshire, the Grandisons, and later the della Porrettas in Italy. The lending and forwarding of long files of letters, so that one group may be informed about the other, is part of the pattern of the book. The groups ramify into the casual contacts of actual society. Letter-writing thus loses dramatic intensity and sometimes becomes a pastime for young ladies, while the protestations about long letters become conventional: "What a length have I run! How does this narrative Letter-writing, if one is to enter into minute and characteristic descriptions and conversations, draw one on!" [24] Thus Richardson moves in the direction taken later by Fanny Burney and Jane Austen. The danger is that such a record will be too trivial and discursive. The age was ready to call almost any batch of sketches or essays "letters." Richardson had already fallen into this trap in *Pamela II,* however, and is generally aware of the danger. Though at the beginning of *Grandison* he is capable of reporting a long argument about ancient and modern learning, he tries to make it part of the social record; we may well feel that there is too much set discussion here, but the dialogue is well dramatized.[25]

In general, Richardson keeps to the relatively simple plan already described: one major correspondent is likely to dominate a considerable section of the book, and other documents are taken into this sequence. The correspondent may send installments numbered as letters ("Harriet in continuation") which are really chapters or long entries in a record kept journal-wise. The attempt of Sir Hargrave Pollexfen to abduct Harriet and her rescue by Sir Charles Grandison introduce new characters and potential correspondents, but Harriet continues to transmit the mail. In presenting the ideal gentleman Sir Charles, Richardson has a new problem; the hero cannot report *in propria persona* all his noble deeds and thoughts. Others must chant his praise, as in Voltaire's *Zadig:*

[24] *Gr.,* I, 86.
[25] *Gr.,* I, x–xiv.

> Que son mérite est extrême!
> Que de grâces! que de grandeur!
> Ah! combien monseigneur
> Doit être content de lui-même!

Harriet at times becomes a collector and transcriber of records about Sir Charles and the history of the Grandison family. The novelist is at some pains to provide her with documents. Thus, when Sir Charles answers Sir Hargrave's challenge to a duel, Sir Charles's own copy of the letter is shown to Mr. Reeves, who shows it to Harriet, who in turn sends it to Lucy Selby. Reeves also gives Harriet a copy of the record of the dialogue between Sir Charles and Sir Hargrave's friend Bagenhall, made by the young clerk whom Bagenhall had brought with him. When Sir Charles comes to breakfast with Sir Hargrave, he likewise brings along a precautionary stenographer.[26] The natural inclination of Richardson's busy bodies in our own enlightened times would be to tap telephones and plant dictaphones.

But these are extreme cases; Richardson usually falls back on the assumption of a ready journal-keeper and letter-writer, perhaps seconded by an industrious assembler and editor of memoranda. When the Grandison sisters tell Harriet the story of their father's tyranny, Charlotte seems to be using notes—"But what say my minutes?"[27] Characters regularly provide one another with files of letters; thus Harriet furnishes the Grandison group with the record down to the time of her abduction, letters already given in the text.[28] When letters not already given are thus provided, the effect is that of a cut-back in the narrative. After Sir Charles has told Harriet directly the earlier part of the Italian story (she remembers it word for word, of course), Dr. Bartlett, Sir Charles's tutor and revered friend, sends Harriet successive "pacquets" of letters recounting the story of the della Porretta family and the early stages of the long negotiations and parleys about a possible marriage of Clementina and Sir Charles. His nephew and amanuensis extracts the story from his papers.[29] But when Sir Charles makes his second journey to Italy, and the match with Clementina seems imminent until her religious scruples come to be decisive against it, the hero himself, for the only time in any long sequence, relays the account to Dr. Bartlett in a one-way correspondence. Clementina herself is never a Richardsonian heroine in the full sense, for she never becomes a major correspondent. Her story was intended to pro-

---
[26] *Gr.*, I, 319–20, 337–43, 378.
[27] *Gr.*, II, 79.
[28] *Gr.*, II, 385.
[29] *Gr.*, III, 42.

vide dramatic suspense and a note of tragedy, but Richardson never allows her to write letters "to the moment" on a large scale. Thus the one character in *Grandison* who shares in some degree the tragic isolation of Clarissa is denied epistolary dominance. Somewhat similarly, though Richardson presents the jealous Olivia as a rival both to Clementina and Harriet, she does not develop as a character or a correspondent, and we may conjecture that the novelist at first intended to give her a larger place in the story and then prudently dropped her. It is almost startling to find the indefatigable Dr. Bartlett telling Harriet that it will not be necessary to give Olivia's story at length.[30]

While Dr. Bartlett is sending his consignments and later while Sir Charles is reporting at length from Italy, Harriet and the English story might seem to be outweighed. There is a mechanical set-up by which Harriet sends the Bartlett installments to Lucy Selby; later Sir Charles's sister Charlotte likewise forwards his advices from Italy to Harriet in Northamptonshire. But the Italian story does not keep the social comedy from developing in England, and this gives a new importance to Charlotte Grandison, now Lady G. She is obviously an extension of the character of Anna Howe, and her letters also elaborate the suggestions for a comedy of manners contained in Harriet's London-to-Northamptonshire letters at the beginning of the story. With the Italian plot kept at arm's length, and Harriet's affairs at a stand, Charlotte is given more freedom to develop her wit and her temperament than Anna Howe ever had. Her husband Lord G., she feels, leaves much to be desired, and she becomes perverse, whimsical, and "arch" to a degree, and is duly rebuked by the more sedate Harriet. Her letters are of major importance in keeping us in the well-bred English world, and for the first time in the story we have a genuine two-way correspondence, Harriet and Charlotte both carrying weight.

After Clementina's renunciation and Sir Charles's return to England, this social tone still dominates. Richardson's problem is to maintain interest now that the way is clear for the union of Harriet and Sir Charles. He still strives for dramatic range, and to this end Clementina and the della Porretta family invade England. When this irruption falls short, as it does, one would expect padding and digressions, along with tedious eulogies and congratulations such as we find in *Pamela II*. Some of our fears may be realized, but not our worst fears; Richardson does not, for example, give us extended travel letters when Harriet and her party take a tour in Northamptonshire, and even the

[30] *Gr.*, III, 406.

glories of Grandison Hall are largely reported, we are told, in letters by Lucy Selby which "do not appear." [31] There are some rather set general conversations, one on the possibility of the intellectual life for women and another on young girls' romantic notions and the folly of a first love,[32] but Richardson does not sink his story by interpolation. The more serious difficulty is that he does not succeed in blending the Italian story and the English social comedy as they converge. Clementina and Charlotte are "scarce cater-cousins."

The vein of social notation does, however, produce ingenious variations of the device of making dramatic play with letters, and this sometimes stands in contrast to the plodding and mechanical provision of documents. At the very beginning, one of Harriet's Northamptonshire suitors, Greville, reads the company passages from a letter from Lady Frampton about Harriet, and "passages from the copy of his answer." He then lends a copy for Harriet to read, scratching out some sentences, but, it is added, only faintly.[33] There is a good deal of by-play of this kind. Letters that are being written may be shared with friends at the elbow of the ready writer; Harriet may begin a letter and Lucy finish it. Charlotte can tantalize Harriet with the possibility of reading a letter from Sir Charles to Dr. Bartlett, though Charlotte of course had no right to pick the letter up in the first place.[34] The surface of the story is rippled with feminine curiosity about the contents of letters. Sir Charles has great reserve; he does not tell all his affairs to his sisters (a piece of masculine psychology ingeniously used by Richardson), and inquisitiveness adds point to the insistent questions as to what has been written, what should be written, what should be sent, read, shown, and to whom. The opening and extension of social relationships, the growth of friendship and love, are figured in this endless process of divulging letters and deciding just how much may be conveyed in confidence at a given time. Negotiations about letters admit of very fine shading. Thus, when the Grandison sisters ask to see Harriet's letters with the proviso that Harriet may omit certain passages, she resents even their assumption that some things she has written should be kept from them.[35] Again, Sir Charles picks up a stray sheet of a letter in which Harriet says that his young ward Emily Jervois secretly loves him; he is of course too much of a gentleman to read it, but the fact that Harriet

[31] *Gr.,* VI, 32, 75, etc.
[32] *Gr.,* V, lviii; VI, lxii.
[33] *Gr.,* I, i, ii.
[34] *Gr.,* II, xxxiii.
[35] *Gr.,* II, xix.

doesn't want him to read something she has written about Emily carries appreciable weight. . . .[36]

Perhaps the most common criticism of Richardson is that he had an imperfect knowledge of his own principles and themes, that he was in part duped by convention, entrapped by his underlying interest in sex, and constantly in danger of being swamped by his own verbosity. But if he falls short of classic control of his themes, the reason may be, not that he was inept or incompetent, but on the contrary that his use of the letter form led him in one direction toward a specific analysis of the enmeshing complexities of life, and in another direction toward a heightened awareness of the discontinuities and blockages, the frustrations and loose ends, that seem to make up the plight of man.

[36] *Gr.*, V, 255-56.

# "Writing to the Moment": One Aspect

## by George Sherburn

Samuel Richardson was justly proud of his lively technique of "writing to the moment"—a technique that transcribed emotional tensions instantly as they arose and not (to use a later phrase) when they were recollected in tranquillity. He used various devices for attaining this sense of presence, and perhaps the fact behind his success is that he had a naturally strong visual imagination: small details show that in his mind he actually *saw* the episodes that he depicted.

Obvious limitations to vividness in his work may be recalled. He wrote uneasily and at times did not clearly convey what he evidently saw. He had little interest in environmental detail or in objective description. Of the stately homes found in all three of the novels, only Grandison Hall got much description.[1] In general, interiors are furnished only with vague chairs and an occasional table—whatever the action really requires, but no more. Clarissa may sit in an "elbow-chair," but the piece is never described further. Persons tend to sit side by side, but practically always in chairs. There are almost no settees or sofas, and when one occurs, as at Mrs. Moor's in Hampstead, it is used as a stage property.[2] A very frequent arrangement places three persons in three chairs, with the principal person flanked, as in a court drawing-room, by subordinates of importance.[3]

Such details, given explicitly but not very vividly, seem in themselves of little interest to Richardson; but at times, curiously, he does pause for almost superfluous details—Lovelace's disguise at Hamp-

---

"'Writing to the Moment': One Aspect" by George Sherburn. From *Restoration and Eighteenth Century Literature: Essays in Honor of Alan Dugald McKillop*, edited by Carroll Camden (Chicago: University of Chicago Press for William Marsh Rice University, 1963), pp. 201–9. Published for William Marsh Rice University by the University of Chicago Press. Copyright © 1963 by William Marsh Rice University. Reprinted by permission of the University of Chicago Press.

[1] *Grandison*, VI, 21–27. All page references to the three novels here given refer to the Shakespeare Head Edition (Oxford: Blackwell [1929–31]).
[2] *Clarissa*, V, 260.
[3] *Pamela*, II, 73, 77; *Clarissa*, II, 217, 225; *Grandison*, III, 102; IV, 237, 342; V, 104.

stead,[4] or Singleton's appearance as a sailor,[5] or Clarissa's room at the bailiff's,[6] or Harriet Byron's masquerade gown[7] (Richardson's own creation?). These are useful but excessive details. Normally the focus is on emotional tensions, such as may be conveyed through physical or bodily attitudes. It is those that are here to be considered as one aspect of this method.

At first sight, these attitudes may not seem much particularized. Most of them have to be the physical reactions of gentlefolk of Richardson's day. A facility in fainting, in the shedding of tears (by either sex), and of bending what Shakespeare had called the pregnant knee are to be expected. All three novels are drawing-room dramas: it is even quaintly pathetic to find the dying Clarissa complaining of Lovelace's persistence in his persecutions: "He will not let me die decently! ... He will not let me enter into my Maker's presence, with the composure that is required in entering into the drawing-room of an earthly prince!"[8] The decorum of the drawing-room implies conventional behavior, but Richardson usually modifies the demeanor of his persons nicely to suit the coloration of the moment.

One may observe that there are various small episodes in which the depiction of tensions seems awkward or false—at least at first sight. *Pamela* doubtless furnishes the best-known examples. Mr. B's first attempt at rape (Letter XXV), it will be remembered, is frustrated by a somewhat tardy fainting fit when Pamela becomes aware that, while Mr. B "expostulates" in her bed, his hand finds its way into forbidden regions. The failure here is less in imagination (Richardson has a pretty gift in imagining attempts at rape) than it is in expression. Almost any reader could improve the arrangement of details in this, Pamela's first real peril, but the disarrangement does not destroy the reader's avid attention.

Another episode that strains a pedestrian reader's sense of presence is the scene in which Pamela of an evening is ordered to wait upon her master at supper.[9] She is too tremulous to be efficient, and, upon wicked suggestions by Mrs. Jewkes, Pamela, while her master is at table, begs for mercy: "Sir, said I, and clasp'd his Knees with my Arms, not knowing what I did, and falling on my Knees, Have Mercy on me, and hear me. . . ." This may be writing to the moment, for if Mr. B's knees are under the table, clasping would be awkward. But

---

[4] *Clarissa*, V, 74, 79.
[5] *Ibid.*, IV, 153.
[6] *Ibid.*, VI, 296–98.
[7] *Grandison*, I, 172–73.
[8] *Clarissa*, VII, 413.
[9] *Pamela*, I, 251.

if Mr. B is envisaged as sitting sidewise at a small round table—he is supping in a parlor—the acrobatics of this kneeling might be possible. Richardson normally *sees* what he is writing. He here imagines rather better than he writes. Another bit of strangeness with the knees occurs in *Clarissa*, where Dorcas kneels hypocritically to Lovelace in order to win favor for and from Clarissa, "bustling on her knees about me." [10]

One again suspects a lack of attention to actuality in the scene toward the end of *Pamela* where, disbursing nuptial largesse to the servants, Pamela is encouraged by Mr. B, who "pulling out his Purse, said, Tell out, my Dear, Two hundred Guineas, and give me the rest." [11] One wonders from what part of his elegant attire a gentleman could "pull out" a purse containing well over two hundred gold coins. This problem of pockets is thus fascinating for men as well as for ladies. A damsel because of her long full skirt could be suspected of concealing voluminous correspondence in pockets (one had two) that (according to Lovelace) "are half as deep as she is high." [12] Pamela, fearing that a pocket might be too easily searched, had stitched her journal to her "under-coat" next to her linen.[13] Ordinarily, ladies placed their generous, tear-moistened handkerchiefs in their pockets.[14]

Much apparently casual imagining can be explained by attention to minute customs of the day, which have long since disappeared. Awkwardnesses among novelists who write with a flowing pen, as Richardson certainly did, may be frequent; but in the case of Richardson, the imagining is likely, upon examination, to be sound and evocative.

Facial expression is perhaps too overt an indication of emotion to require the author's closest attention. Yet see what may be done: Solmes "rising, with a countenance whitened over, as if with malice, his hollow eyes flashing fire, and biting his under-lip, to show he could be *manly*." [15] Clarissa, more conventionally, in the penknife scene, thanks God that she is saved from self-destruction, and "her charming cheeks [Lovelace tells us], that were all in a glow before, turned pale, as if terrified at her own purpose." [16] Clearly it is the emotional coloration that fixes the vividness in these cases. By implication, the same is true when Harriet Byron's desperate admirer, Greville, threatens, "You know what you have declared—Angel of a

[10] *Clarissa*, V, 377.
[11] *Pamela*, II, 312.
[12] *Clarissa*, IV, 46; cf. *Pamela*, I, 319.
[13] *Pamela*, I, 322.
[14] *Grandison*, II, 202; III, 156.
[15] *Clarissa*, II, 235.
[16] *Ibid.*, VI, 70.

woman! said he again thro' his shut teeth."[17] Some emotions do not, as seen in a face, easily translate themselves into words. When Uncle Antony is firmly told by Clarissa that she values his money less than she would kind looks and kind words, he is stupidly nonplussed and angry: he falls into vague wonderment, and, in silence, "looked about him this way and that."[18]

Small details are made to count, especially in the full-figure descriptions. Lovelace (19 June) records:

> At day-dawn I looked thro' the key-hole of my Beloved's door. She had declared she would not put off her cloaths any more in this house. There I behold her in a sweet slumber . . . sitting in her elbow-chair, her apron over her head; her head supported by one sweet hand; the other hand hanging down upon her side, in a sleepy lifelessness; half of one pretty foot only visible.[19]

Again, when in prison, Clarissa is seen in a special posture: "Her face . . . was reclined, when we entered, upon her crossed arms; but so, as not more than one side of it to be hid."[20] The first view of her by Colonel Morden is of course similarly pathetic.[21] Stereotyped attitudes, but with variations, are bound thus to be frequent.

Not all Richardson's attitudes are stereotypes; and even stereotypes may express different emotions. In the *History of the English Stage* (1741), published as if by Thomas Betterton, it is specified that uses of hands may express "accusation, deprecation, threats, desire, &c."[22] Such emotions somewhat imply dramatic action. Richardson's more vivid passages are content to be pictorial and are tableaux rather than violently active situations. Clarissa, for example, reports with almost phenomenal explicitness: "My Father sat half-aside in his elbow-chair, that his head might be turned from me; his hands clasped, and waving, as it were, up and down; his fingers, poor dear gentleman! in motion, as if angry to the very ends of them."[23] This painful picture of the beginning of a family tea is paralleled by the family conclave (typical of the Harlowes and of Richardson) when Clarissa is on the carpet at her return from her stay with the Howes—where she had seen Lovelace, contrary to family injunctions. This scene, preserved to us by the brush of Highmore, shows the family seated in a long row listening to the harsh reproaches of brother James:

[17] *Grandison*, I, 151.
[18] *Clarissa*, II, 218.
[19] *Ibid.*, V, 357.
[20] *Clarissa*, VI, 298–99.
[21] *Ibid.*, VII, 449.
[22] Page 99.
[23] *Clarissa*, I, 51.

> My Brother seemed ready to give a loose to his passion: My Father put on the countenance which always portends a gathering storm: My Uncles mutteringly whispered: and my Sister aggravatingly held up her hands. While I begged to be heard out;—and my Mother said, Let the *child,* that was her kind word, be heard.[24]

This brief passage (as first perceived by Duncan Eaves) furnished Highmore with sufficient matter so that he has depicted in color each attitude of every Harlowe, here given in words, even to the hands of Arabella.

Richardson is very fond of mentioning gestures involving raised hands. Arabella raises her hands more than once "aggravatingly" and frequently raised hands express vague or difficult emotions, such as might reflect the common "words-fail-me" reaction—or they are raised in prayer. Arabella's maid Betty is ironically "astonished (her hands and eyes lifted up)" that Clarissa objects to going to her Uncle Antony's house.[25] But normally sincere and prayerful emotions are thus expressed. Colonel Morden, for example, when, upon his arrival in London, he is informed that Clarissa is dying, exclaims "Good God! . . . with his hands and eyes lifted up." [26] Clementina similarly "prays . . . with lifted-up hands." [27] The Grandison sisters both pray with hands uplifted: Charlotte in gratitude to her brother,[28] and Caroline, earlier, in "pray-pray-fashion" to her unsympathetic father.[29] Clarissa, failing in an attempted escape from Mrs. Sinclair's establishment, raises the window sash and, "clasping her uplifted hands together," cries to the passers-by for help.[30] The raising of hands is indeed very common, but the emotional coloring is so varied and so appropriate that one can feel assured that Richardson saw the circumstance as he recorded it.

Prayers apart, hands are to be kissed and held—graciously or forcibly. When the two Grandison sisters try to lead Harriet Byron to confess that she loves their brother and are seated on either side of her, in sympathy with her speechless predicament, they "vouchsafed, each, to press with her lips the passive hand each held." [31] Pamela, naturally, gets kissed more often and more profusely than any of the ladies in the other novels. A late case is seen in the garden alcove to

---

[24] *Clarissa,* I, 42–43.
[25] *Clarissa,* II, 39.
[26] *Ibid.,* VII, 447.
[27] *Grandison,* III, 60.
[28] *Ibid.,* II, 143.
[29] *Grandison,* II, 72.
[30] *Clarissa,* V, 360.
[31] *Grandison,* II, 204.

which Mr. B has led her: "For he began to be very tiezing, and made me sit on his Knee, and was so often kissing me, that I said, Sir, I don't like to be here at all, I assure you. Indeed you make me afraid." [32] This loving behavior doubtless amused Henry Fielding. Nothing like it occurs in the other two novels.

A gesture prized by Richardson, and evidently by him visualized, is the contemptuous *twirl* of a hand. Arabella grandly says to Clarissa, "'Ask them; ask them, child,' with a twirl of her finger." [33] Later Clarissa in disparagement of Lovelace's rakish friends is reported as saying, "'If ever again'—And there she stopt, with a twirl of her hand." [34] That the gesture is regarded as expressive is seen in Lovelace's added comment, "When we meet, I will, in her presence, tipping thee a wink, shew thee the motion; for it was a very pretty one." [35]

What has already been called the pregnant knee may also convey a considerable variety of emotion. Knees are possibly more active in Italian episodes (thanks to the emotional state of the Lady Clementina?) than in England; but even in England the twentieth-century reader is likely to think knees excessively flexible. Worship or entreaty is the common objective in kneeling, but within these limits there is much variation. Knees may give way as part of a total collapse, as in the case of Clarissa, where the fall adds a gruesome detail of a bleeding nose.[36] Kneeling may become a matter of policy. Mrs. Giffard, the exposed mistress of Lord W, kneels, as Sir Charles Grandison tells us, "Not from motives of contrition, as I apprehend; but from those of policy." [37] In such circumstance, the normally punctilious Sir Charles, far from helping the lady to rise, steps coldly back and lets her get up by herself. Lovelace, as Clarissa reports, "threw himself in the way at my feet," but the move purposed as much to keep Clarissa from leaving him as it did to express unselfish entreaty.[38]

Naturally there are examples of kneeling that are felt to be improper. A gentleman of Sir Rowland Meredith's age and status should not, Miss Byron felt, kneel to her in entreaty for his nephew.[39] Clarissa at St. Albans ironically reproves Lovelace for hypocritically kneeling:

[32] *Pamela*, I, 285.
[33] *Clarissa*, I, 50.
[34] *Clarissa*, III, 360.
[35] The projected imitation is typical: Lovelace is practically always, with varying degrees of insincerity, acting a part. He is hardly ever and never for long truly sincere: his frequent outcries that he suffers more than Clarissa cannot, of course, be believed.
[36] *Clarissa*, V, 378.
[37] *Grandison*, II, 357.
[38] *Clarissa*, I, 258.
[39] *Grandison*, I, 132–33.

"That you are *your own mistress*, thro' *my* means [Lovelace says], is, I repeat, my boast. *As such,* I humbly implore your favour . . . *thus humbly* [the proud wretch falling on one knee] your forgiveness. . . . O Sir, pray rise!—Let the obliged kneel . . . ! " [40]

Clementina, curiously, is on one occasion ashamed of kneeling to Sir Charles, for on many other occasions she feels no such qualm. Still imperfectly recovered from her madness, she is conscious of having caused much trouble. At first she begs forgiveness of her mother (kneeling): she then, Sir Charles tells us:

> came to me; and to my great surprize, dropt down on one knee. . . . I raised her; and taking her hand, pressed it with my lips! . . . She hesitated a little; then turned round to Camilla, . . . and running to her, cast herself into her arms, hiding her face in her bosom—Hide me, hide me, Camilla!—What have I done!—I have kneeled to a man! [41]

Later Clementina is involved in another tableau, one that is hard for the present-day reader to visualize, but evidently not too hard for Richardson: "Dropping down on one knee, God preserve and convert thee, best of Protestants. . . . I would have raised her; but she would not be raised. . . . I kneeled to her, clasping my arms about her: . . . I raised her, and arose; and kissing first one hand, then the other. . . ." [42] Here we have a theatrical picture of two eminently decorous but overwrought lovers both kneeling and both (one trusts Clementina co-operated!) clasping their arms about each other. It must be pure emotional drive or imagined Italian manners.

One may note that kneeling is almost sure to involve added gesture, or added detail, that may enrich the picture. When Emily Jervois is induced to ask her mother's blessing, she reports: "Down on my knees dropt I. . . . (And she kissed my hand, and bowed her face upon it). . . . And she kissed me *too,* and wept on my neck." [43] Complexity of mood as well as of detail is usual in Clarissa's private kneelings, witnessed perhaps through keyholes or by an onlooker in the sponging house, or often seen in filial-parent poses.[44] A final, most conventional kneeling is seen at the end of Harriet Byron's wedding ceremony: "Sir Charles . . . did credit to our Sex before the applauding multitude, by bending his knee to his sweet Bride, on taking her Hand, and saluting her." [45] "Applauding multitude" suggests a theater rather than a church, but the kneeling and the nuptial kiss were apparently

---

[40] *Clarissa,* III, 13.
[41] *Grandison,* IV, 164–65.
[42] *Ibid.,* IV, 407; cf. *Clarissa,* I, 342.
[43] *Ibid.,* III, 310.
[44] *Clarissa,* I, 53, 104; II, 221; V, 4; VI, 298.
[45] *Grandison,* V, 379.

the usual final touch for a "right" wedding before the couple left the altar. In this case, the applause was due: it recognized a suspense that had run through almost six volumes. It is fluently concluded: one feels that not even Sir Willoughby Patterne could have surpassed Sir Charles in grace when "making a leg."

Most readers will agree that Richardson is effective in the small detail, emotionally fused. Certainly it is the small bit that normally clinches the effect. When Betty rushes up to summon Clarissa to a meeting with Solmes: "Miss! Miss! Miss! cried she, as fast as she could speak, with her arms spread abroad, and all her fingers distended, and held up, will you be pleased to walk down into your own parlour?" [46] When asked who is there, Betty replies: "Why, Miss, holding out her left palm opened, and with a flourish, and a saucy leer, patting it with the forefinger of the other, at every mentioned person, There is your Papa!—There is your Mama!" [47] And she proceeds to pat off seven persons—including Solmes. The "arms spread abroad and fingers distended" may seem awkward and superfluous, but the details (assuming the language to be competent) are very precisely what Richardson saw.

In the big scenes, it must be confessed that there is rather less physical detail expressed. In the famous penknife scene,[48] there are few vivid expressions of posture: it is all done in conversation. Yet one feels himself present. Actually more in accord with the technique here being emphasized is the scene between Lovelace and Clarissa after the terrifying cry of *Fire!* [49] Present-day readers sometimes feel that Clarissa was excessively outraged emotionally by the conduct of Lovelace here. They are wrong. Nowadays the language in novels may be more "realistic": four-letter words are in vogue, and we wish far less expostulation and argument. It remains true, however, that if one has merely a small part of the visual imagination that Richardson had, this scene is as lurid as anything in modern fiction.[50] The two persons are almost naked: Lovelace repeatedly clasps his arms about Clarissa, and he trusts that he has not "hurt the tenderest and loveliest of all her beauties." More than once she slides away through his encircling arms, and there is no reason to be surprised that she felt something like complete dishonor; the surprise is that (through romantic worship of innocence?) Lovelace allowed her to escape. He somewhat resembles Pamela's admirer in his frustrations. With the techniques at

[46] *Clarissa*, II, 200.
[47] *Clarissa*, II, 201.
[48] *Ibid.*, VI, 65–71.
[49] *Ibid.*, IV, 388.
[50] *Ibid.*, IV, 393.

his disposal, Richardson made the scene impressive, but there are obviously too many words, too much emotional as well as physical and argumentative wrestling.

There is no end to the examples of vividly seen posture that might be cited. Most "uses" of arms and hands are conventional of necessity, but in these novels most uses are appropriately discriminated and varied in particular detail. Arms, for example, may be clasped by one female about another—and less often by a male; arms may be folded to show restraint or desperation; they may be akimbo to show arrogance; and they may be locked, as in Lovelace's dragging Clarissa from Harlowe Place[51] and again as in the chamber scene where Mrs. Jewkes (preparing to aid Mr. B) says to Pamela: "Here, . . . put your Arm under mine, and you shall find the [keys] about my wrist. . . . So I did, and the Abominable Designer held my Hand with her Right-hand, as my Right-arm was under her Left." [52] Here Richardson shows himself astonishingly knowledgeable.

There can be no doubt that even when Richardson's language is not quite clear, he saw with precision what he expressed with restraint or awkwardness. There were many other aids in his "writing to the moment." Perhaps the best as an aid to suspense is the one that he makes Belford specify in a letter of 4 August, which was adapted as part of the Preface of 1759. A mere memoir, Richardson thought, that shows a personage safe in port after various desperate experiences has less appeal than a story told in letters, where each letter is tentative, suspenseful, and inconclusive.

> *Much more* lively and affecting . . . must be the Style of those who write in the height of a *present* distress; the mind tortured by the pangs of uncertainty (the Events then hidden in the womb of Fate); *than* the dry, narrative, unanimated Style of a person relating difficulties and dangers surmounted, can be; the relater perfectly at ease; and if himself unmoved by his own Story, not likely greatly to affect the Reader.[53]

In his central aim (if we discount that of moral instruction)—to be "lively and affecting"—Richardson was always trying to write to the moment. It is not difficult to see, though it is easy to overlook, the fact that he was much helped by a keen visual gift, commonly evident in the physical contacts and gestures of his persons.

[51] *Clarissa,* II, 359.
[52] *Pamela,* I, 276.
[53] Preface to *Clarissa* (1759), I, xiv.

# Richardson and the Bold Young Men

## by Morris Golden

Even more than most novelists, Richardson is limited in his characters to a few staple types, which are stretched and chopped to fit various molds in his three novels. Unlike such writers as Fielding or Jane Austen in whose books character types recur, it is not Richardson's achievement, whatever his ostensible aim, to show certain intellectual or moral conceptions of human character working themselves out under differing circumstances. Rather, like Lawrence or Dostoevski or Faulkner, he seems to conceive of character as essentially passional; whatever moral arguments he claims to be making are purely superimposed, as witness the great discrepancies between his editorial comments on the first two novels and the effect and nature of the novels themselves. For two hundred years critics have doubted Pamela's "signal veracity" and have questioned whether it was really her virtue that was rewarded; we suspect that *Clarissa* is not primarily a treatise on the enlightened governance of daughters or a homily against running off with rakes. We know that there is something else in these books, particularly the latter, that perennially fascinates us. As a number of critics have been arguing lately, it is the conflict of wills, even more of psyches, that gives these novels their power; and it seems to me, as it has seemed to others, that this direct perception of psychological reality derives from Richardson's own nature, which affected his view of the constitution of the society around him and impelled him to create his lurid emotional effects and his occasionally more lurid characters.

It was long believed, largely on the basis of Richardson's own claims, that he was unparalleled in drawing the hearts and minds of women, perhaps because, in Dobson's phrase, he was a "feminine man."[1] Latterly, much more emphasis has been placed on his self-

"Richardson and the Bold Young Men." From *Richardson's Characters* by Morris Golden (Ann Arbor: The University of Michigan Press, 1963), pp. 1–28. Copyright © 1963 by the University of Michigan. Reprinted by permission of the publisher. The pages reprinted here are the first chapter of the book.

[1] Austin Dobson, *Samuel Richardson*. English Men of Letters (London: Macmillan, 1902), p. 36.

identification with the rakish mental make-up (an emphasis which goes back with a minority of critics, like the Fielding of *Shamela,* to Richardson's earliest notices). David Daiches, perhaps too simply, says that Lovelace "is a mild and timid man's picture of the ideal rake, of Satan as gentleman, witty, boisterous, adventurous, courageous, ruthless";[2] Ian Watt, whose insight into Richardson's mind in this instance seems to me the most perceptive, believes that the treatment of the fallen women in the first two novels (to which may be added that of Lord W.'s mistress in *Sir Charles Grandison*), "the fact that both these novels require the tacit assumption that the passions of his heroines are aroused by rakes, together with his own interest in fallen women and in the 'Magdalen Charity'—all these suggest an obsessional interest in criminal sexuality, an incompletely mastered striving for the kind of experience that 'Mr. B.' and Lovelace represent. It is likely that Richardson had a deep unconscious investment in his hero's sadistic attempts to violate Clarissa. . . ."[3] Richardson does have this "deep unconscious investment," and it manifests itself in his most interesting young men characters—not only the bad ones, like Lovelace, his pale shadows in *Sir Charles Grandison* (Sir Hargrave Pollexfen, Greville, and Fenwick), and the earlier Mr. B., but also in the model of philanthropic gentility, Sir Charles Grandison himself.

By extension, the same preoccupation pervades Richardson's whole view of character, of whatever sex, position, or age. In a letter to his Dutch admirer and translator Stinstra Richardson wrote: "Men and women are brothers and sisters; they are not of different species; and what need be obtained to know both, but to allow for different modes of education, for situation and constitution, or perhaps I should rather say, for habits, whether good or bad."[4] Though no law requires novelists to phrase exactly the theories of character which they have used, or even to have such theories, this is an extremely important passage. It suggests that for Richardson, preeminent at least in his time for

[2] *Literary Essays* (New York: Philosophical Library, 1957), p. 48.
[3] "The Naming of Characters in Defoe, Richardson, and Fielding," *RES,* XXV (1949), 333.
[4] Samuel Richardson, *Correspondence,* ed. Anna Laetitia Barbauld (London: Richard Phillips, 1804), V, 263. This collection will hereafter be referred to as *Correspondence. Cf.* also a comment on Shakespeare in a letter to Lady Bradshaigh of February 14, 1754, a comment which the feminist Mrs. Barbauld seems to have crossed out when she prepared the letters for publication: "He knew them [women] better than they knew themselves; for, pardon me for saying, that we must not always go to women for a *general* knowledge of the Sex. Asks me now with disdain, my dear Lady B., if *I* pretend to know them? No, I say—I only guess at them: And yet I think them not such mysteries as some suppose. A tolerable knowledge of men will lead us to a tolerable knowledge of women." Forster Collection, Vol. XI.

the delineation of the distinction between the sexes, this distinction was essentially made by society and upbringing; that the constituents of character that Richardson saw when he looked within himself are the constituent elements in all human beings; that life, if this is so, is at the bottom of the psyche a wild conflict for dominance; and that moral differences among people will depend on the degrees to which they can restrain the violence of their urges in the interest of social living. But, as I hope to show, for Richardson the merit of a character is not directly and only proportional to the degree of restraint; complete lack of restraint, as in Lovelace, is close to complete evil, but on the other hand even Lovelace is immensely attractive, and the ideally genteel Grandison achieves, with his author's complete approval, total dominance over the society around him. It is true that Grandison is much praised for repressing what he insists is a highly passionate nature, but it is important that Richardson does give him this nature and does make a point of letting him show it at times.

Of the variety of rakish traits which Richardson shared with his major male characters, the least objectionable socially was an aggravated tendency to study young women—a trait leading to his purported "mastery in the delineation of the female heart." When he was thirteen, as he wrote to Stinstra, he had been let into the secrets of the girls for whom he wrote love letters (*Correspondence*, V, 263–64). When he became famous and surrounded himself with a platonic harem of honorary daughters, he not only constituted himself a chief dispenser of advice on all problems of the heart but also very consciously observed the girls in relation to himself (*Correspondence*, III, 222–25). He admitted, in a perceptive self-analysis, that "it is inconceivable how much advantage, in my proud heart, is given me, of peeping into the hearts of my readers, and sometimes into their heads, by their approbation, and disapprobation, of the conduct of the different persons in my Drama. . . ."[5] His attitude toward the young women who were his preferred friends, as revealed both in his letters and in his novels, resembles that of a psychologist toward a particularly endearing lot of guinea pigs. The basic situations of the bold young men in the novels are very similar: Lovelace, the boldest and most powerful of them, keeps Clarissa under constant and predatory surveillance. Mr. B., who is not so persistent a watcher (he has a surrogate in Mrs. Jewkes), nonetheless admits that for months before his mother's death he had been steadily observing Pamela and waiting for her physical and emotional ripeness for seduction. Sir Charles Grandison, the good man, is again and again rapturously praised by

---

[5] Letter to Lady Bradshaigh, February 14, 1754, in Forster Collection of MSS at the Victoria and Albert Museum, Vol. XI (Vol. I of the Richardson MSS).

both his biological and adoptive sisters for his keen observation of women: in a few of the most important scenes of his lax book he is shown with his eyes fixed on Harriet Byron (e.g., just before their conference in his library), who herself is hypersensitive to the responsiveness of her blushes.

Lovelace, Richardson's best-realized character, makes the clearest connection between the timid personality that Richardson believed himself to have and the rake's professional knowledge of the natures of women:

> But I was *originally* a bashful mortal. Indeed I am bashful still with regard to this Lady—Bashful, yet know the Sex so well!—But that indeed is the *reason* that I know it so well:—For, Jack, I have had abundant cause, when I have looked into *myself,* by way of comparison with the *other* Sex, to conclude, that a bashful man has a good deal of the soul of a woman; and so, like Tiresias, can tell what they think, and what they drive at, as well as themselves.
>
> The modest ones and I, particularly, are pretty much upon a par. The difference between us is only, What They *think,* I *act.* But the immodest ones out-do the worst of us by a bar's length, both in thinking and acting.[6]

Of Richardson's own diffidence one need not write—he recurs to it incessantly in his correspondence, perhaps most amusingly in his letter to Lady Bradshaigh, then incognita, on his arrangements for the rendezvous that she never kept. In accordance with the general canon of neoclassicism which Professor Lovejoy has called uniformitarianism,[7] Richardson looked into himself for truth about mankind; unlike most of his contemporaries but Rousseau, he extended the technique to include the universal aspects of sexual fantasy.

Many writers have commented on Richardson's sadistic treatment of his female characters. It is easy enough to document, in the big scenes which would now appear on the dust jackets of his books: Pamela howling as Mr. B. attempts rape, throwing herself at his knees at other times, fainting to the floor at his threats; Clarissa thrashing about the floor half naked begging Lovelace not to violate her, and later undergoing violation before a noisy audience of prostitutes; Harriet Byron gagged and struggling in Sir Hargrave's coach while her kidnapper leers, and afterwards, from the floor of Grandison's

---

[6] Samuel Richardson, *Clarissa, or, The History of a Young Lady,* Shakespeare Head Ed. (Oxford: Blackwell, 1930), III, 115. Subsequent references to *Clarissa* are to this edition.

[7] Arthur O. Lovejoy, "The Parallel of Deism and Classicism," in his *Essays in the History of Ideas* (New York: George Braziller, 1948), pp. 79-82.

chariot, piteously crying for help. All four heroines (allowing for two in the last novel) are threatened with beatings and at times suffer them, sometimes gratuitously—Clarissa, for example, falls on her nose when a door that she is storming in her home is suddenly opened. The similarity to Richardson's own temperament in this respect is everywhere evident; moreover, he was himself aware of the connections between his sadistic fantasies and his sort of art: on March 25, 1751, he wrote to Mrs. Sarah Chapone, "What a deal of Wickedness may it be infer'd was in my Mind to draw from *thence* such a Man as Lovelace:—Indeed I put the Iniquity of two or three bad Characters together in my Mind in order to draw his. . . ."[8]

Richardson's correspondence yields frequent indications of his mildly sadistic delight in teasing the women whose admiration he sought. In a letter of August 21, 1752, he told his friend Thomas Edwards that "I have frighted Miss Mulso, Miss Highmore, Miss Prescott, &c., with allowing them to think I intended a tragical Ending to Sir Charles." To Sophia Westcomb, Richardson wrote on February 1, 1751, "I hope, on receiving my last Letters, you will find me affect only a pretendedly serious Humour, in order to startle you and alarm." In response to Miss Mulso's question whether Sir Charles Grandison did not love teasing, he wrote on July 11, 1751, "No, he does not. Another person, perhaps, may. But it is a fault too ungenerous for Sir Charles Grandison to be guilty of. But here is the thing: you ladies, some of you, scruple not to deserve blame; and then, truly, it is teasing to tell you of your faults in a pleasant way" (*Correspondence*, III, 167). On July 27, 1751, he again told this favorite (the model for Harriet Byron and, in later life, the pious blue-stocking Mrs. Chapone) that

> "Your pride feels for Harriet." Prettily said! But your pride, my dear, must feel, I doubt, a little more than it has felt. A serene man has great advantages over a girl who finds herself, after roving about in the field of liberty, and defying twenty fowlers, just caught. She must part with a few feathers, I doubt. For she will not perch in quiet in her golden-wired cage (*Correspondence*, III, 174).

A whole series of letters to Miss Westcomb is almost amorously tender, though the manner is paternal; but to judge by his letter of November 1, 1750, the purpose of this early delicacy seems to have been to get this young lady into the same position as Miss Highmore and Miss Mulso, in which she could be archly teased. There is practically a lover's quarrel in the next few letters: when the girl is annoyed

[8] Forster Collection, Vol. XII.

because he is so captious, he justifies himself, and then she apologizes and begs forgiveness. All this is exactly Lovelace's technique, though its external aim here is unexceptionable.

With Lady Bradshaigh, Richardson's epistolary wooing is at its most pronounced, as is his similarity to Lovelace:

> "Do not provoke me," say you. Will you forgive me, Madam, if I own that I really have so much cruelty in my nature, that I should wish to provoke you now and then, if I knew what would do it, consistent with respect and decency? For, as I have often said, I admire you even in the height of that charming spirit which you exert with so much agreeable warmth, in a cause in which you think it becomes a tender and humane nature to exert itself (*Correspondence*, IV, 232–33);

further to the same lady,

> I affect to be thought a plain speaker and a plain dealer; but yet I think myself ever under obligation to those who bear with my bluntness; while to those who do not, I owe the less; and contenting myself with my consciousness of meaning well, and not to offend, I take down the dear friend a peg lower than I had raised her, and yet hold myself ready, with joy to lift her up again, as she gives me the wisest reasons for it (*Correspondence*, IV, 339).

Richardson relished Lady Bradshaigh's emotional involvement in the plot and characters of *Sir Charles Grandison* and his consequent power over her. In a letter of December 8, 1753, he exulted over her suspense about the fate of Harriet and Sir Charles. On February 8, 1754, he gleefully wrote her that he could easily get all his readers to pity Harriet at the end by killing her off: "I can draw, I fancy, a charming Child-Bed Death," he says, striking an attitude inconceivable for that more famous literary slaughterer Dickens. Lady Bradshaigh having apparently become ill with fear that he was in earnest, he sent her the last volume of the novel, apologizing much for the joke in a note of February 25, 1754; in the same note, he says that his intention in *Grandison* is to present a wide variety of debatable issues and enjoy the perplexed arguments of his readers. On August 30, 1756, he admitted to her that his occasional needling of correspondents was deliberate: "God forgive me! I love to be a little spiteful, now-and-then."

Quite evidently Richardson, like his chief villain, prided himself on his manipulatory skills, particularly with women. An early biographer in the *Universal Magazine* writes that Richardson's women friends

> would often attack some part or other of his writings, which he always defended so well, as to convince his fair opponents that they were wrong.

If the ladies did not begin with him, he would artfully lead them to the subject himself; for female opposition animated him most, and seemed a greater cordial to his spirits than any flattery which they could bestow upon him and his works.[9]

There is no need to document the sadistic delight in torturing women, and in lighter moments in teasing them, that the bold young men like B., Lovelace, Greville, and Sir Hargrave exhibit; but it is perhaps not so readily apparent that Sir Charles Grandison, like Richardson,[10] steadily harasses the women surrounding him. Whenever his irreverent sister Charlotte begins with him, he pays her double; to Lady Beauchamp he seems one of the most impertinent young men in England; he tricks and lures Lord W.'s mistress into moderating her demands; and, in conformity with Richardson's view of male sexual impetuosity, he pesters Harriet, with the indulgence of her elders and indeed herself, into naming an early wedding day. Unintentionally (but consonant with the same drive on Richardson's part), Sir Charles is responsible for a good deal of Harriet's mental torture. She must await his decision on Clementina before her own love can be returned—she is, as she painfully knows, in intolerable suspense, and she is quite aware that his expressions of fear that she will not have him are due only to his incomparable courtesy. In lesser situations, he also leaves her to wait apprehensively, as when he does not appear when she believes him to be dueling, first with Sir Hargrave and later with Greville; in all cases, the focus is upon Harriet's fears far more than on Sir Charles's dangers.

If the bold young men are expressions of Richardson's fantasies, it is not surprising that the conspicuous ones among them have in common a manner which makes women come to them despite their lordliness—the full desire of the sadist is not satisfied until the girl both loves and fears, until she is hurt but continues loving nonetheless, or perhaps even as a consequence. Pamela, after Mr. B. has attempted her bosom, wants to leave partly because she is not sure that she can withstand his temptations;[11] after he has tried to rape her, had her kidnapped, and placed the odious Mrs. Jewkes over her,

---

[9] "Memoirs of the Life and Writings of Mr. Samuel Richardson," *Universal Magazine*, LXXVIII (1786), 21. According to Alan Dugald McKillop, *Samuel Richardson, Printer and Novelist* (Shoe String Press, 1960; a reprint of 1936 ed., University of North Carolina Press), p. 285, the writer of this memoir was probably Richardson's son-in-law Edward Bridgen.

[10] The equivalence of the names Richardson and Grandison suggests an almost conscious identification of author and hero, despite Dottin's assurance that the character's name derives from that of a pious friend of Lady Bradshaigh.

[11] Samuel Richardson, *Pamela, or, Virtue Rewarded*, Shakespeare Head Ed. (Oxford: Blackwell, 1929), I, 46. Subsequent references to *Pamela* are to this edition.

she hears that he has nearly drowned while hunting and thinks, "O what an Angel would he be in my Eyes yet, if he would cease his attempts, and reform" (I, 243). Adding intolerable insult, he sends up to her prison room proposals for making her his mistress, to which she answers, "I know not the Man breathing I would wish to marry; and . . . the only one I could honour more than another, is the Gentleman, who, of all others, seeks my ever-lasting Dishonour" (I, 257); after the next rape attempt, "now I begin to be afraid, I know too well the Reason why all his hard Trials of me, and my black Apprehensions, would not let me hate him" (I, 294). As much as Pamela, B. has his cake and eats it—not only the pleasure of torturing her, but also the satisfaction of gaining her love.

Lovelace is so well received among women that he can indulge his ego to the extent of singling out one from a crowd of them, to make the others jealous (*Clarissa,* I, 213). Anna Howe writes that

> his *Pride,* and the credit which a few *plausible qualities,* sprinkled among his *odious ones,* have given him, have secured him too good a reception from our eye-judging, our undistinguishing, our self-flattering, our too-confiding Sex, to make assiduity and obsequiousness, and a conquest of his unruly passions, any part of his study (V, 39).

His great aim in *Clarissa* is to get the girl to admit love for him despite his ill-usage of her. It is her triumph that she does not do so, but there are a good many places where Richardson, digging to the equivocal sources of her emotions, leads us to believe that she does love him.[12] And though Grandison does not delight overtly in his mastery, he nevertheless is loved by a huge number of women (all the unmarried ones that have met or even heard of him); and, as his sister points out, twenty hearts will break when he marries. Though hurting Clementina is the farthest thing from his wishes as Richardson has consciously developed him, it is for love of him that she goes mad; for love of him, Harriet Byron languishes in ill health, with her unhappiness exacerbated by a correspondence almost exclusively devoted to his virtues. While I do not argue that Grandison seeks the same response from women that Mr. B. and Lovelace do, Richardson as his creator nevertheless provides it as the only completely satisfying one. Richardson himself, as his letters frequently show, not only wanted those women with whom he established familial contact to suffer his teasing, but he was genuinely hurt and genuinely apolo-

---

[12] *Cf.* Diderot's comment on the hidden, dark motives that Richardson uncovers beneath the ostensible and meritorious ones, in his "Eloge de Richardson," *Journal Etranger,* Jan. 1762, p. 11; *cf.* also Ian Watt's perceptive analysis of her feelings in *The Rise of the Novel* (Berkeley: University of California Press, 1957), pp. 229–30. [See p. 71 in this volume.]

getic if they did not continue to love him or respond to his desire for love.

In view of this sadistic element in their constitutions, it is not surprising that all of the bold young men characters (echoing Richardson's own domestic arrangements, though in an exaggerated way) wish to maintain dominance over their women, wish to be their sole supports, wish to have the women's exclusive regard, both in the future and retroactively. Here, despite the complex analyses of Richardson's social thought which have recently been made by Daiches, Watt, McKillop, and Fiedler, is the prime reason for the uniformly superior social positions of the male lovers in the novels over the female ones: the make-up of Richardson's mind is far more important in determining these positions on the basis of a fantasy of dominance than is some scheme of symbolism involving the relations between the aristocracy and the bourgeoisie. Though an endearing quality of *Pamela* is the heroine's triumph over her lover, Mr. B. is frequently seen in positions of physical mastery over Pamela. He stands over her while she cries on the floor (I, 248); he orders her to wait on him at table, attending behind him "out of my sight": "Sir, said I, and clasp'd his Knees with my Arms, not knowing what I did, and falling on my Knees, Have Mercy on me, and hear me, concerning that Wicked Woman's usage of me—" (I, 251). When he finally proposes marriage he is accepted in language which is most soothing to his ego and to that of his creator:

> . . . I hope it will be always my Pride to glory most in your Goodness; and it will be a Pleasure to me to shew every one, that, with respect to my Happiness in this Life, I am intirely the work of your Bounty; and to let the World see from what a lowly Original you have raised me to Honours that the greatest Ladies would rejoice in (II, 42).

The wedding ceremony pays due regard to the fantasies of dominance: B. said afterwards "That when he had done saying, *With this Ring I thee wed,* &c. I made a Court'sy, and said, Thank you, Sir" (II, 144). The next day she is grateful first to B. and then to God, and hopes "that I may preserve an humble and upright Mind to my gracious God, a dutiful Gratitude to my dear Master and Husband. . . ." (II, 165–66); and though Pamela is amused by the forty-eight rules for her behavior as a wife that Mr. B. lays down, she nonetheless accepts them. The refractory attitude of Lady Davers further enables B. to show his dominance; and although his actions are childish, Pamela is forced to consider them seriously, the point being that even an irrational husband is to rule:

Presuming *Pamela*! replied he, and made me start, Art thou then so hardy, so well able to sustain a Displeasure, which, of all things, I expected, from thy Affection, and thy Tenderness, thou wouldst have wished to avoid? . . . And, *Pamela*, I'll forgive you too, if you do not again make my Displeasure so light a thing to you, as you did just now (II, 271–73).

B. was himself aware of his need to be unquestioned ruler, and had once said to Sir Simon Darnford that "he thought he should hardly have made a tolerable Husband to any body but *Pamela*" (III, 73), since he must have his way and be the superior. Reporting on his having frightened Pamela when she attempted to manipulate his attitude toward his bastard daughter, B. takes a typical dominance-fantasy view of her: "What have I done? Let me know, dear good Sir! looking round, with her half-affrighted Eyes, this way and that, on the Books, and Pictures, and on me, by Turns. . . . I still held one Hand, and she stood before me, as Criminals ought to do before their Judge. . . ." (III, 132); the attitude is much like Lovelace's, though the situation is even more repellently sadistic, since it is arranged purely for fun. In the only continuous argument between the couple, over whether Pamela should suckle her young, B. has his own dominance in the family in mind in his objections: he admits that he would be jealous of Pamela's being distracted by his own child and does not want to be awakened at night when she feeds it. Miss Darnford, observing the B.'s at the time of the first childbirth, writes that B. "is lofty, and will not be disputed with; but I never saw a more polite and tender Husband, for all that" (IV, 127).

*Clarissa,* which emphasizes situations involving the expression of urges toward dominance much more than do the other two novels is built on the contentions of aggressive spirits, several of them young and male. James Harlowe is immediately characterized by his arrogance toward all around him, and a good part of the first movement of the work involves his struggle for mastery with Lovelace, Clarissa serving as the battleground. At least part of Lovelace's success, we are early to infer by contrast with James, lies in his courtly though superficial repression of his ego when he deals with women: the cruder James, according to Anna Howe, will not marry easily because of his naked insistence on ruling (I, 60). But very close to Lovelace's surface are overwhelming urges toward dominance. When he has lured Clarissa away from her family, for example, he is so excited that he cannot sleep as fantasies race through his mind:

> How it swells my pride, to have been able to outwit such a vigilant Charmer! I am taller by half a yard in my imagination than I was. I look *down* upon everybody now. Last night I was still more extravagant.

I took off my hat, as I walked, to see if the Lace were not scorched, supposing it had brushed down a star; and, before I put it on again, in mere wantonness, and heart's-ease, I was for buffeting the moon (III, 33).

Unlike Mr. B., Lovelace sees the nobility and strength of the object of his aggression as added stimulants, since to defend his image of his own greatness he must despise easy game. However, his intention is to bring her down to his level—his dominance, as he comes to realize, is based purely on power and experience, not on innate greatness of character. He is merely blinder, and not braver than B., and his real need, as Richardson has Clarissa point out, is for lording it over his inferiors, the members of his gang.

In a passage that again betrays his creator's identification with him, Lovelace boasts of his love of dominance: "I am half-sorry to say, *that I find a pleasure in playing the Tyrant over what I love*," as women do, "And why should it be thought strange, that I, who love them so dearly, and study them so much, should catch the infection of them?" (V, 123). In the scenes preceding the rape, Richardson is at pains to emphasize the weakness and pathetic lowness of Clarissa: she complains about her head all evening, and then, to give a good sadistic preliminary, sinks at Lovelace's feet, begging mercy. He lifts her to a chair, she says she is ruined, "And down on her bosom, like a half-broken-stalked Lily, top-heavy with the over-charging dews of the morning, sunk her head, with a sigh that went to my heart" (V, 309-10).

In the last novel, the outward arrogance and impetuousness are qualities of the villainous bold young men Sir Hargrave and Greville; but even Sir Charles shows a good many traits of dominance, while the action of the story depends exclusively upon his imposing his virtuous will on everyone with whom he comes into contact. He is the universal settler of domestic problems (a role in which, to judge by Richardson's correspondence, the author saw himself), and his decisions determine the fates of the two heroines. Sir Hargrave, on the night in which we meet him, says that he will kill any man competing for Harriet Byron, thereby initiating a subplot which had merely been hinted at in the other two novels; Greville, a somewhat more engaging ruffian, grabs one of Harriet's hands, after leaving tooth marks on the other with his kiss, and says, "You may be glad you have an hand left. By my soul, I could eat you."[13] In the bruising scene after Harriet's kidnapping, Sir Hargrave is shown with

---

[13] Samuel Richardson, *The History of Sir Charles Grandison*, Shakespeare Head Ed. (Oxford: Blackwell, 1931), I, 150. Subsequent references to *Grandison* are to this edition.

Harriet at his feet begging, praying, and generally subordinated, and he responds with "your very terror is beautiful! I can *enjoy* your terror, madam" (I, 230). But note that it is in Sir Charles's coach, after he has beaten Sir Hargrave and saved Harriet, that she lies moaning to be saved, and it is in his household, which is under his absolute rule, that she has her fainting spells and is restored to mental health.

Grandison's paternalism is not limited to subordinated young women: he has been "more than a father to his *uncle*" (II, 333); when he imposes reason upon the Beauchamps, Lady Beauchamp complains that "I thought a good man must of necessity be bashful, if not sheepish: And here your visiter is the boldest man in England" (III, 263). During negotiations for his marriage to Harriet, his sister Charlotte, who has been irritated by Harriet's female delicacy, warns her that he does not like to waste time and will soon have her on a reasonable schedule (V, 203); and in an echo most specifically of B., but also of Lovelace, Grandison will not take a seat in Parliament now because he might be indebted to a politician for help and wishes to be above all parties. In general, Grandison no less than Lovelace is a projection of Richardson's dominance fantasies; the fantasy here, however, takes the socially attractive form of imposing order on mankind, an imposition to be achieved through a variety of virtuous means (mostly through the dissemination of money, though also at times through a show of power), but almost as absolute as Lovelace's naked enforcing of his demonic urges. The motive of most artists may well be identical with this fantasy, but rarely has it been more explicitly affirmed than in a letter of Richardson's:

> The world is not enough used to this way of writing, to the moment. It knows not that in the minutiae lie often the unfoldings of the Story, as well as of the heart—; & judges of an action undecided, as if it were absolutely decided. Nor will it easily part with its first impressions. . . . But when this hasty-judging world will be convinced that they have seen the *last works* of this too-voluminous writer, they will give what he has done, more of their Attention—*perhaps* . . . Then, madam, will be discovered and approved, if I am not a false prophet, . . . those delicacies occasioned by the difficult Situations of my principal Characters, to which now they will not attend.[14]

Note, by the way, the fantasy here, powerfully objectified in *Pamela* and *Clarissa,* of the angered child that takes revenge on stern parents by imagining its death and their subsequent grief.

The pervasiveness of fantasy in the creation of character is, I be-

---

[14] To Lady Bradshaigh, February 14, 1754. Forster Collection, Vol. XI.

lieve, Richardson's preeminent contribution to the novel; and the fantasies are mainly of dominance and subordination, as seem to have been those of the author himself. Lovelace is the most conspicuous weaver of fantasies, but both the major men and women partake in them—sometimes through transparent dreams, sometimes in incoherent raving, sometimes in more or less rational elaborations of plans, and sometimes by virtue of their situations as actors of the fantasy in Richardson's mind. Mr. B. even has his fantasy detailed by his early female alter ego, Mrs. Jewkes, who tells Pamela that he

> has found out a way to satisfy my Scruples: It is, by marrying me to this dreadful *Colbrand,* and buying me of him on the Wedding-day, for a Sum of Money! . . . She says it will be my Duty to obey my Husband; and that Mr. *Williams* will be forced, as a Punishment, to marry us. . . . But this, to be sure, is horrid romancing! (I, 243-44).

In the garden scene which prefigures B.'s reform, he insists on having the remainder of Pamela's journal (her most secret thoughts must conform to his dream of himself as her master); at her refusal to tell where it is, he proposes to strip her in search of it, promising himself considerable amusement. Pamela, no martyr, provides the papers immediately.

In the generally sane world of *Pamela,* the naked adolescent sexual dream is recognized for what it is, "horrid romancing"; but in the lurid nightmare of *Clarissa* such dreams become Lovelace's overt motivations. He is so dominated by his fantasies of superiority that almost any incident or train of ideas in which he engages develops into one of them. When his creature Leman begs him to be more merciful to Clarissa than he had been to a Miss Betterton, Lovelace's justification is that "I went into mourning for her, tho' abroad at the time. A distinction I have ever paid to those worthy creatures who died in Childbed by me" (III, 250). Particularly annoyed by Anna Howe's interference in his attempts on Clarissa, he develops a complicated plan for obtaining a boat, attacking and kidnapping the entire Howe party on the high seas, and parceling out the women to himself and his gang (IV, 271). This dream leads on to another, in which he envisions himself in court on trial for raping the boatload of women; in a transparent recollection of passages and scenes in *Jonathan Wild,* he sees himself paraded to jail, and argues that in comparison to Caesar and other conquerors he is innocent of evil (IV, 276). His fantasies, dictated as they are by the current situation, often feed on pictures of himself and Clarissa in the future. At one point, he elaborates at length how, with Clarissa's will broken, she would live with him as his mistress and dote on him, fearing his anger (IV, 21); at another, he foresees Clarissa, suckling his twins, begging for marriage, which he can provide or not as he chooses (IV, 355); at yet another he describes what the story of himself and Clarissa might have been, after ten years of marriage, if no one like Belford knew the details of their courtship: a peaceful idyll, except that he would have tried a number of other women but always returned to Clarissa, "And what is there so very greatly amiss, AS THE WORLD GOES, in all this?" (IV, 383); contemplating marriage again, he sees a procession of his huge family trooping to church, as in the effigies of families on old monuments (VI, 108). Perhaps his most amusing fantasy is of a society in which people change marriage partners every year, an arrangement which, he argues, would end rape, adultery, fornication, and polygamy, and might destroy the reason for many duels and murders (V, 292–96). Again and again, Richardson invites Lovelace away from the world of here and now and into exactly that pit of fantasy that most frightened Swift and Johnson when they looked within themselves. Johnson feared to look on the bosoms of Garrick's actresses, lest his imagination be overly stirred; Richardson was proud of an imagination that unaided could furnish him with his brothel scenes. Here may be a central difference between the moralist whose restraints are so great that he does not even try to introduce people into his novel and the novelist who concocts a suitable morality to cover his imaginings.

Everything is grist for Lovelace's mill of sexual fantasy: having met the women at Hampstead with whom Clarissa has sought safety, he develops a plan for luring them to London and serving them to himself and his followers (V, 341). After the rape and Clarissa's heightened detestation of him, he spins a plan, half dream and half program, of letting her escape and win the help of an old woman who, in a bed they are to share, turns out to be himself (VI, 9 ff.). This particular episode is one of the most conspicuous keys to the kind of trickery that Richardson wishes to perpetrate on the reader through the character of Lovelace: we do not know, until several pages have passed, that Lovelace is more serious here than in, say, his plan for stealing the Howe party or for instituting yearly divorces. For Lovelace, in large portions of the book, reality is completely distorted by his urges toward domination; he is technically mad—but the world on the whole accedes to his mad plans, with Clarissa the only person in it who, after the madness culminates in rape, insists on seeing reality. As the reports of Clarissa's lingering illness and imminent death fall thickly upon him, he becomes aware that only in the world of fantasy can he completely have his own way: he yearns to be told what he knows is not true, that Belford and Clarissa are merely plotting to get him worked up to the utmost and then to arrange for the marriage (VII, 398). When reality is forced upon him through her death he becomes violently insane—a more perceptive psychological stroke than the routine madness of Clarissa immediately after the rape.[15]

In *Grandison,* the fantasies are more subdued, except for the one which dominates the novel and which coyly and interminably recurs in Richardson's private correspondence—polygamy. Besides forming the central situation in the novel—the contention in Grandison's mind between the "twin excellences," Harriet and Clementina—the issue is both implied in a number of symbolic situations and explicitly discussed. Lord W., for example, says to his nephew that "I was told, within this month past, that no fewer than Five Ladies, out of one circle, declared, that they would stand out by consent, and let you pick and choose a wife from among them" (II, 342). The fantasy, though not ramified and elaborated as it is with Lovelace, is a pure and ideally satisfying one, since for Grandison women languish unasked: aside from the two heroines, the women whom he has casually met in his travels, and the five ladies known to Lord W., there are also the developed characters of Lady Olivia and Emily Jervois, as well as such suitors as Lady Anne S. and Lady Frances, who yearn off stage. His sister Charlotte believes that a special law should be passed in Parliament to permit him to marry both Harriet and Clementina (V, 330); in the last volume, when Clementina has run to England after his marriage there with Harriet, we see the two girls interminably arm in arm, either engaged in praising him or standing in a tableau on either side of him, with the inescapable result that he is impressed on us as a sultan with his two preferred wives (e.g., VI, 153, 312). And Harriet's wise old grandmother jokes that his favorite scheme of Protestant nunneries would serve a useful purpose if they only held all the women who were made desolate by his marriage (VI, 220): a convenient arrangement which would concentrate the exclusive homage that the author's psyche demanded and would reject the polluting bodies so repugnant to the conscious moralist.

Richardson's own correspondence is full of references to polygamy, which, with ponderous jocularity, he defends as a rational and pious scheme. In a letter to Lady Bradshaigh of December 8, 1753, he says that it might be a good indication of Harriet's generosity if, after the ceremony, she offers Grandison the right to spend half of each year with his Italian wife. With this same lady he had engaged in a run-

---

[15] *Cf.* Goldsmith's comment in *Citizen of the World,* Letter XXI, that "fits are the true aposiopesis of modern tragedy."

ning argument over polygamy after the publication of *Clarissa*, in which he insisted, not completely in fun, that neither the Bible nor the "law of nature" prohibited the practice (however, wishing to live at peace with the laws of his country, he said he would neither advocate it in print nor engage in it).[16] His style of living, while technically chaste, involved surrounding himself with an intellectual harem, blue-stockings whose minds he continually attempted to dominate. In *Pamela* and *Clarissa*, it goes without saying, the male protagonists contribute their share toward the explicit advocacy of polygamy, B. in his affair with the countess, and Lovelace *passim*.

A burlesque of the socially acceptable version of this fantasy—the double standard in sexual behavior—appears in one of Lovelace's most amusing peculiarities, his aversion to sleeping with any woman who has ever slept with another man. Of his response to the offers of the doxy Sally, he says (a variation of what he often repeats): "This, thou knowest, was always my rule—*Once any other man's*, and *I* know it, and *never more mine*" (IV, 283). Repellent as Richardson intends this sort of nonsense to be, is it immensely different in author's motivation (or reader's susceptibility) from all the nonsense in *Grandison* about the "divided heart," all of the variations on the question of whether the girl who had once loved, albeit innocently, could be a satisfactory wife? All the major bold young men created by Richardson (who wrote all of his novels after his first wife had died and he had remarried) have loved before—B., not innocently but rarely; Lovelace, a host of deflowered virgins with whom he has stocked brothels in several countries; Grandison, Clementina Porretta —while his heroines have previously untouched hearts, whatever may be said of their heads. In general, Richardson and his heroes (and villains) are more than usually fascinated by a subject of reverie and speculation that was peculiarly characteristic of their century but is, of course, unlimited by time.[17]

As a concomitant to the sadism either exhibited by the bold young men in their thirst for dominance or implied in their actions, situ-

---

[16] For his defense of polygamy, see especially *Correspondence*, VI, 190–91, 218ff., 235 ff.

[17] As a few indications of contemporary interest in the subject, *cf.* Montesquieu's playing with the idea of the harem in the *Letteres persanes*, Goldsmith's occasional use of it in the *Citizen of the World*, Cowper's "Anti-Thelyphthora," and Johnson's speculation, recorded in Boswell's *Journal of a Tour to the Hebrides*: "'I have often thought, that, if I kept a seraglio, the ladies should all wear linen gowns'" (Collins Classics ed., 1955, p. 152). For discussion of this interest, see Alfred Owen Aldridge, "Polygamy and Deism," *JEGP*, XLVIII (1949), 343–60, and Ian Watt, *Rise of the Novel*, pp. 147–49.

ations, or dreams, these characters show also, like their creator, the complementary guilt feelings that at times are extreme enough to constitute masochism. Again Lovelace, Richardson's prime psychotic, most clearly manifests this symptom, but the others also have traces. Mr. B., for example, takes a curious pride in having Pamela tell his genteel circle about his mischievous and malicious actions (II, 104); he assures her, after their marriage, that she is his superior mentally (II, 152); he describes how, while planning her seduction, he had despised himself (III, 207); and several times he enjoys reading repentantly those passages in Pamela's diaries and letters in which she has described his viciousness (e.g., IV, 199).

Lovelace is most explicit in his masochism, which strikes a modern reader as amazingly authentic, though (or perhaps because) irrational: at one point he clasps Clarissa's knees and cries, "Darkness, light; light, darkness; by my soul!—Just as you please to have it"; he goes on to say that he is all crime, she all virtue; he wants her to give him laws, put a halter about his neck, and lead him where she will, and he is willing to beg forgiveness at her father's feet (III, 151). When he comes upon her in Hampstead, she is so pathetic that

> I forgot at the instant all my vows of Revenge. I threw myself at her feet as she sat; and, snatching her hand, pressed it with my lips. I besought Heaven to forgive my past offences, and prosper my future hopes, as I designed honourably and justly by the Charmer of my heart, if once more she would restore me to her favour (V, 234).

After the rape he says, kneeling and holding her dress, that she is his sovereign, and "My destiny is in your power!—It depends upon your breath!—Your Scorn but augments my Love!" (VI, 27). As he had triumphed, wallowing in dominance, in the fire-scare scene and the scene before the rape, so he wallows even more in inferiority in the dagger scene (VI, 69–70), which symbolically places the noble integrity of Clarissa and his own vicious smallness in their proper relationship. After her escape, Lovelace seems to alternate the extremes of these moods—at times arrogantly dominating his family or attempting to dominate society, Belford, or anyone whom he meets, at others overcome by his inferiority to Clarissa. To Anna Howe, for example, he writes that if he is permitted to see Clarissa again, "I will be content to do it with a Halter about my neck; and, attended by a Parson on my right-hand, and the hangman on my left, be doomed, at her will, either to the Church or the Gallows" (VI, 269). Though Lovelace has a deplorable tendency to put his reveries into practice, he nonetheless exhibits the androgynous male-female urges in everyman more clearly and honestly than any fictional character before the time of Freud, more effectively, I think, than any major character in English literature but Bloom.[18]

In *Grandison* it is the bad bold young men who explicitly show the masochistic traits, as might be expected. Greville, for example, wants Harriet to say that she hates him (I, 155), and he grovels in theatrical self-torture when he hears of Grandison's conquest of her heart, just as he makes a special point of abasing himself to the happy couple before the wedding (V, 162). Sir Hargrave, when Harriet fights off his efforts to marry her in the house to which he has brought her, falls like Lovelace, throws his arms around her knees, and adores her greatness (I, 231). The hero himself, though he is too pure for such abandon, takes exquisite delight in his mental sufferings, which arise from his difficulties with Clementina; he voluntarily enslaves his happiness, and presumably the happiness of Harriet, to Clementina's crazed will and enjoys the refinements of delay to which he is thereby subjected. But with this particular aberration it must be granted that Grandison is least affected.

Richardson himself seems to have enjoyed the wilfulness of the girls with whom he surrounded himself; though his reactions to his wife's demands were likely to be pure peevishness, he courted pertness from his adopted daughters and delighted in being attacked by them. In the letter to Edwards in which he describes having frightened three of the girls with an intention of ending the last novel sadly, he adds: "The Supposition has brought me some charming Expostulations from them." [19] In a dispute with Miss Mulso at about the same time, he admits that he has deliberately quibbled "to make you rise upon me, and say right things in your usual beautiful manner. And my end is answered. I suffer.—You shine" (*Correspondence,* III, 190). In his description of a day in the life of one of his young female visitors he self-pityingly refers to himself as "the passive," who is at their call, and mostly disregarded (*Correspondence,* III, 222–25). In general, it seems to me that where he could indulge a socially acceptable version of his masochistic urges he did so—with visitors or correspondents, with whom he had to observe decorum and could therefore allow himself some limited freedom, as against the family, where such freedom might entail deep and dreadful emotional involvement. In his novels, as his alter egos were more or less

---

[18] Though in another connection, Mr. Watt, with his usual perceptiveness, sees Bloom as the culmination of tendencies initiated by Richardson: *Rise of the Novel,* pp. 206–7.

[19] Letter of August 21, 1752. Forster Collection, Vol. XII.

virtuous, they showed less or more of the uncontrolled indulgence of sexual fantasies.

With his bold young men characters, then, particularly with Lovelace, Richardson had much in common psychologically. The similarities extend into various though related habits and actions. Like Richardson with his adopted daughters, Lovelace loves arguments, as he often tells Belford (e.g., III, 304). Lovelace defends his schemes as natural and simple (IV, 375)—so also does Richardson defend his characters, plots, and general writing procedure. When immensely excited, as when he is planning rape on the night of the false fire, Lovelace's knees shake, his limbs are convulsed, his heart beats so loudly that he is afraid all will hear him; though this sort of thing seems no more than appropriate to the circumstances, Richardson's lingering over it may derive from his own nervous hypersensitivity, which led to such finger shaking that in his last few years he could never be sure that when he sat down to write a letter he would be able to hold the pen.

Perhaps the most interesting indication of the similarities between author and character is Lovelace's description of the importance of details in the planning of schemes, which is so close a translation of Richardson's general literary method into terms of action:

> I never forget the Minutiae in my contrivances. In all matters that admit of doubt, the *minutiae* closely attended to, and provided for, are of more service than a thousand oaths, vows, and protestations made to supply the neglect of them, especially when jealousy has made its way in the working mind (III, 201–2).

For both author and character, fantasy is given the appearance of reality through the erection of an immense structure of details. For both the technique works—all the other characters in the novel argue interminably about Lovelace's stratagems and intentions, overlooking his central aim; students for two centuries have worried about such trivia as why Clarissa failed to escape in time, most of them avoiding her overriding function as the appetizing object of the author's fantasies.

Though Richardson's descriptions of his process of character creation are not consistent, he does talk a number of times of his own absorption into the characters (particularly into Lovelace and Charlotte Grandison) and is perfectly aware that he is dredging up from his subconscious material that a respectable bourgeois should not know about: "What a deal of Wickedness may it be inferr'd was in my Mind to draw from thence such a man as Lovelace." I argue, therefore, that Richardson's most lively and effective male characters are modifications, sometimes great and sometimes minor, of certain urges, rather than rational actors chosen for moral or artistic reasons. In his attractive characters, Richardson finds the urge to violence as important as its judicious restraint. Without this urge, men are shown as colorless and faintly absurd. The men with the urge toward dominance achieve the heroines; those without it, consolation prizes of dubious value.

# Chronology of Important Dates

| | |
|---|---|
| 1689 | Samuel Richardson born in Derbyshire. |
| 1706 | Bound apprentice to the printer John Wilde. |
| 1713 | Becomes overseer and corrector of a printing house. |
| 1715 | Made a freeman of the Stationers' Company. |
| c. 1719 | Sets up business for himself as a printer. |
| 1721 | Marries Martha Wilde, daughter of his former master. |
| 1731 | Death of first wife. |
| 1733 | Marries Martha Leake. |
| 1734 | Publishes *Apprentice's Vade Mecum*. |
| 1739 | Publishes his version of L'Estrange's *Aesop*. On November 10, begins *Pamela*. |
| 1740 | Completes *Pamela* on January 10 and publishes it in November. |
| 1741 | Publishes *Familiar Letters* and *Pamela,* Part II. |
| 1747 | Publishes first two volumes of *Clarissa* in December. |
| 1748 | Third and fourth volumes of *Clarissa* published in April and final three volumes in December. |
| 1753 | In July, becomes Master of Stationers' Company. Publishes first four volumes of *Sir Charles Grandison* in November and fifth and sixth volumes in December. |
| 1754 | Completes publication of *Sir Charles Grandison* in March. |
| 1761 | Dies on July 4. |

# Notes on the Editor and Contributors

JOHN CARROLL, the editor of this volume, is Professor of English at University College, University of Toronto. He is the editor of *Selected Letters of Samuel Richardson* and is preparing an edition of *Clarissa*.

WILLIAM J. FARRELL is Associate Professor of English at Marquette University.

MORRIS GOLDEN, Professor of English at the University of Massachusetts, has written *Richardson's Characters* and *Fielding's Moral Psychology*.

CHRISTOPHER HILL is Master of Balliol College, Oxford. His works include *The Century of Revolution, 1603-1714* and *The Good Old Cause: The English Revolution of 1640-1660*.

FREDERICK W. HILLES is Professor Emeritus of English, Yale University. He edited *The Age of Johnson, Essays Presented to C. B. Tinker* and coedited with Harold Bloom *From Sensibility to Romanticism, Essays Presented to F. A. Pottle*. His works also include *New Light on Dr. Johnson*.

A. M. KEARNEY is Lecturer in English at Chorley College of Education, Chorley, Lancashire.

M. KINKEAD-WEEKES is Senior Lecturer in English at the University of Kent, Canterbury. He collaborated with Ian Gregor on *William Golding, a Critical Study*.

A. D. MCKILLOP, Professor Emeritus of English at Rice University, is the author of *Samuel Richardson, Printer and Novelist* and *The Early Masters of English Fiction*, as well as of other works on eighteenth-century English literature.

W. M. SALE, JR., is Professor Emeritus of English at Cornell University. He is the author of *Samuel Richardson, A Bibliographical Record* and *Samuel Richardson, Master Printer*.

GEORGE SHERBURN was Professor of English at Harvard University. He wrote *The Early Career of Alexander Pope* and edited *The Correspondence of Alexander Pope*.

DOROTHY VAN GHENT, late Professor of English at Buffalo, wrote *The English Novel: Form and Function*.

IAN WATT is Professor of English at Stanford University. He is the author of *The Rise of the Novel* and has edited *Tristram Shandy*.

# Selected Bibliography

## I. Editions

The best collected edition of Richardson's novels is that of the Shakespeare Head Press (Oxford: Basil Blackwell, 1929–31). Editions of *Pamela* and *Clarissa* are published by Everyman's Library. His *Familiar Letters on Important Occasions* was reprinted with an introduction by Brian Downs in 1928 (London: Routledge). The prefatory material to Pamela was reprinted in *Samuel Richardson's Introduction to Pamela,* ed. S. W. Baker, Jr., by The Augustan Reprint Society (Los Angeles: William Andrews Clark Memorial Library, 1954). *Clarissa: Preface, Hints of Prefaces, and Postscript,* with an introduction by R. F. Brissenden, was published by The Augustan Reprint Society in 1964. Anna Laetitia Barbauld edited his correspondence in six volumes (London, 1804), and *Selected Letters of Samuel Richardson,* ed. John Carroll (Oxford: Clarendon Press) was published in 1964.

## II. Books and Monographs

Brissenden, R. F. *Samuel Richardson.* London: Longmans, Green & Co., Ltd., for the British Council, 1958.

Bullen, John S. *Time and Space in the Novels of Samuel Richardson.* Logan: Utah State University Press, 1965.

Dobson, Austin. *Samuel Richardson.* London: Macmillan & Co., Ltd., 1902 (English Men of Letters series).

Dottin, Paul. *Samuel Richardson, 1689–1761, Imprimeur de Londres.* Paris: Perrin et cie, 1931.

Downs, Brian. *Richardson.* London: Routledge & Kegan Paul Ltd., 1928.

Kearney, A. M. *Samuel Richardson.* London: Routledge & Kegan Paul Ltd., 1968.

Konigsberg, J. *Samuel Richardson and the Dramatic Novel.* Lexington: University of Kentucky Press, 1968.

Kreissman, Bernard. *Pamela-Shamela: A Study of Criticisms, Burlesques, Parodies, and Adaptations of Richardson's Pamela.* Lincoln: University of Nebraska Press, 1960.

McKillop, A. D. *Samuel Richardson, Printer and Novelist*. Chapel Hill: University of North Carolina Press, 1936. Reprinted by The Shoe String Press, 1960.

Sale, W. M. *Samuel Richardson: A Bibliographical Record*. New Haven: Yale University Press, 1936.

―――― *Samuel Richardson, Master Printer*. Ithaca: Cornell University Press, 1950.

Thomson, Clara. *Samuel Richardson, A Biographical and Critical Study*. London: Horace Marshall, 1900.

Uhrstrom, Wilhelm P. *Studies on the Language of Samuel Richardson*. Upsala, 1907.

## III. Critical Essays and Chapters in General Studies

Bradbrook, F. "Samuel Richardson," *From Dryden to Johnson*, The Pelican Guide to English Literature, IV, ed. Boris Ford. London, Penguin Books Ltd., 1957.

Crane, R. S. "Richardson, Warburton and French Fiction," *Modern Language Review*, XVII (1922), 17–23.

Daiches, David. "Samuel Richardson," *Literary Essays*. Edinburgh: Oliver and Boyd, 1956.

Day, Robert Adams. "Before Richardson and After," *Told in Letters*. Ann Arbor: University of Michigan Press, 1966.

Donovan, R. A. "The Problem of Pamela," *The Shaping Vision*. Ithaca: Cornell University Press, 1966.

Dussinger, J. A. "Richardson's 'Christian Vocation,'" *Papers on Language and Literature*, III (1967), 3–19.

―――― "Conscience and the Pattern of Christian Perfection in *Clarissa*," *PMLA*, LXXXI (1966), 236–45.

Eaves, T. C. D. and Ben Kimpel. "The Composition of *Clarissa* and Its Revision Before Publication," *PMLA*, LXXXIII (1968), 416–28.

―――― "Richardson's Revisions of *Pamela*," *Studies in Bibliography*, XX (1967), 61–88.

Golden, Morris. "Richardson's Repetitions," *PMLA*, LXXXII (1967), 64–7.

Hughes, Leo. "Theatrical Convention in Richardson: Some Observations on a Novelist's Technique," *Restoration and Eighteenth Century Literature*, ed. Carroll Camden. Chicago: Chicago University Press for William Marsh Rice University (1963), 239–50.

Kearney, A. M. "*Clarissa* and the Epistolary Form," *Essays in Criticism*, XVI (1966), 44–56.

Kermode, Frank. "Richardson and Fielding," *Cambridge Journal*, IV (1950), 106–14.

## Selected Bibliography

Kinkead-Weekes, M. *"Clarissa* Restored?" *Review of English Studies,* X (new series, 1959), 156–71.

Krutch, J. W. "Samuel Richardson," *Five Masters.* Bloomington: Indiana University Press, 1959.

Pierson, R. C. "The Revisions of Richardson's *Sir Charles Grandison,*" *Studies in Bibliography,* XXI (1968), 163–89.

Price, Martin. "Clarissa and Lovelace," *To the Palace of Wisdom.* Garden City: Doubleday and Company, Inc., 1964.

Pritchett, V. S. *"Clarissa,*" *The Living Novel.* London: Chatto & Windus, 1946.

Rabkin, N. *"Clarissa*: A Study in the Nature of Convention," *English Literary History,* XXIII (1956), 204–17.

Sack, Sheldon. "The Great, Useful, and Uncommon Doctrine," *Fiction and the Shape of Belief.* Berkeley and Los Angeles: University of California Press, 1964.

Sherbo, Arthur. "Time and Place in Richardson's *Clarissa,*" *Boston University Studies in English,* III (1957), 139–46.

Sherburn, George. "Samuel Richardson's Novels and the Theatre: A Theory Sketched," *Philological Quarterly,* XLI (1962), 325–29.

Taupin, Rene. "Richardson, Diderot, et L'Art de Conter," *The French Review,* XII (1939), 181–94.

Utter, R. P. and G. B. Needham. *Pamela's Daughters.* New York: The Macmillan Company, 1937.

Wendt, Allan. "Clarissa's Coffin," *Philological Quarterly,* XXXIX (1960), 481–95.

Zirker, M. R. "Richardson's Correspondence: The Personal Letter as Private Experience," *The Familiar Letter in the Eighteenth Century,* ed. H. Anderson, P. B. Daghlian, Irvin Ehrenpreis. Lawrence: University of Kansas Press, 1966.

M1111315 78    823.6
                R
               RICHARDSON

Carroll

   Samuel Richardson

KIRN MEMORIAL LIBRARY
NORFOLK PUBLIC LIBRARY
NORFOLK PUBLIC LIBRARY SYSTEM

BOOKS MAY BE KEPT OUT 28 DAYS.
SPECIAL BOOK, TIME 14 DAYS.
OVERDUE CHARGES, 5 CENTS A DAY.